To Liberate and Redeem

To Liberate
and Redeem

moral reflections on the biblical narrative

Edward LeRoy Long Jr.

Foreword by J. Phillip Wogaman

The Pilgrim Press
Cleveland, Ohio

The Pilgrim Press, Cleveland, Ohio 44115
© 1997 by Edward LeRoy Long Jr.

Biblical quotations are from the New Revised Standard Version of the Bible, © 1989 by the Division of Christian Education of the National Council of the Churches of Christ in the U.S.A., and are used by permission.

Printed in the United States of America on acid-free paper

02 01 00 99 98 97   5 4 3 2 1

Library of Congress Cataloging-in-Publication Data

   Long, Edward Le Roy.
      To liberate and redeem : moral reflections on the biblical narrative / Edward LeRoy Long, Jr.
        p.   cm.
      Includes bibliographical references and index.
      ISBN 0-8298-1176-1 (pbk. : alk. paper)
      1. Bible—Criticism, interpretation, etc. 2. Christian ethics. 3. Liberty—Religious aspects—Christianity. 4. Redemption. I. Title.
      BS511.2.L66   1997
      220.6—dc21   97-5601
                                                          CIP

Contents

Foreword

The purpose of this foreword is to help prepare the reader for a very good book. The work of a highly respected teacher of Christian ethics, this volume explores the ethical teaching of the Bible. Those whose thinking has been challenged by Professor Long's writings in ethics over several decades will not be surprised to find here a richly nuanced discussion in ethics. What is exciting about the book is the grace and sophistication with which the Bible is explored. The result is one of the most fruitful discussions of the Bible and ethics that has ever been produced. That is no exaggeration. Until the fairly recent past, the state of biblical scholarship was not advanced enough to permit such a discussion. And in the last few decades, most writings on the Bible and ethics by biblical scholars have not demonstrated equal competence in the literature and methods of ethics.

The Bible is not a simple manual of ethical commandments, even though it is sometimes used in that way by people seeking the security of clearly set forth prescriptions by which to live. The Bible is much, much deeper than that, and this book explores the depths with a trained eye for the ethical nuances. Long wisely remarks that the materials of the Bible "undercut any and all pretensions to quick, simple, or unambiguous solutions to the human enterprise." But every page of the book makes clear that the Bible also richly supports and guides us in our humanity.

I am glad Professor Long uses the word *reflections* in the subtitle. That better prepares us for a book that explores the Bible's richness without imposing upon it any single moral theory. It better conveys the sense that the Bible always has more than we will quite understand. At the same time, it helps us handle aspects of the Bible that ought not to be used slavishly, if at all. In reading the book, an analogy came to mind. The Bible is something like a diamond, with many facets refracting the central core of brilliance in different ways, none of which conveys it all. Edward LeRoy Long's reflections draw us into the most important facets and help us experience the central core, but without any pretense that we will see it all.

Much of the book is organized around the tension between liberation and redemption. Liberation is powerfully represented in the Exodus experience, when the Hebrew slaves were liberated from captivity in Egypt. That formative event is precursor to much biblical material about liberation from other forms of outward oppression, including economic exploitation and political tyranny. It is clear that the Bible is not restricted to any purely nonmaterial realm of spirituality. Outward forms of oppression greatly affect our humanity and cannot, therefore, be excluded from our ethics. Long underscores that point in a well-developed discussion of creation and cosmology, helping the reader experience the drama and importance of God's creation of physical life in a very physical world.

The other part of the tension—redemption—is introduced most deeply through the trauma of the Exile of the Hebrews in Babylon and its aftermath. Through that national tragedy, the Hebrew people came to a profounder understanding of God's redemptive love. They blamed themselves for the tragedy; they had been faithless sinners, so God had punished them. The greatest biblical writings of the period—especially the chapters beginning with Isaiah 40—are about God's forgiveness and healing, the redemption of Israel from its guilt, and the restoration of its relationship with God.

In a sense, both liberation and redemption, as expressed in the Bible and explored by Long, are about freedom. The first is freedom from oppression; the second is freedom from sin. If the first is more external and social, the second is more internal and personal. The two cannot finally be separated, either in the Bible or in an adequate statement of Christian ethics.

The themes are picked up in the New Testament, where Christ, as interpreted in the Gospels and the writings of Paul, expresses both our need for inward redemption and outward liberation. The letters of Paul explore the way in which we are liberated from bondage to external law, either ritualistic requirements or moral legalism. Being grasped by the deep compassion of God, as revealed in Christ, we are free from slavish compliance to externals. Long is clear that our moral fulfillment is in our response to God's compassion, not in the avoidance of responsibility. Long is also clear that the main weight of New Testament teaching is anticipated by what Christians call the Old Testament—the New Testament does not supersede or replace the Old Testament; rather, it amplifies, fulfills, illumines what is central to Old Testament teaching and centers it in Christ.

In exploring the New Testament, Long also helpfully reflects upon the ethical importance of the church. The church, as institution with institutional needs and corruptions, is in tension with the purer life of the spirit—a point that is especially evident in Paul's letters to recalcitrant churches. Yet the life of spirit must find expression in institutions, as Paul also well understood. This New Testament tension is anticipated in the Old Testament tension between leadership by Spirit-led or charismatic judges and the institutionalization of monarchy. Lurking behind these distinctions is the perennial tension between spiritual love as a positive ethical principle and coercive power as protection against injustice.

What makes this book such a helpful contribution is the fact that Professor Long relates these (and other) biblical moral themes to contemporary issues and problems. For instance, his discussions of contemporary movements of liberation—including the Latin American liberationists, movements of racial-ethnic liberation, women's liberation—help us see them as contemporary manifestations of the Exodus and expressions of God's own liberating power. In discussing them, Long is well informed and perceptive. At the same time, the external forms of liberation toward which these movements aspire cannot fully encompass the reality of and redemption from sin. Ultimately, the external and the internal forms of oppression must be resolved together.

I am also intrigued by his discussions of environmental questions and his insight into how the biblical accounts of creation help us work through the dilemmas of how to use the gifts of nature without exploiting them. Here, too, he helps us avoid oversimplified uses of the Bible.

I could go on, but I do not wish to encroach further on Professor Long's time! It is a very good book. Do not expect to find here the easy formulations you might see on a bumper sticker or in some clever new overarching theory about biblical ethics. This book will not start any new theological fads, quickening the pulse for a time but destined to fade quickly. It is deeper, broader, more responsible than that. Perhaps its greatest contribution is that, as a treatise on ethics, it is so very biblical.

J. Philip Wogaman

Preface

This is a book about making moral choices. It looks at the nature and purpose of moral decisions and not merely at the content of such decisions. People are concerned about what is right, good, or fitting for many reasons. Sometimes those reasons are fully as important, if not more so, than what people decide to do about a particular problem or issue.

Consequently, moral decision making is undertaken from a set of commitments that in the aggregate constitute a worldview—a faith stance. Understanding the faith stance from within which moral decisions are made is an important aspect of what Christian ethics is all about.

This is also a book about the Bible. The Bible is a narrative of people and groups whose lives have been shaped by certain historical experiences, conceptual understandings, and ultimate commitments. It tries to look at their experience as a way of helping us to think about our experience from a similar perspective. By understanding how the people of the biblical story responded to the problems and issues they confronted while standing in faithful responsiveness to God, we can be helped to follow their example, although not necessarily to replicate their specific decisions.

Across the years I have written several works that overview Christian thinking about morality and have also made some—often preliminary and explorative—suggestions about possible Christian responses to certain specific issues and problems. However, my last (and only) attempt to set down an overall perspective for understanding Christian moral responsibility was done more than forty years ago.[1] It is time for a fresh set of reflections.

Much has changed in those four decades. In the 1950s, theological reflection took place in a different milieu than it does now. A discrete set of writings framed the issues. The discussions, while by no means marked by agreement, were at least carried on in the framework of a commonly understood set of alternatives—basically the debate between so-called Christian liberalism and neoorthodoxy. The thinking of certain key figures—who have subsequently come to be referred to as "the giants"—was pivotal. To be sure, theological outlooks were constantly changing but usually in a somewhat linear way, with particular perspectives or emphases following one another and sometimes moving back again in something like a pendulum swing. Despite such shifts and arguments, those who kept abreast of the field of Christian ethics could know what books to read and what issues to address in order to be part of the conversation.

Now that I am retired (but not "shelved") I sense a different situation. A veritable plethora of approaches exists—too many for even the person who tries to stay well informed about these matters to master. There is doubt, not only about the central structure of the field, but even about the contours of the disagreements. There are few, if any, clearly outstanding "giants," not because people are thinking less fully or less impressively, but because so many people are thinking in such a variety of ways that it is difficult to know who stands out in contrast with the others. Moreover, theological reflection has not been exempted from the process of deconstruction that has characterized modernity. This has rendered it more difficult to be confident of any particular perspective—not less so because those who are seemingly confident of their own way of thinking are often truculent and insensitive to the complexities and ambiguities that are inevitable in any effort to look at issues with intellectual fairness, scholarly humility, and gracious faithfulness.

As I have tried to think about the moral requirements of Christian fidelity in such circumstances, I have come to see fruitful possibilities in reflecting on the biblical narrative. For a decade I attempted to teach seminary students to think about Christian ethics through the lens of scriptural materials, using them to illumine issues and problems that have attended efforts across many centuries to define what God requires of us. Biblical imagery is powerful, not least because it is accessible to persons with a wide range of conceptual abilities and even to those who are not familiar with the technicalities of moral reflection. Biblical imagery can probe issues profoundly without being pretentious or contrived, without growing obscure or artificially complex. It can allow for a range of perspectives and insights that are loosely structured rather than tightly knit, that engender moral maturity precisely because they relate to such a wide spectrum of human experience. Biblical imagery can be suggestive—even helpful and definitive—without jamming others into looking at moral issues in a particular way that permits little or no differences of opinion and commitment. The biblical materials contain many of the diversities that are needed in order to characterize moral reflection as an invitation to be faithful rather than as a demand to be correct. These materials can be utilized irenically rather than polemically, converting morality into a way of being helpful rather than a way of being demanding or constricting.

Because this book is written by a person who has directed most of his scholarly attention to dealing with Christian thinking about the moral life and not as much attention to the enormous and complex materials that have been written about the Bible, it may not be as perceptive or reliable as an introduction to the literature of the Old and New Testaments as are many other works. But I have made an earnest effort to exercise scholarly warrant for what is said here and to build bridges between knowledge about the Bible and thinking about moral issues.

The reflections in this book are designed to help a wide variety of readers come to their own deeper sense of the nature of moral choice under faithful obedience to the Gospel. They are not written with the intention of trying to advance highly specialized matters of interest only to an elite community. The issues are not simple, but I hope that this presentation makes them clear. If the reflections in this book help readers to think about moral issues with greater perception and sensitivity, that will be gratifying. If the reflections in this book can be accessed by a wide range of readers, all seeking to be faithful, its writing will not have been in vain. If the tone and substance of the insights offered in the reflections help to mitigate the polarities between various contemporary assertions about the nature of Christian obligation—many of which seek to yank everyone else into accepting a particular view or emphasis—perhaps we can all benefit. The New Testament suggests we "see through a glass darkly."[2] Of all the words of the Bible, those may be the most inerrant ones. Christian experience, informed by biblical understanding, also helps us to know that we perceive reality partially, and are morally faithful in but halting and imperfect ways. But such limited understandings and imperfect moral achievements are sufficient—not because ignorance is a virtue or because ambiguity is satisfying—but because the final outcome of the moral task lies not in our accomplishments but in the love of God by which all faithful persons are justified.

Acknowledgments

No author can complete a work without collegial support, not all of which can possibly be acknowledged. Four individuals in particular gave me special help as I worked on the writing of this work: Professors John Petersen and Douglas Oakman of the Religion Department of Pacific Lutheran University; Dr. Neill Hamilton of Drew University (Emeritus); and Dr. Albert Curry Winn, retired from both seminary and pastoral leadership. Each read a draft and provided extensive written observations—a number of which are incorporated into the work—but all of which greatly helped to bring the book to its present form. My son, Roger W. Long, provided the diagrams in chapter 17.

Introduction

On Reading the Bible for Moral Insight

The Bible contains a variety of literary materials that illumine the human situation in a special way. Christians rely on such illumination as guidance in forming their beliefs about the ultimate nature of things and in sensing the moral responsibilities that grow out of those beliefs. The reflections in this book explore the major dimensions of the Bible's perspectives on nature, history, and the human condition and suggest moral responses appropriate to those perspectives.

Reading the Bible is a complex and even difficult undertaking. None of us can be sure we do it with sufficient faith and wisdom. Faith assertions concerning the importance and reliability of the biblical materials—some of which employ terms like "infallibility" and "inerrancy" to emphasize the ultimate character of that importance—provide no guarantees about the abilities of readers and interpreters to understand the import of a biblical perspective correctly. None of us who read the Bible are infallible nor inerrant, and yet the substance of the biblical perspective cannot be apprehended except through the work of interpretation—whether by ourselves or by others.

People read the Bible by various methods and for various purposes. The term "hermeneutics" is widely used to denote the theory and practice of interpreting sacred and literary texts. Although it may not be necessary to employ this particular term to discuss the process of biblical interpretation, it is undoubtedly important to be conscious of our methodology, that is, to be aware of the hermeneutics we use to interpret the rich and varied materials that hold an authoritative place in our faith professions. Yet, curiously, we must not presume to construct a hermeneutics with a rigidity that forces everyone to respond to biblical materials in only one set and predefined manner. To do so would be to place highest trust in a method of reading Scripture rather than in the message and power of the Word itself.

Perhaps the most prevalent approach to interpretation is a hermeneutics that concentrates on particular texts. It is common among those who believe the Bible to be a special source of truth (and even among those who do not) to ask what particular texts say (or mean). Alas, people can turn to biblical texts in highly questionable ways. There once was a popular practice—at least I have encountered people who have done it—of believing one can answer questions about life, even make decisions about what to do about a particular moral quandary, by opening the Bible at random, blindly dropping a finger onto the page, and inferring an answer to some question by reading the text that is thus located. Interestingly enough, this does not always yield results that are as absurd as the assumptions behind this form of pious roulette. But this hardly constitutes a dependable use of the Bible for moral purposes.

Surely a hermeneutics of the text can be almost infinitely more sophisticated than that! Perhaps no book in the world has had greater or more serious attention devoted to ascertaining what it says. Many denominations require their clergy to learn the original languages in which the biblical materials were written so that they can better discern the meaning of the text. Those who interpret the Bible can be further helped to do this by a plethora of commentaries and study guides that present highly sophisticated analyses of the text and its possible meaning or meanings.

Moreover, some of the most common affirmations about the authority of the Bible have been shaped by an emphasis on reading the text. As popularly understood and frequently used, some views about biblical authority imply a concept of "flat equivalency," making every text as legitimate and as significant as every other text. While this popularized version of what plenary inspiration means is adopted in the name of bolstering the authority of the Bible in matters of faith and morals, it may actually have the opposite consequence. Almost all reading of the Bible depends on selections. Although texts are seldom selected by pure chance (as by casually dropping a finger), they are likely to be selected by either inclination or disposition. One need only imagine how certain texts could be chosen and strung together under a presumption of flat equivalency to realize how readily the Bible can be used in ways that mock the fundamental premises of a moral perspective: "Cain slew Abel"; "Go Thou and do likewise"; and "What Thou doest, do quickly." Although we have no difficulty discerning the fallacious consequences of a use of biblical texts when it leads to moral nonsense, how can we be sure that ecclesiastical divines are not doing something analogous when, for instance, they "proof-text" a document like the Westminster Confession of Faith?[1]

Texts lend themselves to prooftexting, but also to sloganizing. Many preachers, in both conservative and liberal pulpits, not infrequently utilize a biblical text as a kind of slogan for giving punch to the theme or thesis of a sermon. In the overall life of a congregation such sermons may well provide guidance and inspiration, which can further personal faithfulness and even inspire people to actions that are important in the overall economy of God, but using a text as a slogan does not necessarily validate a particular sermon as an authentic reflection of a biblical worldview in a broad sense.

Hermeneutics of the text, particularly those that are associated with terms like "infallible" and "inerrant," often claim certainty for some religious perspective. Prooftexting, for instance, is often utilized for hurling vendettas against opponents in theological disputations. Simplistic sloganizing, though frequently less truculent, is not much better. To be sure, no serious scholar of biblical materials dares to dismiss the importance of discerning what a text says—indeed what a great number of texts say—but no serious interpreter of the biblical materials will ever be content to utilize a single text or even a small selected group of texts as the sole and sufficient basis for arriving at moral judgments. Texts should be utilized in relationship to larger and more controlling perspectives on the Bible's encompassing understanding of divine/human interaction.

A second typical hermeneutics focuses concern on the origins of the materials found in the various parts of the Bible. Biblical scholarship has furnished a marvelous body of information—not necessarily representing agreement among all those who concern themselves with such study—that sheds light on the temporal setting, geographical location, authorship, and intended readership of the biblical materials. We have an ever increasing body of information that illuminates the origins of the various books of the Bible, even of various portions of books that modern scholarship suggests were put together from materials originating at different times or from various sources. Biblical scholarship also helps us to understand the social and political situation of biblical times and hence the circumstances out of which a particular part of the Bible came. The intention of a hermeneutics of origins is to be historically accurate, to be as thoroughly aware and as objectively informed as possible about the circumstances that have surrounded the development of given parts of the Bible.

No serious reading of biblical materials can ignore the insights offered by a study of their background and origins. Unfortunately, such a hermeneutics—dependent as it is on the so-called higher criticism of the Bible—has (mainly in the twentieth century) been resisted in some circles as tampering with a revealed deposit of truth. Higher criticism is seen by many as a threat to textual authority in the inerrant sense. Many ecclesiastical groups have been torn asunder by arguments about the legitimacy of higher criticism and thus have been deprived of the contribution that a knowledge of the origins of biblical material can offer.

But a knowledge of origins does not by itself furnish a sufficient guide to moral decision making. Higher criticism may be pursued as a kind intellectual inquiry that does not necessarily involve theological commitments. No person who is reading biblical materials for the purposes of forming faith and guiding moral decisions can rest content merely with learning about the conditions at the time of their writing. Biblical scholarship that is interested only in such matters is not so much a theological as a literary and historical discipline. It deserves to be respectfully utilized but it does not furnish a sufficient basis for arriving at judgments concerning faith and morals. Faith and morals require theological gestation, not merely historical information.[2] A knowledge of the origins of biblical materials can be of some help in discerning their moral significance, but by itself such knowledge does not furnish adequate guidance for moral decision making. For instance, just because a biblical character behaved or acted in a certain way does not bind us to imitate that character.

A third type of hermeneutics depends on a controlling concept or ideal in light of which the disparate and even contending perspectives of various biblical materials are arranged into a coherent and compelling system. Not infrequently this controlling concept has moral overtones. Many of the great advances in the enrichment and extension of Christian understanding have been made under the aegis of such a hermeneutics of a governing ideal. Paul, for instance, made freedom into a controlling principle for interpreting the Old Testament. Thus he could break away from the confines of prevailing Jewish outlooks on the Hebrew Scriptures and make Christianity possible for Gentiles. Luther's adoption of justification by faith as the basis of his understanding of Scripture was the central factor in his ability to get beyond the confines of the Roman Catholic penance system of his time. Today, a tremendous theological dynamic with momentous consequences for understanding Christian faith depends on the idea of liberation as a governing principle for constructing a biblically grounded faith having a fresh urgency.

Although there is always a danger that a particular governing idea may not have sufficient scriptural warrant to justify the place it is given, any significant use of the Bible may well depend, at least to a measurable extent, on the presence of such a guiding idea. In so-called Protestant liberalism the idea of love constitutes the touchstone for judging biblical materials. Similarly, although professing to be primarily faithful to the inspired text, Protestant Fundamentalism utilizes certain key concepts for ascertaining whether Scripture is being correctly understood. Its controlling concepts include, in addition to the idea of plenary inspiration, the full divinity of Christ, the blood atonement, and belief in the Second Coming of Christ.

One of the important contributions made by a hermeneutics of a governing ideal is to counter a simplistic use of proof texts to resolve deep and perplexing moral issues. Some years ago, a task force of a major Protestant denomination charged to make recommendations regarding its denomination's position on sexual matters suggested the importance of what it called a "justice-hermeneutic."[3] It argued that the Bible should be so read as to assure justice to all persons regardless of their personal orientations and dispositions, not as a sourcebook of isolated texts that in and by themselves provide definitive guidance on specific moral issues. This plea for a frank and open embrace of a governing ideal has much to commend it, for surely justice is a central biblical category, and those who read the Bible to develop a rich and sensitive sense of justice are faithful in an important way. But every proposed governing ideal used in a hermeneutics must itself be scrutinized for legitimacy and judged for adequacy in tension with other ideals that have commended themselves as clues for understanding Scripture. Moreover, no single idea is likely to be adequate to grasp the scope, breadth, and diversity of the biblical materials. The discernment of significant ideas is a fruitful venture, but it is important to avoid the use of but one idea as a category into which to jam the biblical message without remainder.

A fourth way of reading the Bible is to understand it in developmental terms. Such an approach is greatly aided by the chronological information available from higher criticism. After all, development can be traced only in relationship to a realization of the sequential order in which the biblical materials emerged. But development is likely to be measured in terms of some governing idea that is taken to be the climactic consequence of the process. For example, Harry Emerson Fosdick, whose book *The Modern*

Use of the Bible was popularly acclaimed in the 1920s, contended that the ideas in the Bible grew and enlarged as they were developed, but he also held that they came to a meaningful fruition in the teachings of Jesus. Speaking of the biblical writings, as these are understood in their historical emergence, Fosdick had this to say:

> Plainly we are dealing with ideas that enlarge their scope, deepen their meaning, are played upon by changing circumstance and ma-turing thought so that from its lowliest beginning in the earliest writ-ings of the Hebrews any religious or ethical idea of the Bible can now be traced, traveling in an often uneven but ascending roadway to its climax in the teaching of Jesus.[4]

It may be, however, that some of the ideas found in the earliest passages from the Bible contain spiritual insights about the nature of divine-human interaction that are clearly as profound as those contained in the later writings. Conversely, some of the writings we know to have been among the last to enter into the canon may be morally less helpful than those from earlier periods. Moreover, despite what Fosdick affirmed, some of the insights in the religion that was developed about Jesus and that entered into the record after he had done his ministry may be as worthy of explo-ration as the ideas contained in the teaching of Jesus himself. Although there undoubtedly is development in the biblical narrative as circumstances change and thus new vistas of understanding open, to think of this process as altogether developmental may be to impose an arbitrary framework on the materials. Biblical ideas are not necessarily valuable for moral insight in direct relationship to their location in a chronological ordering.

A fifth type of hermeneutics involves appeals to the importance of an ecclesiastical setting as the position from which the Bible may be read most faithfully. The Roman Catholic Church has always held that the ecclesiastical tradition offers much needed guidance for reading Scripture, and the church became even more explicit and emphatic about this matter as it countered interpretations being offered by the Protestant reformers under the banner of *sola scriptura*. Arguments have flown back and forth about whether the Bible produced the church, or the church (because it determined the canon) produced the Bible. If the Bible produced the church, then the Bible's authority is, as most Protestants have held, crucial for determining whether or not the church is faithful. If the church produced the Bible, then the church legitimately claims to offer guidance as to how the Bible should be understood. The Eastern Orthodox tradition, in a stance not dissimilar to that of the Roman Catholic tradition, asserts that Christ appeared even before Scripture and that the Church is the locus of his continuing presence.

Anglicanism has, by and large, understood the tradition of the church as a source of authority for faith and morals to be cherished and respected along with Scripture. Its use of Scripture, therefore, reflects some foundational qualities in its spiritual life. Moreover, because Anglicanism has thought of this authority more in terms of creating an ethos than as specifying a particular set of propositional dogmas to be given intellectual consent, there has been relatively little biblical literalism in the Anglican tradition.[5]

Among many Protestants there is a growing sense that the formula *sola scriptura* is inadequate despite its polemical usefulness at the time of the Reformation. Such Protestants see the church as providing an important community in which to discern what the Bible says. For instance, Stanley Hauerwas, whose thinking is influenced strongly by the heritage of the left wing of the Reformation (which has never been limp in its devotion to Scripture), has increasingly emphasized the role of the church as the locus of guidance for the reading of Scripture. Seeking to free the interpretation of the Bible from its cultural imprisonment to American or to purely individualistic values, he affirms what amounts to a new version of a hermeneutics of ecclesiastical setting. He suggests that both the Protestant Fundamentalists and those who embrace higher criticism (between which there has been and is so much antagonism) are committed to a similar premise: that there is a text that is accessible to individual reading, subject only to individual judgment. In contrast, asserts Hauerwas, "If we are to understand Scripture it is necessary that we place ourselves under authority, a placement that at least begins by our willingness to accept the discipline of the Church's preaching."[6]

A hermeneutics of ecclesiastical tutelage offers much to counteract privatized and idiosyncratic misreadings of Scripture, but it may become a hermeneutics of ecclesiastical control to the extent a church becomes self-conscious and even bureaucratized in its claim to offer proper guidance to reading Scripture. History offers ample evidence that ecclesiastically endorsed readings of Scripture have often been morally inadequate, as for instance, when many churches once read the Bible as legitimizing slavery. Merely turning to see how the church suggests Scripture be read provides no assurance of being faithful to the word.

All of the foregoing ways of reading the Bible are called into radical question by a sixth type of hermeneutics, which calls itself a hermeneutics of suspicion. This hermeneutics is aware that the message that is read from Scripture is undoubtedly colored by the standing ground of the interpreter (a phenomenon that is clearly evident in several of the preceding hermeneutics).

Those who read the Bible with a hermeneutics of suspicion examine the governing ideals that have had such influence in the history of biblical interpretation (whether in themselves or through ecclesiastical traditions) and find them inadequate, if not indeed downright erroneous. They come at the text from a radically different standing ground and realize that what has been traditionally read as the message of the text is not necessarily its meaning at all, or certainly not its only possible meaning.

Some of the most astute and powerful contemporary work with the hermeneutics of suspicion is associated with the doing of theology in a feminist or womanist perspective. We see such breakthroughs, for instance, in the work of Elisabeth Schüssler Fiorenza, who reinterprets many biblical materials in ways that release them from the androcentric framework in which they have been customarily read.[7] For example, the church has traditionally designated those who met the resurrected Jesus "apostles," but confined this category to men. Contemporary women scholars, quite correctly, have pointed out that women were the first to see the resurrected Jesus and should therefore be designated as "apostles," and indeed should be accorded the most important of apostolic roles. The biblical material is clear enough on this matter, but that fact seems to have been perceived only when the biblical record was approached with a hermeneutics that brought new and entirely different perspectives to the reading of Scripture.

Despite its usefulness in pointing out problems related to interpretations from the past and persisting into the present, a feminist hermeneutics may become more of a hermeneutics of a controlling idea than a hermeneutics of suspicion. Feminist readings of the Bible are valuable. They stand or fall on their suggestive truthfulness, and do not gain validity from suspicion alone. A hermeneutics of suspicion is possible from a variety of perspectives. Suspicion may be crucially important in keeping the church tradition from forever being a categorical straitjacket that blocks new ways of understanding and interpreting the Bible. Yet those who employ a hermeneutics of suspicion may well need to be suspicious even of suspicion, lest the breakthroughs of one generation become the dogmas of another, and lest mere negation become overly controlling in approaching biblical materials.

A seventh approach toward reading the Bible is more difficult to dub with single, simple terminology. It might be called a hermeneutics of tutored responsiveness. Instead of asking what the text says, one should ask what the text signifies as it is experienced by the reader or by the reading community. It makes a place for the work of the Spirit, not as the surrogate of correctness, but as the catalyst of an openness to a compelling sense of meaning that is bestowed on a reader as that reader (or group of readers) enters imaginatively into the drama of the biblical narrative. Such a hermeneutics may well, like a hermeneutics of origins, see the text in its original setting, not so much to determine what its author meant to say when it was first written, but to enable those who read it today to partake vicariously of the dramatic transformations in spiritual outlook and moral behavior that took place in the lives of the people about whom the text is a narrative. The thrust of this hermeneutics is not necessarily for certainty (as often as is the thrust of the text-centered approach), or for objective accuracy (as often as is the thrust of a hermeneutics of origins), or for a guiding principle (as often operates in reliance on a governing ideal), or merely for spiritual nurture and growth (as in a hermeneutics of growth and development). Fidelity is understood less in terms of correctness than in terms of responsiveness; less in terms of creating an overarching concept than in terms of an exciting sense of having been grasped by a compelling vision. This hermeneutics makes us think of the biblical materials in terms of narrative and drama rather than as a collection of texts; in terms of experiences with which we resonate in the depths of our being rather than in terms of concepts that merely inform our understanding. Those who read the Bible from this stance are capable of being suspicious but also of being surprised, of being grasped by truth rather than merely grasping ideas. In a significant sense this hermeneutics focuses not only on how we read the Bible but on (as Karl Barth once put it) "how the Bible reads us."[8]

The practitioners of each of the foregoing hermeneutics can be tempted to think more highly of their method than they ought to—to regard the method or its conclusions as the one and only valid way to approach biblical materials. Too much theology—and biblical interpretation is no exception—is preoccupied with showing why others are wrong. Strong polemics and hostile stances occur as a consequence. But it may well be that there are aspects of each approach that contribute to a larger whole. The result may not be as neat and orderly, as consistent and as coherent, as the seeming assurance provided by regarding one of the hermeneutics described above as definitive. Our understanding of the biblical narrative may have to change as one or another way of looking at the biblical materials proves at any given time to be no longer satisfactory or especially illuminating or persuasive.

The reflections that follow employ imaginative analogy to relate what can be discerned from the biblical narrative as to how the people about whom the Bible speaks were morally faithful (or unfaithful) in their times and circumstances and then ask how we can be spiritually and morally faithful in our times and circumstances. The reflections in this work are offered without attempting to prove they are the only way in which to garner moral guidance from Scripture. They are indebted in many and various ways to several of the foregoing hermeneutics. Hopefully, the interpretations that follow are more faithful to the Bible as a total narrative than are moral stances backed only by isolated texts—but that does not mean one can dispense with the use of texts. These interpretations may offer deeper insights than can be encompassed by a single governing idea— but that does not mean they avoid conceptual frameworks in which to see issues. Hopefully, they pay attention to the origins from which the biblical writings emerged—but use those origins as a means of interacting with our present situation and not merely as interesting information to satisfy classroom curiosity. Hopefully, they acknowledge changes, even growth, in moral discernment—but do not make chronology a simplistic measure of spiritual progress. Hopefully, they are informed by long association with communities of faith—but see such communities as most healthy if they encourage dialogue about momentous questions of faith and do not insist on particular answers. Yes, hopefully, they enable our experiences to be read by the biblical narrative even as they involve a reading of the Bible from where we stand. They are offered in the trust that a wholesome faith is too much a mystery to provide certainty and too important a commitment to be merely a casual undertaking. It can only be hoped that these reflections commend themselves to those who read them as helpful and faithful ways of understanding the significance of the biblical narrative for making moral decisions and for understanding the importance of moral obligation.

1

Egypt and Exodus

Oppression and Liberation in a Moral Perspective

The Way of Israel—its way of life and its patterns of behavior (that is, what may well be said to constitute its ethic)—has its origins in the experience of liberation. The pivotal dimension is an experience, not an ideal in the sense of an articulated, abstract norm, and not a quality of character for which the term "virtue" is appropriate. Nothing is implied concerning the unique spirituality of those in Egypt—in fact, the unfaithfulness that sometimes marks Israel's life or the actions of its people is actually revealed in the record with remarkable candor. Nor is anything directly claimed for the superior moral virtue of the Hebrews. The central thing about this group that warrants attention is its condition of slavery. And this God does not intend to tolerate!

Although the account of the Exodus is not placed at the beginning of the literary format of the Bible, it is chronologically first in the biblical drama as experienced by the Hebrews. After the Exodus took place, a good deal of other reflection was brought together from memory and by speculation to set Exodus into a historical and even a cosmic framework of meaning. Much of that reflection now appears in the Book of Genesis, though it also finds expression in the Psalms and Wisdom literature. Those materials, including the accounts of creation and the saga of the progenitors as well as liturgical appreciations of the created order, have considerable relevance to understanding the moral worldview of the Bible and will engage our attention in subsequent chapters. But Exodus, not Genesis, is the dramatic beginning of Israel's self-understanding.[1]

The drama of the Bible focuses initially on God's concern about a group that is oppressed. The group is found making bricks under harsh conditions of servitude. The divine concern for the Hebrews who are enslaved in Egypt expresses itself initially through historical events that bring about their release from bondage. The account of this release is a narrative of escape from morally intolerable political and social conditions.

A biblically informed reflection on morality starts, therefore, with the scriptural materials that deal with oppression and the release from that condition. This beginning renders liberation from oppression a central and crucial paradigm for understanding God's will for persons and for social groups. Indeed, it renders liberation the initial moral category from which a biblically informed ethic springs forth. Liberation implies that there is a divine opposition to conditions of oppression wherever they are encountered. Exodus suggests that God wills liberation; that God breaks the rod of oppressors; that God opposes every illegitimate imposition of authority by which one group subjugates another.

This is a stunning claim, the implications of which have momentous consequences. It speaks directly and powerfully to groups that are subjugated and warrants their efforts to break the bonds that keep them down. Those who are relatively well off, who enjoy freedom and privilege, may not grasp the full impact of the narrative. For instance, what many of us probably remember from hearing the story of the Exodus as taught in Sunday school is the astonishing parting of the Red Sea so that the Hebrews could pass safely out of Egypt on supposedly dry land. That event grasped our imaginations as children because it signifies God's mighty power—a mighty power that aided the escape in a seemingly miraculous way. Similarly, we may have focused attention on how Moses used the threat of the plagues to smite the oppressor in ways that infer (albeit possibly less spectacularly than does the parting of the waters) the hand of God working supernaturally in the process. But to focus primary attention on these aspects of the story may be to miss the central meaning. Not only can it obscure the centrality of liberation by concentrating attention on the miraculous aspects of divine intervention, but it can obscure the difficulties that attended the overcoming of oppression. Not all releases from bondage are overcome in stunning ways. Not even the Exodus event wafted the Hebrews out of Egypt with such apparent ease. Other dimensions to the account reward careful scrutiny because they supply far more important moral insights.

For instance, the story reveals the uncertainties and arduous difficulties involved. It suggests the agony experienced even by those destined to be liberated. Moses, for instance, was not ecstatic about his commission. When told of it he replied, "Who am I that I should go to Pharaoh, and bring the sons of Israel out of Egypt?" (3:11) Many an ethical mandate to work on behalf of righteousness has prompted a similar hesitation. Few people relish the prospects of confronting oppressive power, even if they feel divinely commissioned to do so. Sunday school lessons would be more realistic if they pointed to the parts of the narrative that tell of the difficulties that inhere in liberating activity instead of dwelling on those parts of the story that seem almost to glorify the event with seemingly miraculous overtones.

Moses also recognized that his leadership might be either resisted or repudiated by the people. He inquired of God how he should answer if the people queried him about the identity of the God who was sending him to be their liberator. Moses asked to know God's name because a name is a source of assurance and a means of commending some person to others. Surely, we ask a person who comes promising us something, Who has sent you and what is your name? We may even ask for references, check credentials, and demand some evidence that the person who is reported as making the promise is so positioned as to be able to deliver the results. According to the story, Moses was given more than the divine name with which to impress the people with the authenticity and validity of his commission (4:1–9), but even the bestowal of those special powers did not entirely alleviate the hesitation and anxiety of Moses. He protested, even after having been given such special powers, "I have never been eloquent, neither in the past or even now that you have spoken to thy servant, but I am slow of speech and slow of tongue" (4:10).

We might give these hesitations of Moses a more contemporary twist. We can imaginatively suppose a modern Moses having to ask, "Suppose Pharaoh is a philosophical naturalist or an anthropological relativist and simply laughs at the claim of so feeble and subjugated a minority?" "Suppose Pharaoh ridicules the plagues as merely accidental coincidences between the making of a political demand and some natural calamity?" Or, "Suppose Pharaoh is a political realist who thinks that naked coercive power alone affects the outcome of historical events, and like the leader of a modern totalitarian state resorts to the use of technologically sophisticated techniques to quell the whole enterprise?"

Terry Waite, the Anglican envoy who some years ago went to the Middle East seeking the release of hostages held by Islamic militants undoubtedly had to ask questions having this kind of import. How could Waite expect to get the hostages released when those who held them obviously were adept at making hard-headed rejections of claims advanced by Western religious leaders? How could Waite expect the mandate for liberation to be honored when so much religion since the time of Moses has seemed more to sanctify the authority of political leaders than to support the work of those who work for the release of captives? Moses is portrayed by the biblical narrative as being able to demonstrate that the God who had commissioned him was more powerful than the deities to which the pharaoh responded. In an age of religious pluralism and even of secularism that sort of claim was less possible for a Terry Waite to make. But alas, if we draw a line too sharply between what we believe the Bible tells us about the backing Moses had for his mission and the backing we believe Waite had for his, we may undercut the belief that liberation is divinely sanctioned and hence abandon a centrally important aspect of biblical faith.

Still other insights emerge from a careful reading of the story. For instance, Megan McKenna examines how the midwife role that the pharaoh assigned to the Hebrew women played a part in the drama. Since it was assumed that any leadership that might arise to lead the Hebrews to freedom would be male, the midwives were told to see that all the male infants born of the Hebrews were to be killed (1:16). The midwives disobeyed the pharaoh, and lied a little to cover up their transgression of his edict. According to McKenna, "The Exodus event and all that follows from it begins with an act of disobedience to authority that is oppressive, destructive of life, dangerous for children, and only intent on securing its continued existence."[2] McKenna's observation suggests nothing less startling than the realization that the Exodus was made possible by women who engaged in civil disobedience. Their disobedience was approved by God, and although many a Sunday school child knows about the infant Moses floating in the basket among the bulrushes, not all of them get told explicitly that this event involved lawbreaking. This latter dimension has been quietly overlooked (or at least underemphasized) by much traditional teaching about the Exodus story, particularly in those church groups whose conservative disposition prompts them to extol law and order rather than a divine mandate that transcends the claims of worldly authority.

Had Moses been foresighted, he might also have asked, "What shall I do when the people get tired of the journey while still in the wilderness and want to turn back?" Or, had he been prescient, he might also have asked God what to do if they blaspheme the event through some great apostasy. By looking carefully at the experience of Moses, we can learn something about the difficulties involved in seeking liberation. No leader of a social cause is ever given a group of perfect persons with whom to carry out a liberating agenda. Perhaps it is good that Moses did not foresee how the people would behave once they were beyond the clutches of the pharaoh. He might have reneged on his commission!

All of these questions pose matters of logistics and strategy, and frequently present themselves whenever a social venture is proposed, whether as a political cause or a religious odyssey. Pragmatically, they may call a proposed exodus into question for tactical reasons, but they don't abrogate the moral legitimacy of the undertaking, nor do they add up to a negation of the bold conviction that God wills liberation.

But our reflections must move to another level. As the scope of moral inquiry is expanded, questions such as these arise: Why should the God of Moses be concerned to obtain the release of the Hebrews from Egyptian slavery and not also be concerned with securing the liberation of groups caught in oppression or slavery in other parts of the world of the time? To explore that question in any depth would take us to a complex level of reflection—one that produces a problem of theodicy. From within the experience of liberation, however, it is not necessary to weigh the warrant for release from bondage in comparative terms or to regard a particular cause as morally paramount to all other causes. The Hebrews do not have to put the Exodus on hold in order to consider whether or not another oppressed group somewhere in the world is even more deserving of release from its bondage. Questions like that do have to be faced in reflective moral analysis, but they do not come up in the throes of a liberation experience itself. But before we examine that question in all its vexing implications—which in a profound sense permeates the whole biblical story—we turn to another set of questions prompted by the Exodus as a model for thinking about God's work.

How many different kinds of human experience can be subsumed under the rubric of "Egypt"? The experience of the Hebrews in Egypt was one of slavery—of being "put upon unjustly" by hard taskmasters. They were victims of political subjugation. They suffered an imposed servitude attended by harsh demands.

Certainly, many groups have found themselves in situations almost identical to the plight of the Hebrews in Egypt. Their enslavement in a political/structural sense has been, or still is, obvious. In eighteenth- and nineteenth-century America the slaves understood their plight in terms of the biblical model, and their hymnology—much of it based on the imagery of Exodus—legitimately expressed this understanding in clear and unmistakable ways. They were concerned about liberation and turned to the biblical narrative to interpret their predicament and to bolster their hope it would be redressed. In twentieth-century South Africa, blacks were victims of a system of deliberate subjugation and degradation—a system that had grown progressively repressive over many decades and seemed resistant to many efforts to abolish it. *Apartheid* is relatively easy to recognize as an instance of blatant injustice, but it is appalling to see how privileged persons remained blind to its oppressive nature for so long. The horrendous victimization of the Jewish people in the Third Reich was a form of oppression even worse than that in Egypt: the pharaoh only imposed harsh servitude; Hitler engaged in genocide.

Throughout the world, and particularly in the Third World, political oppression and economic hardship create conditions easily identified as Egypts. It is no accident that the resurgence of liberation as a central theological category should be most strongly articulated by Christians in this Third World.

But other conditions of oppression have different structural contours—although this fact does not make them any less onerous nor make them less easy to put up with than coercively enforced slavery. It does, however, make it less likely that they will be clearly recognized as blatant forms of oppression. Those who are sick and handicapped suffer oppression—albeit in a somewhat different way than do slaves. The Exodus paradigm may not immediately and directly correspond to their plight, although concepts subsequently developed in both the Old and the New Testament do help to sensitize us about their needs. Widows and orphans need an exodus, but perhaps in slightly different ways than do slaves. The horror of the Holocaust is easy to discern, but the various subtle forms of anti-Semitism that abound in the modern world are variations on the Egyptian condition, as are the conditions imposed upon black people even in a country that supposedly grants them equality under the law but denies them equality of opportunity in the economic order and equality of respect in the cultural ethos.

The oppression of women, particularly those battered and/or contemptuously subjugated, disturbingly parallels the model of imposed servitude, and perhaps even exceeds it since the oppression occurs largely in private, making detection and redress less likely. But other oppression of women, who may consciously or unconsciously regard themselves as less important than men or fail to acknowledge the importance of their contribution to human well-being, requires more imaginative insight to recognize all its complexity and disturbing dimensions. It may be the more difficult to recognize precisely because it does not obviously exhibit the features of a systemic slavery and deliberately imposed oppression.

Certainly it is the task of ethical reflection to see the many forms that "Egypt" can take. The common thread that links all of these forms is that they find persons subject to an external will or to a set of circumstances for which the oppressed have no responsibility, and from which release is necessary for those persons to be free. Usually those circumstances have to be altogether changed rather than merely modified. (We will suggest later in this discussion that other forms of human disablement may not fit under the rubric of "Egypt"—the rubric, that is, of overtly imposed oppression—and that biblical understandings of those other forms of disablement is no less important to take into account with a Christian understanding of morality than the model of externally imposed oppression.)

Still other issues are raised by the Exodus story. One of these issues concerns the factors that made the liberating events "get going" in the first place. What are sufficient engendering conditions for a liberating event to arise? If the events of Exodus are judged as a purely natural enterprise, there isn't any guarantee that Moses will solicit a response from the people. The people do not send Moses on a mission to explore the possibility of getting help, though one strand in the record suggests that the people cry to God about their plight and Moses is commissioned in response to their cry. But another strand suggests that God sees their predicament and becomes concerned and takes the initiative in sending Moses. (After all, Moses does ask God what to do if the people don't respond to him, meaning that Moses himself isn't exactly persuaded that the people are standing on the brink of expectation for him to arrive as their leader.)

Oppression (i.e., the experience of being in "Egypt") moves to Exodus only under certain conditions. Not only must the outrages of oppression be felt, but the possibility of release must become plausible. There must be some dynamic that moves the situation of people from mere oppression to an articulated discontent with oppression and then on to a sense of the possibility of liberation. A theological term for this would be *prevenience*—that which comes before in order to crystallize the potential and elicit the response. (Oppression remains unchallenged as long as such a prevenient dynamic is entirely absent.) In modern parlance, this involves something like what Paulo Freire, in *The Pedagogy of the Oppressed,* calls "conscientionization"—that is, rising to an awareness of one's oppression and achieving the resolve to repudiate it.[3] The motivation for release from oppression does not necessarily come solely from inside the oppressed group. Very little liberation is initiated merely from being stepped on. Those who experience oppression have to become aware that there is something unacceptable about being stepped on before they are likely to yearn for liberation. In a profound sense such awareness is something of a gift.

An issue analogous to this is involved in the discussion (even debate) that has attended the understanding of salvation throughout much of Christian history. Is release from bondage to sin and death sought entirely at the initiative of the sinner, or does the very seeking of such release already exhibit a movement of grace toward the sinner that the sinner has not autonomously (that is, entirely by the power of the self) initiated? The idea of prevenience contends that the power to wish redemption is already a bestowed consequence rather than a self-initiated movement. The biblical record does not settle this issue as regards the Exodus with any finality because the story suggests a crucial role for both the initiative of God and the cries of the people. This issue is never finally settled in Christian moral reflection about salvation either, since the mystery that surrounds the instigation of salvation is dissolved into a barren rationalism both by those schemes that make the yearning for salvation totally dependent on the divine foreknowledge and those schemes that insist it has to come from an autonomous human initiative. Similarly, a spiritually sensitive awareness of liberation will recognize the difficulty in determining whether the yearning to be free is already a gift of God or merely the result of human resolution.

The ethicist will ask, "What is necessary for people to come to the realization they are illegitimately oppressed?" A particular instance of oppression can be so long-standing and so complete that people endure it without the sense of outrage that prompts a movement for release. Only when a sense of hope brings the disadvantaged to the recognition that things might be different do they begin to yearn for an Exodus. This means that the Christian is called, not merely to side with those who are already seeking to break the bounds of oppression, but to stir up those who are caught in situations of oppression to look forward to leaving their Egypts.

The trick is to do this in a way that discerns the difference between legitimate and illegitimate conditions of restraint. There is no condition that cannot be interpreted from within as oppressive if one is predisposed only to resent it. All participation in community involves some subordination of the self or of small-group interests to the needs and welfare of the larger community. It is possible to chafe against limitations on one's freedom even when those limitations are legitimate aspects of group belonging. The task of moral reflection is to provide that contextually conditioned wisdom by which persons who are illegitimately oppressed will seek an appropriate Exodus without at the same time causing persons whose privately defined desires are legitimately subordinated to the needs of public order to think they have a license for rebellion. Needless to say, the historical record of doing this is not replete with balance and effectiveness.

Still another point implicit in the story of the Exodus is the importance of group destiny. Exodus happened to a group, not to individuals. It involved a political act, not private emancipation; it entailed historical changes, worked out within historical flux by political leaders and subjugated groups. Rather than advancing some abstract teaching, in liberation God takes action—concrete, specific, historical action. There is, certainly as the drama opens, little rationalization or intellectualization of the situation. Rather than analyzing and talking about the problem at length, persons in the biblical narrative do something about it.

Of course moral analysis cannot stop with the realization that a situation is intolerable. The movement known as "political theology" stresses the importance of the dynamic and functional aspects of God's doing in contrast to the focus of metaphysical or speculative theologies on the aspects of God's being. As exemplified by the writings of Johannes Metz, Jürgen Moltmann, and Dorothee Sölle, it has been an effort to overcome a speculative and reflective modality for expressing faith with an activistic one.[4] Its practitioners seek to counteract the relegation of faith to the private individualized sphere (where, it is felt, both social individualism and existentialistic philosophy have pushed it) and to work out what faith means in terms of action (or, using the "in" word, in terms of *praxis*.) But, alas, political theology is also—to the extent it is a mode of theological reflection—analytical and conceptual rather than operational.

Even so, political theologies take the model of Exodus seriously, particularly that aspect of the model that portrays the divine reality in acting rather than in being. The ethics of such a perspective are the ethics of a particular agenda or event rather than those of reflection and analysis.

The question posed earlier intrudes again, "By what considerations is the liberation warranted, and even more pointedly, the liberation of this particular group of people?" There is a little ditty that runs:

How odd, of God,
to choose, the Jews.

That ditty forces the issue. What grounds are there for choosing this particular group? Exodus is about a specific historical choice of a special and identifiable group behind which the whole power of transcendence is placed to accomplish a special result. Can this be warranted, and if so, on what grounds?

Kant's categorical imperative, which is the foundation of much contemporary ethical reflection, admonishes us: "So act that you might wish your action to be universal." Would that be a sufficient impetus to warrant an Exodus or to prompt the search of an oppressed group for liberation? Slaves and servants often feel an obligation to be obedient to their masters. There is something in all of us that may well resist the idea that breaking away from fiduciary responsibilities should be a universal impulse, even if those responsibilities involve elements of oppression. Greek philosophical rationalism probably could never have warranted an Exodus (just as overly rationalistic concepts of justice in our day can't legitimize programs of affirmative action). Liberation occurs when a special dynamic—a particularity of impulse—says, "In the name of God this condition of oppression has got to be broken. Never mind what kind of possible precedent it sets!"

This problem arises whenever the claims of particularity are pitted against those of universality. Is any group that is disadvantaged by the economic/political realities of a cultural setting entitled to be singled out for special action? How oppressed must a group be to warrant an Exodus? It is no accident that, as we have suggested, African American songs in pre–Civil War America were built on Exodus imagery, not on a rationalistic concept of impartial justice. Similarly, it is no accident that the rationalism of the Enlightenment, which stresses the importance of the universal over the claim of the particularistic, symbolizes justice by the blindfolded lady holding a pair of scales—an image carved on the front of many a courthouse. A blindfolded lady won't see the condition of the oppressed, but will only judge between the claims of the articulate ones who make their cases in a court.[5] Many events in human history, as well as the deepest struggles we observe in our time, are to some extent caught in the tension between these two ways of understanding what it means to be concerned about justice, between attempts to weigh conflicting claims impartially and the impulse to break unjust oppression wherever it is found.

Certainly we need to realize that the pharaohs of history don't voluntarily release their captive brickmakers out of some sudden enlightenment about the claims of justice. Despite all the heritage of Britain and its strong profession of democratic principles (which clearly made its professed ideals morally superior to those of any pharaoh), it granted India independence only when Gandhi forced the issue. Despite all the ideals of equality given lip service in the America civic heritage, strides toward freedom of the black people did not begin until an oppressed lady refused to give up her seat to a white man or to sit in the back of a bus. Then her identity group rallied behind her.

A liberating event is more apt to be instigated through the dynamics of historical impulse than in response to the logic of principled ideals. When the time ripens, movements take off both from their inner drive and the legitimation that they are given by some historical warrant. An Exodus is more likely to emerge because a Moses is shocked to see a kinsman beaten (2:11–14) than because he has taken a course that deals with various theories of justice.

Finally, the relationship between God and the people is not conditional on the achievements of the group to be liberated. The choice of the group does not follow some period of apprenticeship in fidelity, some testing of the worth or capacities of the oppressed group for religious commitment or moral achievement. God deals with all the members of the oppressed group much as does, for instance, a fire department or a rescue squad with the victims of a calamity. (It is not standard operating procedure for rescue forces to run back to the school principal and ask for the scholastic records of the people involved in a calamity in order to decide which of several injured individuals should be rescued first, or seek out the scoutmaster to see which of those who need attention once earned the greatest number of merit badges.) The very condition of being victimized creates an unconditionality of claim. Moreover, all members of the needy group are considered eligible for the benefits—no distinctions are made between different persons in the group, except perhaps in terms of their need for attention. Standing in the oppressed group is enough to legitimize the claim; being severely hurt warrants immediate attention.

This may seriously erode the usual assumption that the reason for having a morality is to provide the criteria by which the worthy are distinguished from the unworthy so that just rewards can be meted out according to merit. Religions often get to the stage where they do exactly that, but the *fons et origo* of Israel's life (and we will, by extension, also come to include the New Israel as committed to the same dynamic) is an experience where such distinctions within the oppressed group are simply unknown. To be a Hebrew is to be within the orbit of liberation's benefits. To be oppressed or needy is enough to warrant God's concern and to warrant inclusion in the group that is destined to be the beneficiary of freedom and release.

2

Genesis History

Exodus in the Context of Historical Reflection

A momentous event like the liberation of the Hebrews from Egypt prompts reflections—reflections that look for historical precedents in the context of which the momentous event can be understood, that push toward a discovery of deeper meanings in the event, and that eventually articulate more adequately the nature and purpose of human experience in the larger sense. Just as Alex Haley, almost a century after the slavery of his people officially ended, went in search of his roots and by doing so shed new light on the experience of both slavery and emancipation, so the Hebrews may be thought of as searching for their roots as the events of the Exodus opened for them possibilities of being a people with a new destiny. The search for origins is part of any drama, a reflective part that serves as a lens through which meaning is perceived, not only by those for whom the momentous event is an experience but also for those for whom it has become a heritage.

Chapters 12 to 50 of the Book of Genesis constitute a body of material that suggests how early Israel understood its past in relation to the events it was experiencing in its present (i.e., the time of the Exodus). These chapters give us a clue to the substance of an oral tradition (or traditions) that may well have been present during the working out of Israel's liberation but came to be written down only much later. Various stories in the oral tradition were woven into the narrative as it now appears in Genesis—but even the process of redaction is complex. Most scholars find the hand of three editors evident in the material, each of whom had a particular perspective on the events in question. The earliest of these editors, whom scholars called the Yahwist, provided the main framework for the patriarchal narratives (or "prehistory" of Israel), starting with the stories of Abram/ Abraham, Isaac, and Jacob (Genesis 12–35 and 48–49). A second editor, working some two centuries later, whom scholars call the Elohist, provided additional materials that are scattered throughout the Yahwist's framework but stand alone in a coherent body of material that constitutes chapters 20–22. A still later writer, whom scholars call the priestly writer, added some chronological and genealogical materials. The remainder of the Book of Genesis (chapters 37–48), also put together by the Yahwist and the Elohist, consists of stories about Joseph.[1]

This material gives possible clues to why Israel should have been chosen for release from Egyptian bondage by tracing the relationship between God and the Hebrews back to the situation before they were caught in bondage. Thus it sheds some light on the phenomenon of prevenience, as discussed in the previous chapter—suggesting that the choice of Israel was not merely arbitrary. This material also contains interpretations of what it means to respond faithfully to God in ways that have intrigued subsequent thinkers down to the present. In the first century, Saint Paul went to the story of Abraham in order to conceptualize the meaning of Christianity in terms that opened it to a wide range of potential converts; in the nineteenth century Søren Kierkegaard used the account of Abraham and Isaac to write a powerful and possibly disturbing exploration into the relationship between religious faith and moral obedience. Today, women theologians are finding that accounts of women's lives in this portion of the Bible—such as those of Sarah, Hagar, and Tamar—yield fruitful new insights concerning the meaning of fidelity to God. Although some of the uses to which this material has subsequently been put may extrapolate beyond the drama as experienced and understood by the Hebrews, these explorations are legitimate parts of biblical interpretation utilized as a source of theological understanding. Nor has the mining of these narratives for theological and moral meaning necessarily come to an end.

Paul D. Hanson has suggested that the early narratives of Israel's history are a probable source of the important realization that the predicament of the Hebrews in Egypt was a contradiction of the very destiny that had been promised to the Hebrews in the covenant made with Abraham. As Hanson observes,

> While the deliverance from Egypt was the revelatory event though which early Israel grasped the most distinctive aspects of her faith, the ancestral narratives of Genesis, interpreted within the larger sociopolitical matrix of the village and pastoral tribalism of the second millennium, help us to recognize the alternative view of reality

that maintained in the Hebrew slaves in Egypt an openness to a divine act of deliverance.[2]

According to Hanson, one of the powerful elements in the maintenance of the realization that their present plight was not their intended destiny was the fact that the God who was worshiped by the Hebrews was not a member of the Egyptian pantheon and could not therefore be controlled by the gods of their taskmasters.

This provides a profoundly theological dimension to the warrant for liberation. The Hebrews gained their freedom, not merely because they were oppressed, but because they were loyal to a deity that could not be controlled by the oppressors. Hence, liberation had a theological and not merely a sociopolitical warrant. The Hebrews were destined to escape enslavement, not merely because slavery as such was looked upon as a social wrong (as we today would probably assume) but because the slavery of this particular group contradicted divine promises made to the forebears. Indeed, the Hebrew forebears whose lives are recounted in the Genesis narratives themselves held slaves, so the import of these accounts is not so much a moral condemnation of a particular social institution as a theological promise to a particular group.

The patriarchal portion of the Genesis narrative opens with a passage giving striking instructions and offering mind-boggling predictions. Abram is to leave Haran, the place where he has settled, and go to an unknown land. Although remarkably old, he is also told that he will be the progenitor of a great nation, and that both he and the nation will be blessed with good fortune (12:1–3). The migration of Abram in response to this promise involves a departure from familiar territory. In this account an enormous promise is found coupled with a demand to take an enormous risk. We should not read this account casually. It is not easy for well-established householders like Abram (even if they are relatively pious) to give up all their ties to a particular location and all the amenities and securities they have created in that location and to take off into parts unknown—trusting only in a divine promise.

We cannot tell for sure whether this story was told in its present form to the Hebrews in Egypt who were facing the coming Exodus. Perhaps it was, and if so, perhaps it was significant in helping them face the prospects of moving to a new land. Although Abram is asked to give up a land in which he is established, the Hebrews in Egypt are asked to leave a situation in which they are oppressed. In both cases the future has to be ventured into with faith, trusting almost entirely in God. In both cases promise and risk are inseparably joined. Those in Egypt may well be given courage to make the leap to freedom by hearing the story of Abram, who made a leap to a new land under conditions that offered less reason to leave than the reasons the Hebrews have for seeking escape from bondage.

There are vignettes in the chapters that follow in which God provides Abram with further nudgings and further promises. He goes to Egypt temporarily to escape a famine. He makes a false inference about the identity of his wife, Sarai, in order to gain entrance into the pharaoh's house (12:10–17), although when the ruse is discovered he is sent away from Egypt. Later, he is assured that, though old, he can be the father of many offspring (15:4). At first Abram's wife bears him no children but instead arranges for Hagar, her Egyptian maid, to be the surrogate (16:3f.). These stories affirm that God moves to fulfill his promise through people who act in various ways—not necessarily in ways that in all instances would be considered morally proper.

Finally, God made a covenant with Abram. This was considered so momentous it was tied to a name change (17:5). With that name change came a new and everlasting promise that God would always accompany Abraham in his journeys. This promise was cemented in a covenant, which was accompanied by the institution of circumcision for male members of the tribe (whether born within it or adopted by it) (17:11–14). The making of this covenant was immediately followed by the prediction that Abraham would have a son by his wife Sarah (Sarai's new name). Moreover, Abraham was told that the land of his present sojournings would eventually be inherited by his descendants. Each of these promises has momentous potential significance; each raises a set of moral issues.

These chapters of Genesis provide a possible explanation of why Israel can legitimately think of herself as destined to inherit Canaan as a promised land. The story of Abraham indicates that the forebears of the Hebrews once lived in the land of Canaan, indeed even possessed the land. When the Hebrews left Egypt in the Exodus to move to the promised land, they were, in a certain sense, returning home. Although Abram had left Canaan voluntarily, seeming thereby to have relinquished a claim on the land, the movement of his descendants from Egyptian slavery to the land of Canaan was not an entrance into entirely new territory. To be sure, so many years had elapsed between the time of Abraham and the time of the Exodus that the sense of ownership undoubtedly has shifted—perhaps several times. But that does not cancel out the fact the Hebrews once called Canaan home even though their reentrance into it would undoubtedly be disruptive of life for those presently living there.

But establishing the claim to the new land by citing the presence of forebears does not necessarily eliminate the moral problems. In order to leave Egypt, the Hebrews have to enter a land they do not presently own. To do this, they must either displace other people or at least intrude on territory that had come to be more or less legitimately occupied by others. The Exodus model was used in colonial times by the English Puritans as a way to think about their pilgrimage to the New World. Religiously oppressed in England, they interpreted their trek across the Atlantic as something analogous to the trek of the Hebrews across the Red Sea. This also involved entering land that they did not own, and in this case there was no corresponding presence of their forebears in the New World. The Puritans made what later developed into the idea of Manifest Destiny into a legitimation for the occupation of a land with which there was no possible prior connection through their forebears. That land clearly belonged to others, and some of America's problems as a nation have stemmed from the way this sense of particularized chosenness was used to legitimize the subjugation of a population native to the New World.

Indeed, contemporary Native Americans, confined in squalor to reservations that were carved out for them among the least promising geography of the New World, possibly can claim that their situation is more nearly similar to that of the Hebrews than was that of the Puritans. Suppose the descendants of some American Indian tribes were to come to the many places in America that were once owned by their forebears and displace the people who now live there on the grounds that the land is historically theirs. The consequent disruption would be enormous. The claim of Israel on Canaan raises—from a perspective looking at these matters from outside the commitment circle of the biblical "in-group"—a scandal of particularity. If particularity warrants special claims that are immune from scrutiny according to universally acceptable measures of justice, the very nature of human relationships will be fundamentally different than if there are grounds by which all claims can be adjudicated within a larger context of decision. When the justice of redress (which is not at all difficult to legitimize as a ground for breaking the bonds of injustice) is shifted to the idea of specially destined benefits, the problem becomes inescapable. Whenever a group that God chooses (or one that believes God has chosen it) feels that it does not have to answer to anybody else because its claim rests on a special destiny that cannot be tested in the arena of public debate (i.e., universal discourse), it is bound to raise problems. Of course, the group can point out that no claim can really be tested in this way because what is asserted to be a public arena of discourse is simply the rationalized preeminence of the prevailing oppressive system taken as normative. That argument can legitimize its action to itself, but it cannot make it credible to others. It is necessary to be cautious about using a situation of oppression as a warrant for making unrestricted claims against all other groups.

The problem inherent in the scandal of particularity would be further complicated if the claims of two or more special groups came into conflict with one another. Suppose that another group—equally thinking of itself as chosen by God and equally entitled to escape servitude and oppression—had simultaneously marched toward the promised land of Canaan? We don't have that problem posed by the biblical story—but it isn't clear that such a problem can't arise when more than one group reads the biblical story as a warrant for pursuing its own version of Exodus to buttress a claim for its own relief from oppression. One of the really difficult problems confronting all liberation theologies today is to mesh the plausible particularity of their claim to the righting of some wrong into some harmony with the claims of others who also feel that their oppression warrants some special treatment. Because it doesn't explicitly address this issue, the biblical narrative at this point is not profoundly helpful in dealing with this kind of moral quandary—but, alas, this issue cannot be indefinitely ignored.

When the covenant is made between God and Abraham, it is accompanied with the promise that Abraham will become the forebear of a great nation. Although an old man, he is promised an heir through Sarah. This promise is so momentous in its implication that both Abraham and Sarah greet its prediction with derision, though Sarah later denies having reacted in that way (18:15). But a son, Isaac, is born and is circumcised according to a newly commanded ritual (21:1–4). Isaac is chosen to become the progenitor of Abraham's descendants in place of the son born to Abraham through Hagar as a surrogate.

The son that is born to Abraham and Sarah figures in one of the most traumatic stories in the Old Testament—a story that has intrigued many interpreters in different ways. According to the story, Abraham is ordered by God to take his son Isaac into the land of Moriah and offer him there as a burnt offering (22:1–18). As a purely sociological exercise in etiology this story can be read as an explanation of how animal sacrifice replaced human sacrifice in Hebrew cult practice. But in a book, *Fear and Trembling*, the nineteenth-century Danish theologian Søren Kierkegaard pushed the theological implications to far more radical implications. Kierkegaard's treatment of the story escalates the risk associated with obedience to God to an almost unlimited degree. Nothing is to be held back, not even the very son most cherished and already destined to become the channel of God's promises. Nothing is to be secondary to obedience, not even the claims of morality. Kierkegaard spoke of this as requiring an "infinite resignation" involving a "teleological suspension of the ethical." Speaking of those who use the story to show that God is ultimately merciful and does not require the sacrifice (which would undoubtedly include those who interpret the myth as an explanation for the substitution of animal for human sacrifices) Kierkegaard has this blistering observation: "If people fancy that by considering the outcome of this story they might let themselves be moved to believe, they deceive themselves and want to swindle God out of the first movement of faith, the infinite resignation."[3]

When Kierkegaard lived, one of the most prevalent intellectual trends was represented by Hegelian philosophy. Hegel sought to create a system of universality grounded in morality and reason. Kierkegaard was fighting this system, and his book *Fear and Trembling* was one of the treatises by which he did so. The story of Abraham's possible sacrifice (and Kierkegaard's musing about its meaning) still invite reflections on the complex relationship between religious faith and moral integrity.

In some situations the insight of Kierkegaard illumines an issue profoundly. At times, a staunch allegiance to moral norms may very well block a more promising historical accomplishment, even an accomplishment in which God seeks to do some momentous work. Had the Hebrew midwives, for instance, insisted that civil disobedience is morally unacceptable, they would not have prepared the way for their people to escape oppression. Had the Hebrews been convinced that it is unexceptionably required of slaves to be faithful to their master's commands, there would have been no Exodus. At times it is necessary to "teleologically suspend the ethical" in order to be profoundly obedient to God. In our day it might just be that we must suspend what are asserted to be invariable standards about lifestyles in order to be open to a liberation that God is working out for an oppressed group in our very midst.

But if faithfulness involves a risk that even moral expectations may need to be bracketed, how can we be sure it will not lead to incredible and bizarre consequences? If morality is to be suspended for reasons of devoted commitment to some new work of God, how are we to avoid a use of faith to legitimate destructive actions? In February of 1994 a religious zealot broke into a Muslim mosque in the city of Hebron on the West Bank and opened fire on worshipers at prayer. He may have remembered that in 1929 Arab riots took nearly seventy Jewish lives at that same location, but merely citing that hardly eliminates the moral problem. Today there are growing instances of religious behavior that is all too prone to suspend normal ethical expectations in the dynamics of being obedient to fanatically espoused causes or to cult leaders who are followed with infinite resignation. Kierkegaard would probably not regard such behavior as an expression of infinite resignation, since a human cause or a human leader rather than the divine ultimate makes the claim for obedience. But such distinctions may not be easy to sustain in practice. Any form of religiosity that deliberately puts morality aside in order to demonstrate its total (unconditional) character is potentially dangerous and most certainly must be questioned. Religiously inspired extremism is a form of behavior in which there is something of a "teleological suspension of the ethical."

How do we know when such a suspension of moral standards is legitimate and when it is not, when it is commendable in the Kierkegaardian sense and when it is dangerous and destructive beyond all measures of civil responsibility? Any society, whether a family, a nation, or even an international order, seeking to be faithful to the highest vision of what is good, cannot automatically accept appeal to religion as a blanket and unassailable defense for actions that have momentous destructive consequences for either the self or for others. A biblically grounded moral sensitivity may provide clues that help sort out these vexing issues, for thinking about how to determine the difference between a suspension of the normally ethical that deserves to be honored and such a suspension that is an abomination. But this insight will never be so clearly offered as to bypass entirely all the complex risks involved. We hazard ethical decisions by faith and do not make them by infallible guidelines.

Meanwhile, we are required, not only to hear from Kierkegaard on this story, but from those for whom it conveys entirely different meanings. Ellen Umansky has retold the story of Genesis 22 from a woman's perspective. She recounts Sarah's anguish when, upon awakening in the morning, she finds both Abraham and Isaac gone. This highly unusual event fills Sarah with dismay, and she waits and then screams. Finally, she sees them return, and senses what has happened even without an explanation from Abraham. Indeed she refuses to let Abraham offer an explanation, which (according to Umansky) would probably only have involved assumptions crucial to male domination. Umansky prefers to interpret the return of Isaac as the preservation of that by which Sarah's covenant with God had been sealed. Commenting on this story, Umansky writes,

> Sarah's belief, which I experienced as my own, offers me another
> way of looking at the *Akedah* (the story of the binding of Isaac). As I
> retell my vision, I become more and more convinced that the *Akedah*
> as contained in the Bible is only half of the story. Perhaps Abraham
> did believe that it was his responsibility, as a man of faith, to do what-
> ever he felt God commanded. But the vision I received from Sarah is
> that God does not take back his gifts and that perhaps those who
> hear such commandments should question whether they have heard
> him correctly.[4]

How can we know whether or not we ever hear God correctly? How
do we know whether Kierkegaard's reading of the story is valuable as
productive of a faithful capacity to lay aside moralistic hang-ups (including
some that are woven into the very fabric of androcentrism) in order to
move faithfully in new and divinely mandated ways, or Umansky's reading
of the story is a necessary safeguard against the very fanaticism that too
often does so much to render religion dangerous? It may not be given us,
particularly as individuals, ever to know with certainty what is morally the
most faithful stance. If there is a meaningful set of insights on this, it will
probably be found in the context of a community that realizes and articu-
lates the depths of this problem and seeks to make responses of faith that
eschew fanatical certainty in offering answers to it.

Moral actors at times have to wrestle seriously with a tension between
the requirements of conventional moral rules and the requirements of
human justice and compassion. Another story in the historical section of
Genesis highlights this kind of wrestling with poignant intensity. The conventional moral standards of the time called for women caught in harlotry
to be put to death, either by stoning or burning. This was a provision for
enforcing the moral standards of the time. But in the story of Tamar in
Genesis 38 we find this standard scrutinized in a shattering way. Judah,
Tamar's father-in-law, is told that Tamar appears to be a harlot. He says, not
yet knowing the full context of Tamar's story, "Bring her out and let her be
burned" (38:24b). But when Judah learns that Tamar's rights had been
denied to her by his own sons and when she demonstrates by exhibiting a
signet ring, cord, and staff belonging to Judah that Judah himself is unwit-
tingly the father of the foetus, he repents and declares, "She is more righteous than I, in as much as I did not give her to my son Shelah" (38:26). In
commenting on this story, suggesting that it explores the relationship between law and grace in ways that are similar to later New Testament stories
and even the writings of Augustine, Paul Hanson observes, "It would be

too much to say that all God's teaching on the relation between law and grace was completed within the Hebrew Bible. But it would be an act of insensitivity and ingratitude to our Jewish heritage to miss the deep roots · of that teaching in Hebrew scripture."[5]

We have been contending that any reading of Scripture involves some selectivity, and that such selectivity is often guided by the life situation of the reader. An interesting illustration of how this works out in specific terms is present in some recent commentary on the significance of the sections of Genesis dealing with Hagar (16:1–15 and 21:8–21). As she worked with these texts Dolores S. Williams came to realize that the story of Hagar is often cited in African American thinking about the Bible. She came to feel that this was the case because Hagar's experience as a slave almost directly parallels that of African American women under slavery and consequently provides great insight by analogy to the experience of African American women, both during slavery and after it had been legally abolished.

In a fascinating and detailed exegesis of the materials in Genesis that deal with the Hagar story, Williams shows how the treatment of Hagar in her times, governed in large measure by the patriarchal customs and laws of her world, forced Hagar to be a surrogate mother for Abram's first child, yet also permitted Abram to concede to Sarai's demand that the child be disowned once Sarah had become the mother of Isaac.

> The African-American community has taken Hagar's story unto itself. Hagar has "spoken" to generation after generation of black women because her story has been validated as true by suffering black people. She and Ishmael together, as family, model many black American families in which a lone woman/mother struggles to hold the family together in spite of the poverty to which ruling class economics assign it. Hagar, like many black women, goes into the wide world to make a living for herself and her child, with only God by her side.[6]

Although the story of Hagar is mentioned in commentaries that treat the Bible in an integral manner on a verse-to-verse basis, it is instructive to examine how infrequently the story of Hagar (and Ishmael) has been treated in scholarly overviews of the Old Testament written by men. In such overviews materials can be presumed to be selected according to the importance attached to them. Neither Hagar nor Ishmael are mentioned in at least three books that overview the Old Testament, including two that are particularly concerned with ethical issues.[7] In two others these figures are mentioned in passing but not examined as important symbols.[8] In still another work, more extensive references are made to the accounts of Hagar and Ishmael, but mainly in exploring the documentary sources in Genesis rather than as symbols of theological/ethical significance.[9] These observations are not meant to discredit the use of biblical stories by any of the authors in question, but rather to show how much the social location of writers affects their judgment concerning the importance of this or that part of the Bible.

The remaining part of Genesis history that calls forth our attention involves the stories about Jacob and his family. These stories complete the background account of the Hebrews' plight in Egypt, yet they also suggest that the purposes of God in history are carried out even by persons whose moral character is not necessarily exemplary and whose interactions are not necessarily most desirable. To Americans, raised on stories about their forefathers, like that of George Washington and the cherry tree—stories designed to portray a level of moral integrity far beyond that of normal expectations—the stories of Jacob and Joseph can be shocking.

In the story of Jacob and Esau, two sons of Isaac who are forever at odds, we have a series of morally troublesome episodes. In Genesis 25:29–30 we are told that Esau willingly sells his birthright, that is, the privilege that attends being the firstborn son. The birthright passes to Jacob, who grasps it for all it can mean to him, and who tricks Isaac into bestowing on him the blessing that custom and morality reserve for Esau (27:19). In this instance, instead of suspending the specificity of the legal requirement which, as we have seen, had been done in other accounts, Isaac appeals to the binding letter of the law as the reason for not correcting his error. This story is apparently intended by the writer to account for Israel's triumph over the Edomites, since Jacob is the progenitor of the former and Esau the progenitor of the latter, and is used to introduce a series of accounts concerning Jacob's sojourn in Haran. This venture results in a period of prosperity that enables Jacob to acquire the wealth with which he proposes a reunion with Esau (33:1–17). Although these accounts do help to reinforce a presumption of Israel's claim to the promised land (as do the earlier Abraham stories), they hardly provide the material out of which a strong, morally grounded concept of international law might be conceived. They do not evaporate the scandal of particularity. Perhaps the writers sensed this, because in the story in which Jacob wrestles with the nocturnal visitor (an angel) and wins the blessing, he is left with a wound that seriously disables him without taking away his standing (33:24–31).

A major cycle of stories in Genesis concerns the figure of Jacob's son,

Joseph. The stories of Joseph and his brothers are an especially complex weaving together of several sources, which creates difficulties for those who are concerned with reading the materials for origins. Joseph is a talented sibling who is something of a special favorite of his father. This makes his older brothers jealous, and they seek to deal with Joseph first by threatening to kill him and finally by arranging to see that he is sent off to Egypt. There Joseph suffers a series of contrasting fortunes, ranging from successful service to the Egyptian official to whom his brothers sell him, to imprisonment for disloyalty that is falsely alleged against him by the wife of the official. Because his skills, which include the ability to interpret dreams, are considerable, Joseph manages to deal with both situations successfully for a considerable period of time. Although Joseph is subject to much malfeasance, he refuses to take vengeance on his brothers after Jacob dies (50:20).

These accounts do suggest the depths to which sibling rivalry can go, but also that God can make use of such rivalry to bring about a providential outcome. This saga, to which most scholars accord a reasonable degree of historical warrant, is used by the narrator both to provide an account of how the Hebrews found themselves in Egypt and to suggest the role of divine providence in the life of the Hebrews. According to Walter Harrelson, "the narrator wished particularly to account for the fact that Israel had settled in Egypt, had first prospered greatly, but then had been subjected to a severe test of faith by Yahweh in order to make this people disciplined for the coming task: entrance in the Land of Promise, establishment as a faithful convent people through whom all the families of the earth would be blessed."[10]

The disciplined testing to which Harrelson refers suggests that a blessing from God does not result in an immediate prosperity that comes from a happy grasping of a special benefit. As the narrative moves from Genesis to the first chapter of Exodus, we are told that the temporal destiny of the Hebrews changes when a new king comes to power, a king fearful of the multiplying presence of the Hebrews and the status that Joseph has managed, for a time at least, to secure for them. This leads to the oppression that creates the occasion for the Exodus. The Exodus, in turn, is the beginning of a new and complex continuation of the biblical narrative in which freedom leads to obligation, liberation is followed by covenant, and faithfulness involves acceptance of moral responsibility.

3

Exodus and Sinai

Liberation and Moral Obligation

The biblical drama begins with liberation but quickly comes to involve moral obligation. The juxtapositioning of promise and risk that is evident in the stories of the patriarchs becomes a juxtapositioning of freedom and obligation in the accounts of the making of the Mosaic covenant and the giving of the Law at Sinai. This means that the experience of liberation quickly shifts from an orientation focused on escape and freedom to one that entails dutiful response. The part of Exodus that recounts the giving of the Ten Commandments and other laws by which Israel is to govern its life becomes an essential complement to the part of the book giving the story of the escape from Egypt.

Whereas while they were slaves in Egypt the Hebrews had to do things because they were afraid of the punishment that would follow if they failed to perform the tasks demanded of them, in the relationship that grew out of the Exodus they come to ask what they should be doing to celebrate the new relationship that has changed their lives. Instead of the hostile authority represented by the Egyptian taskmasters, which rendered the experience of obligation oppressive, the mighty acts that God has performed for the people lead naturally to a welcome response in which obligation is associated with appreciation. Such a context engenders the joyous doing of what is appropriate out of gratitude for a blessing that has already been bestowed rather than a fearful doing of what is required out of a necessity to head off retribution.

This creates, to employ terminology that is frequently invoked in theological ethics, an ethic in the indicative rather than the imperative mode. In the imperative mode the ethical requirement is set forth as a requirement, and one's standing or status is made conditional on meeting the requirement. The action of God in bringing the Hebrews out of Egypt might have been portrayed in the imperative mode. Had that been the case the story might have been written differently. God would have sent Moses to the group in Egypt with a message like this:

> I see your plight and am sympathetic to your cause. But I need to know you are capable of meeting the conditions for being true followers. Here are some requirements I expect you to abide by for a probationary period. Moses will keep accurate records of your achievements and report to me how well you do. If you are faithful for the period of the test, if you show the requisite resolve, prove capable of the quality of life I want those who bear my name to exhibit, and otherwise live up to these expectations, then I will come back and arrange to get you out of Egypt.

In contrast to that imperative scenario, in the indicative mode the experiences of liberation and acceptance are initial, and the ethical requirement is subsequential. Moral response is a means of expressing gratitude for a relationship or experience that is already operative. Acceptance of moral law can even become a means of celebrating a relationship gratefully acknowledged. That desire for celebration is no less valid (and surely as powerful) as a motivation for acting morally as are threats mounted by oppressive rulers or conditions set up as requirements for obtaining benefits.

This difference between the imperative and indicative ways of viewing moral obligation might be recast for illustrative purposes into contemporary terms by contrasting how two imaginary sets of parents send a child off to college. One set of parents sets out a whole series of do's and don'ts and makes it very clear that their support will be forthcoming only if the obligations are followed. The other says, "You have been in this household all your life. We want you to act now that you are on your own so that we will always be proud to say that you are ours. You are going to be free— only use your freedom as a means of celebrating the relationship that is already 'indicated' as having been established between us." (Or, to put the matter differently, in the imperative mode the operative assumption is "We will be your parents if . . .," whereas in the indicative mode, it becomes "We are your parents, therefore . . .")

If we look at the giving of the Ten Commandments in the Exodus account we find that they are set forth in the context of "I am your God, therefore . . ." Morality enters as an opportunity for gracious response, not as the obligatory precondition of being accepted. (Actually the very same set of Ten Commandments introduced in Exodus 20 with an indicative framework is repeated later in Deuteronomy 5 with a somewhat more imperative context. In Deuteronomy the verses that surround the Ten Commandments talk about obeying them "that your days may be long in the land which God gives you," and even "that you may live." That reintroduces imperative conditionality into the equation and dilutes the indicative premise.)[1]

Imperative and indicative moralities may consist of the same specific indications of what is proper behavior, although indicative moralities tend to be suggestive about the requirements of faithful behavior under the conditions of newly achieved freedom, whereas imperative moralities tend to become rigidly prescriptive about moral obligations so that rewards can be had from following them precisely. If the destiny of the faithful is already assured by release and liberation, people can rejoice in the guidance offered by morality without having to be bound to every jot and tittle of the requirements. However, if the destiny of the faithful is dependent on conformity to what is expected, then it becomes extremely crucial to have the Law spelled out just right and to obey it without deviation or equivocation.

The Ten Commandments have as much to do with describing the quality of obedient gratitude and response as they do with putting down ethical principles that are universally valid on independent grounds. They do not warrant the premise that it is possible to make a clear and neat separation of religious devotion from moral intentionality. The Ten Commandments give no comfort to the premise that it is possible to agree upon morality without regard to so-called "overbeliefs."

For example, the Ten Commandments make the avoidance of idolatry equal in importance to not stealing. Morality and fidelity are inevitably bound together. Thus the whole ethical enterprise is made far richer and broader than it could ever be on the basis of moral prohibitions alone. One can be idolatrous—that is, be guilty of giving a first loyalty to something other than God—without ever being immoral in the narrow sense of breaking some ethical code. The story of the rich young ruler in the New Testament, for instance, is not an account of someone who has done some serious moral wrongs—as did, for instance, the wicked servant—but it is an account of someone who has let secondary concerns get primary—or ultimate—attention (which is the gist of idolatry). According to the Ten Commandments misplaced allegiance is as dangerous as deliberate malfeasance; failure to maintain covenantal relationships is as serious as the breaking of some specific rule of conduct.

In popular piety (as found in civic religion, for example) it is not uncommon for people to suggest that while they do not wish to be bound by religious dogmas, they are quite willing to acknowledge the claims of morality. They may even profess to acknowledge the importance of the Ten Commandments as foundational parts of a public morality. Such thinking explains, for instance, why some people believe that the Ten Commandments can be posted on the walls of public school classrooms without in the least breaching the wall of separation between church and state. Such thinking has little warrant in light of the Ten Commandments themselves, for in the Ten Commandments matters of belief in God and singular loyalty to the ultimate are given the same weight as matters of moral behavior.

Moreover, by understanding the Ten Commandments as responses to a mighty liberation already enacted, it is possible to take them seriously as moral guides without making them absolute injunctions. Actually, the Bible contains more than one set of ten rules that accompany the making of the covenant between God and the people. A decalogue in Exodus 34, for example, has to do with dietary and ceremonial requirements—the foundational premises of Jewish ritual law. Christians ceased to feel bound by those, largely because in the first century it was decided that Christians are not obligated to obey all the Laws of Moses (see Acts 15). Instead, Paul, who helped to obtain this decision, held that the members of the new Christian community were bound only by the ethical laws of Moses. That kind of decision would have been less possible had the decalogues been viewed as rules for ensuring fidelity rather than as the outgrowths and the celebration of a liberating redemption. However, it hardly behooves Christians to think their religion is somehow superior because it stresses moral obligations rather than cultic practices. Religions that include ceremonial obligations as part of their self-definition often have a richness in their common life that simply isn't present in religions that define themselves merely by correct doctrinal beliefs or proper moral requirements. While most of us are grateful that Christians are not obligated to follow the ritualistic set of ten commandments, we might well ask ourselves if our corporate life wouldn't be richer if we were.

Following very closely the commandments as set forth in chapter 20 of the Book of Exodus come a series of specific admonitions that appear in a quite different form. These admonitions are frequently called "the ordinances" and are portrayed in the account as having been bequeathed to Israel in much the same way as the Commandments were bequeathed. These constitute what is often called the Book of the Covenant, or Covenant Code—running from Exodus 20:23 to 23:19. The provisions in this material are much more detailed, culture specific, and hypothetical than those in the Ten Commandments.

The material from Exodus21:1 to Exodus 22:16 has a clearly identifiable form, running "If . . . then . . ." [This is occasionally varied as "When . . . then . . ."] This is case law, consisting of a specific proscription followed by the specification of an appropriate retribution or punishment for any breech of that proscription. In many instances case law arises as a secondary development following the declaration of a general norm, and so it might seem natural to assume that the Covenant Code is an amplification of the Ten Commandments. However, according to many biblical scholars, the case law set forth in the Covenant Code was drawn largely from materials present in the cultures of Mesopotamia from the late third millennium B.C.E. on and actually appeared in Israel's life before the final redaction of the Decalogue. "The Book of the Covenant," observes Paul Hanson, "is a fascinating source for the study of community in early Israel because of its rough-hewn nature. Unlike the Decalogue, it has not been worked and reworked over the centuries so as to emerge as a polished jewel."[2]

While, to use Hanson's term, these laws have a "rough-hewn" quality, a number of the provisions constitute directions for governing a social order with a no-nonsense realism about how people behave and what is sometimes necessary in order to obtain their obedience to moral requirements. These laws might even be considered to represent something a bit closer to the imperative mode used for setting forth demands, thereby contrasting somewhat with the magnificent portrayal of the indicative in the giving of the Ten Commandments. Nevertheless, the ordinances warrant attention, not only because they undoubtedly were considered important by the redactors of the biblical materials but because a good deal of contemporary Western law continues to embody many of their provisions.

The first part of this material (21:1–11) consists of instructions governing the treatment of slaves—including a provision for setting them free at the end of six years [academicians among us will be tempted to draw an analogy with the timing of sabbatical leaves for faculty members]. It may be that the Hebrews introduced an element of compassion into the codes that were found in the other cultures—thereby affording some degree of humanization into the slave system as practiced by the Hebrews in contrast to how it was carried on by other groups.[3]

Moving to verse 12, we read an ordinance governing the matter of taking life. Remember the commandment merely says: "You shall not kill!" But the ordinance says: "Whoever strikes a person mortally shall be put to death. But if it was not premeditated, but came about by an act of God, then I will appoint for you a place to which the killer may flee. But if someone willfully attacks another and kills another by treachery, you shall take the killer from my altar for execution." This ordinance clearly draws a distinction between premeditated murder and involuntary manslaughter—and even today these are considered different levels of offense.

Verse 16 provides that "Whoever kidnaps a person, whether that person has been sold or is still held in possession, shall be put to death." In some jurisdictions that is still the law. The so-called Lindbergh Law makes kidnapping punishable by death.

The commandment says "Honor your father and your mother." But the ordinances—once in verse 15, another time in verse 17—say, "Whoever strikes father or mother shall be put to death," and "Whoever curses father or mother shall be put to death." Most people will have no problem thinking of the commandment as representing the better wisdom here. There is probably no jurisdiction in the world today, including those composed of people who believe themselves to be strictly governed by biblical imperatives, that would apply this ordinance literally. Even those who currently advocate the death penalty for capital crimes do not propose it as a punishment for childhood rebellion.

Sometimes the provisions for penalties in these case laws work, not to intensify or to heighten the sanctions, but to hold them within bounds. Several of the ordinances limit the revenge that can be extracted for torts (injuries done by one person to another). For instance, verse 18 says "When individuals quarrel and one strikes the other with a stone or fist so that the injured party, though not dead is confined to bed, but recovers and walks around outside with the help of a staff, then the assailant shall be free of liability, except to pay for the loss of time, and arrange for full recovery." And, similarly, verse 22 specifies, "When people who are fighting injure a pregnant woman so that there is a miscarriage, and yet no further harm follows, the one responsible shall be fined what the woman's husband demands; paying as the judges determine. If any harm follows, then you shall give life for life, eye for eye, tooth for tooth, hand for hand, foot for foot. burn for burn, wound for wound, stripe for stripe." This *lex talionis* restricts the usual desire to respond to injury by doing the attacker one better—to knock the other person's teeth out even if that person has only skinned your knuckles.

The various ordinances reflect an attempt to regulate social interaction by what in jurisprudence would be called the application of precedence and equity. There is a lot of experientially based common sense in them. For example, verses 28–32 deal with what to do if cattle get out and do mischief.

> When an ox gores a man or woman to death, the ox shall be stoned, and its flesh shall not be eaten; but the owner of the ox shall not be liable. If the ox has been accustomed to gore in the past, and its owner has been warned but has not restrained it, and it kills a man or a woman, the ox shall be stoned, and its owner also shall be put to death. If a ransom is laid on the owner then the owner shall pay whatever is imposed for the redemption of the victim's life. If it gores a boy or a girl, the owner shall be dealt with according to the same rule. If an ox gores a male or female slave, the owner shall give to the slave owner thirty shekels of silver, and the ox shall be stoned.

Except for the differentiated treatment afforded free persons and slaves, the general principle of liability enunciated in that passage is still very much a part of contemporary tort law.

Or, verse 33: "If someone leaves a pit open, or digs a pit and does not cover it, and an ox or a donkey falls into it, the owner of the pit shall make restitution; giving money to its owner but keeping the dead animal." The essential logic of that law still governs cases of this type today, which is why contractors put stanchions around excavations to keep people from falling in and to avoid liability suits.

Verse 22:2 says, "If a thief is found breaking in, and is beaten to death, no blood guilt is incurred; but if it happens after sunrise, bloodguilt is incurred." In the law today breaking and entering by daylight is a lesser offense than breaking and entering at night.

The idea of liability for wrong is expressed in other provisions of the Covenant Code. For example, verse 22:6 says, "When fire breaks out and catches in thorns so that the stacked grain or the standing grain or the field is consumed, the one that started the fire shall make full restitution."

The several provisions for dealing with breaches of trust are very interesting, and have about them a certain wholesome "realism" about the way people are apt to behave. Verses 7 and 8 provide this advice.

> When someone delivers to a neighbor money or goods for safekeeping, and they are stolen from the neighbor's house, then the thief, if caught, shall pay double. If the thief is not caught, the owner of the house shall be brought before God [that is, cast the sacred lots, called

Urim and Thummin], to show whether or not the owner had laid hands on the neighbor's goods.

Or verse 9:

> In any case of disputed ownership involving ox, donkey, sheep, clothing, or any other loss, of which one party says, 'This is mine,' the case of both parties shall come before God; he whom God condemns shall pay double to the other.

Verses 10–13:

> When someone delivers to another a donkey, ox, or any other animal for safekeeping, and it dies or is injured or is carried off, without anyone seeing it, an oath before the LORD shall decide between the two of them that the one has not laid hands on the property of the other; the owner shall accept the oath, and no restitution shall be made. But if it was stolen, restitution shall be made to its owner. If it was mangled by beasts, let it be brought as evidence; restitution shall not be made for the mangled remains.

Although it is no longer required that people determine their guilt or innocence by casting sacred lots, anyone who runs a lost-and-found realizes that those who inquire whether their property has been turned in must be asked to describe the property for which they are looking before they are allowed to see it. Although those who care for property are no longer required to swear oaths, they are required to post bonds to ensure they do not misappropriate that for which they are guardians.

In these many different ordinances we can see the same logic at work that we see operative in the development of common law—that is, the law that decides cases by considerations of equity (a common idea of what is just and appropriate in various cases of wrongdoing—even if there is no statutory rule dealing with a particular kind of problem). These ordinances were attributed to Moses to give them the sanction of special origin—but it stretches the credibility to believe Moses wrote down these provisions *de novo* in some sudden moment of inspiration.

Another body of material found within the ordinances is quite different from the case laws just examined. Paul Hanson calls this material, found in Exodus 20:22–26 and 22:17–23:19 *Yahwistic law*,[4] and contrasts it sharply with the more general case law that composes the other part of the Covenant Code. These laws appeal explicitly to the experience of the Exodus as their foundational reason for being. Within this material are found some instructions for appropriate worship of God, but of greater interest are the several provisions that "set forth patterns of behavior that constitute a quality of life in keeping with the nature of the God revealed in the [Hebrews'] own deliverance from slavery, a life of compassionate justice."[5] These laws admonish the people to remember their own bondage and subsequent wanderings and consequently to show special compassion for the poor, the stranger, widows, and orphans. The spirit of compassion governing this Yahwistic law prompts the admonition to return stray animals even to enemies (23:4) and to relieve animals of inordinate burdens (v. 5). Moreover, in a very explicit command that is honored far more in the breach than in fidelity even among those who profess to obey the Bible literally, the lending of money at interest is prohibited within the covenantal group (22:25). Because it cites God's liberation as a model for human behavior, this part of the Covenant Code is far nearer the Ten Commandments in its indicative thrust than is the case law.

Many of these laws, particularly those in the first group, suggest a process known as moral casuistry—that is, a way of dealing with specific cases in light of codified requirements that have to be rethought in order to render them fitting. This is a continual and controversial feature of religious morality. Many people think of casuistry as a quirk that reached its height under the Jesuits—who employed it in the confessional to legitimize actions that might upon first reflection seem to be almost immoral. But that is too simple. Casuistry is a perennial feature of moral reasoning. People constantly ask how the didactic provisions of codes and commandments are to be applied in a given set of circumstances. For example, the commandment calls for Sabbath rest. If somebody writes a term paper on the Sabbath, does that violate the commandment? (Some religions today would say it does; others would say it doesn't. This difference in the "if . . . then" is a difference in the casuistry of the two groups.) Should tithing be on gross income or on income after taxes? One can imagine both answers being offered by persons interpreting the meaning of the law.

Any effort to deal with questions like these involves casuistry, whether applied on an ordinary commonsense basis or with great learning. Nobody engages in casuistry unless the commandment is taken as obligatory—but there is always a danger that casuistry will dilute or contradict the intentions of the law.

Some technical terminology is valuable for understanding casuistry. The Jesuits developed a doctrine known as probabilism for advising Christians in the confessional. According to that doctrine, if the tradition has within it a strand of thought or precedent that would serve to make a possibly questionable procedure legitimate—it can be undertaken even if it seems morally shaky. Some of the authorities argued that a given course of action has to have as weighty a set of precedents for it as against it for it to be permissible—that position is known as equiprobabilism. Still others, critics of the Jesuits and their probabilism, argued that the action could be approved only if the weight of the case history favored it. Their position is known as probabiliorism.

It is easy to suppose that those who engage in such reasoning are guilty of moral equivocation. But before doing that it is well to ponder how often we too must deal with questions of conscience that the specific law or code does not directly answer. What, for instance, do we say to a person really troubled by whether or not it is lawful for a Christian to pay taxes to a state engaged in military activities? We might say, based on a reading of the history of the tradition, that it is probably legitimate to pay the taxes. We might also say, based on reading other parts of the tradition, that it is morally legitimate to refuse to pay the taxes (providing the refusal is open and aboveboard, not done by subterfuge).

Although the ordinances are not themselves casuistical treatments of the commandments, the differences between these two forms of moral injunction help us to reach a more sophisticated understanding of religiously grounded morality. It is well to have commandments, highly refined and authoritatively given statements of general norms; it is equally important to have ordinances, rough-hewn indications of how people seeking to be faithful deal with a host of complexities that confront them in ordinary experience. The comparison between these two forms of moral guidance also sheds light on the difference between authoritatively enunciated injunctions and experientially based admonitions. Both have a valid role to play in morality; it is well to know the difference and even more important not to confuse them.

The Book of Exodus is not merely concerned with moral law. Much of the book is given to setting forth a basic perspective on what is involved in the worship of God. The covenant is portrayed as involving ceremonial and ritual dimensions, not merely the didactic setting forth of moral obligations, and guidance is offered for continuing to observe the covenant with ceremonial reenactment.

The twelfth chapter of Exodus institutes the celebration of Passover, one of the important and richly observed ceremonies of the Jewish calendar. The twentieth chapter details how an altar of earth shall be used for offerings, but not an altar constructed of hewn stones or fashioned with tools. But, in contrast, the twenty-fifth chapter begins a long section of many detailed instructions for creating a place of, and paraphernalia for, worship. Such artifacts for worship could only be constructed by the extensive use of tools. Indeed, the detailed instructions for creating cultic practice, including a priesthood and all the accoutrements thereof, that occupy the section of Exodus through chapter 31 hardly confirm the view that moral earnestness and ritual observance are somehow at odds with each other. To the extent that religious ceremony recalls the mighty act of God in the liberation of the people and rehearses and reaffirms the covenant that attended that liberation, it has an important and legitimate role— a role that reinforces morality.

But religious ritual is no guarantee against corruption. The biblical record juxtaposes the giving of the tables of the law and the making of the golden calf as simultaneous events—even as Moses is on the mountain receiving the tables of the Law, the people are in the valley making substitute deities. The contrast between these two vignettes in the Book of Exodus suggests some profound truths about religious behavior.

The story of the making of the golden calf under the leadership of Aaron suggests that priesthood can mislead and rituals can corrupt just as much as they can appropriately celebrate covenant. The depth of this account is marvelous—as reading only a small part helps us to realize. After the calf has been made, Moses confronts Aaron, seeking to find out what had gone wrong. He asks:

> "What did this people do to you that you have brought so great a sin upon them?" And Aaron said, "Do not let the anger of my lord burn hot; you know the people, that they are bent on evil. They said to me, 'Make us gods, who shall go before us; as for this Moses, the man who brought us up out of the land of Egypt, we do not know what has become of him.' So I said to them, 'Whoever has gold, take it off'; so they gave it to me, and I threw it into the fire, and out came this calf." (32:21b–24)

The story suggests that something deeper than a mere violation of a proscription against making a graven image is entailed in this event. Ritual is resorted to as a substitute for the celebration of covenant and may even become an end in itself. When that happens ritual is an offense. That is no less a possibility today than it was in the time of the Exodus. As a means of celebrating something beyond itself, ritual is a legitimate means of expressing devotion. It may even keep alive the sense of covenant. But when it becomes a substitute for covenant, the resulting apostasy is disastrous.

Moreover, there is an instructive contrast between the way in which God finally deals with this apostasy and the way in which Moses deals with it.

When Moses hears of the event, he implores God and says:

O LORD, why does your wrath burn hot against your people, whom you have brought out of the land of Egypt with great power and with a mighty hand? Why should the Egyptians say, "It was with evil intent that he brought them out, to kill them in the mountains, and to consume them from the face of the earth"? Turn from your fierce wrath, change your mind and do not bring disaster on your people. Remember Abraham, Isaac, and Israel, your servants, how you swore to them by your own self, saying to them, "I will multiply your descendants as the stars of heaven, and all this land that I have promised I will give to your descendants, and they shall inherit it for ever." *And the Lord changed his mind about evil that he planned to bring on his people.* (32:11b–14, emphasis added)

That, to a religious consciousness raised on terms such as "immutable" and "unchangeable" as the best adjectives with which to think about God—has always been a stunning passage. It suggests that the capacity to "repent" (as the older translations put it)—that is, to change one's mind in light of circumstances—is actually a higher quality of being that unchangeableness. Why, indeed, should it strike us as odd to think of a God who has that quality as less profoundly ultimate than a God that doesn't ever change?

But there is another passage, in the very same chapter as this account of God's decision to relent the punishment, that relates how Moses behaves—or, more precisely, how the people behave under his leadership. Moses stands in the gate to the camp and says, "Who is on the LORD's side. Come to me" (32:26). And the sons of Levi do so, and (supposedly at God's command) they slay all the other people. That is traditionally taken as the origin of the priestly order, though it need not be taken as a proof that all priesthood is necessarily rooted in a act of terror.

This contrast is not the first instance in human history when the mercy of God has proven more evident than the capacity for forgiveness in religious devotees. Indeed, fanaticism is one of the potential outcomes of uniting moral conviction with religious zeal, and many a cultural despiser of religion thinks of this as compelling evidence that human life is more human and tolerable when it is conducted without the benefit of doctrinal loyalties.

The story of the golden calf also reveals that there was a strong tendency among the people to distrust wilderness as much as they resented oppression. Oppression makes life uncomfortable in one way; wilderness threatens it in another. We can think of wilderness as a condition in which there are no leaders—when a Moses figure has disappeared—and when there are no standards to provide life with the possibility of order. Wilderness can be as threatening as oppression. In one, authority is intolerable because it is oppressive; in the other, life is threatening because there is too little structure to authority. There are groups whose religious outlook is built on the sense that we are in one of these circumstances; there are also other groups whose religious outlook is built on the feeling that we suffer from the other.

The religious situation in contemporary America is marked by a contrast between two such groups. On the one hand there are those who feel the reality of the continuing structures of oppression and of repression that deny to so many persons in our time the economic justice and political (not to mention the cultural) freedoms to which they are entitled. That impulse produces theologies of liberation and calls for social change. On the other hand there are those who feel that the loss of moral guidelines, faddish vacillation in faith systems (particularly in theology), and a dissolution of the cements of civility and decency that make community possible, are so great that we live in wilderness. Such a feeling often engenders a desire to return to previous conditions of imagined stability or to create harsh and oppressive restraints. It may even produce a desire to establish law and order even without being duly concerned for how nonconformists get hurt.

The contrast between these two impulses runs very deep and is creating a polarization in the religious scene that has momentous consequences. It is difficult to resolve the tension between these two stances by appealing to evidence alone in order to settle the issue of whether any particular cultural condition is an Egypt or a wilderness. Either condition is traumatic by itself, and the fact that people see the same historical circumstances as evidence for either of these problems to the exclusion of the other may be still more traumatic.

Perhaps the religious situation has become so modernized, so devoid of a sense of its historical roots, that some people want nothing to do with either Exodus or wilderness. Some people even appear to prefer that the ethical and moral questions not arise. If morality entails the possibility of Exodus, and Exodus leads to the discomforts of wilderness, perhaps life would be better without morality. But the only possibility of having life without those complications would be to be content in Egypt—or in what Søren Kierkegaard once called the aesthetic stage—which is a pre-ethical condition. "If ignorance is bliss, 'tis folly to be wise"—but it is also subethical and in a profound sense, subhuman. The biblical story simply wouldn't be the same story had it been only a recipe for contentment—a learning to live in cultural "Egypts" without feeling the oppression or yearning for liberation. God did not send a Norman Vincent Peale to the Hebrews either in Egypt or in the wilderness, toting a copy of *A Guide to Confident Living*. And, by implication, any interpretation of religion—even if advanced in the name of Christianity—that thinks of peace of mind as a self-authenticating value is grossly incompatible with the biblical worldview. We should be thankful that the Hebrews were not furnished with religious leaders whose primary interest was in teaching people merely how to cope with circumstances rather than changing them.

The life of the Exodus pilgrims slowly begins to require some sort of social and organizational cohesion. The people involved in the experience of liberation eventually have to deal with questions about getting along together as a social group and not simply reacting against oppressors. What they do about that as they seek to remain loyal to the covenant will be the focus of the discussion in the next chapter.

4

Promised Land and Holy Kingdom
Habitat and Governance

Israel's history following the time of Moses is a long and not untroubled series of events that involved a generation of wandering in places that its people could not call home (traditionally, forty years in the wilderness) and a tumultuous process of coming into a place they could consider their own (the promised land). These events were attended by the task of determining how to govern Israel's internal affairs (including the relations between the twelve tribes) as well as how to deal with threats from neighboring nations. These matters, which take several books of the Bible to recount,[1] prompt moral reflection on some of the most perplexing issues addressed by social ethicists. To deal with them requires us to reexamine the role of land (and by inference the proper use of all physical and tangible resources that provide a stable setting for human life) and issues related to governance (which by extension involve suitable ways of enabling people and groups to live together). Some of the most troublesome questions for religious ethics—questions that are still debated after centuries of concern about them—are implicit in these parts of the biblical narrative.

The events through which Israel moved were indeed traumatic. Even in the twentieth century political refugees still face enormous dislocations when they give up everything that both binds and supports them in an oppressive regime and venture to a new land without friends and without resources. That is a momentous odyssey and we should not necessarily be critical of those who find it simply too much to contemplate making, or of those who find it impossible to emerge from such a transition with hopes and promises fulfilled. Moreover, we should not be surprised by the difficulty of finding easy moral meanings in such events, whether among the persons whose stories are found in Scripture or among those whose stories are found in contemporary newspapers.

A central motif in the biblical narrative is the movement of the Hebrews toward the promised land. Bernhard Anderson observes, "In the faith of ancient Israel 'the guidance out of Egypt' was inseparably connected with 'guidance into the arable land.'"[2] Walter Brueggemann suggests that Israel was always wrestling with its relationship both to Yahweh and to land, and that these cannot be separated without destroying a unique and necessary dialectic.[3] The relationship to Yahweh involves fidelity and obedience; the relationship to land involves possession and management. Few challenges to moral reflection are more difficult and demanding than to work out a suitable relationship between these two aspects of human responsibility.

The biblical narrative suggests that Yahweh, the God of Israel, destined the people to possess the land of Canaan. In an earlier chapter we have already suggested the difficulties that arise from taking this mandate as overriding the claims of all others to the same territory. But there is another tension persistently evident in the biblical materials. The Hebrews were instructed to possess the land but to have nothing to do with its inhabitants: to eschew interchange with the Canaanites, particularly to shun their religious practices. For many years scholars contended, following Julian Morgenstern, that there were socioeconomic differences between the Hebrews and the Canaanites, differences between a culture in which the shepherd is a prototype figure and a culture in which the farmer's role is more dominant. More recently a different thesis has been advanced: that the tension arose between two classes, a ruling class and a revolting peasantry. Whatever is the case, it is clear that political and economic factors were involved in the pressure to maintain religious separatism and that questions concerning the use and possession of land (tangible property) strike deep chords of concern and commitment.

Modern thinking about land is dominated by a concept of property rights. John Locke made the ownership of property the most important of three innate—that is, God-given—rights: the right to life, the right to liberty, and the right to property. According to Locke one of the most important functions of government is to protect and conserve property rights, which are in principle inalienable.[4] Much modern practice with respect to property grows out of Locke's perspective. Property is treated as an impersonal, inert resource that can be used in whatever manner best advances the interest of its owner, even if that use entails depletion of the property's intrinsic worth. An industrial corporation, for example, may strip-mine land that it owns for coal. It may only need to own the mineral rights under the land in order to do this, in which case it destroys important qualities of a property it doesn't even own in order to get to the part of the land that it does. In this modern concept the functional definition of property tends to be "that which I can use however I please."

The biblical idea of land stands in contrast to this modern attitude toward property rights. In the biblical narrative land is to be possessed only as a gift or trust from God. It is to be used and enjoyed but not exploited. It does provide habitat and location, without which persons are less fully human than they otherwise would be. But in the biblical perspective, habitat and location are qualified standings that involve no right of despoilment. Thus, several concepts that guide Israel's life serve as qualifications of the modern concept of land as mere resource to be exploited as owners see fit. An important symbol of this alternative manner of possessing land is the concept of the Jubilee.

The Jubilee year, as described in Leviticus 25:8–17, provides that any member of the community who had become a slave during the previous fifty years will be freed and that any property that had been sold to a fellow countryman shall be returned to the original owner or his family. This idea boggles the modern mind. What would it mean to organize the use of land according to such a concept?

It would mean, on the positive side, that land could not be despoiled or exploited. If a landowner, for instance, uses up the nonrenewable resources of a piece of the earth (whether a small parcel or a broad countryside), then it cannot be returned to the original owner in full. A requirement that the land is to be returned to the original owner (by inference in its original state) at stated intervals can thus protect land from despoilment. On the negative side, the idea of the Jubilee might well mean that landowners would hesitate to improve land, to build on it anything more than minimal structures destined to disintegrate at or about the time of the Jubilee. This could easily lead to tawdry construction (of which we have all too much even without the threat of a Jubilee year!) and would render unlikely anything like the technically sophisticated building of highly enduring structures that are found in the more impressive sections of a modern city. It is probably no surprise that the idea of the Jubilee was never implemented. This has led some scholars to declare the idea to be "completely obsolete."[5] But that declaration may be as wrong in one direction as the literal implementation of the concept might prove to be in the other.

The idea of the Jubilee year requires that the land be treated with the same beneficence as human beings are supposedly treated. A related provision in Leviticus (25:1–7) extends the concept of sabbatical rest to the land, requiring it to lie fallow and allowing it to rejuvenate every seven years. The idea of the sabbatical year, which embodies the same principle of respite for a shorter time span than does the Jubilee, also requires the land to be rested even as human beings are accorded repose. As a general principle, the idea that the land (and by extension every other material resource) is to be treated with the same consideration as human beings are to be treated, is not necessarily an impossible one and certainly not outdated. It surely would transform the manner in which human beings relate to the earth and it might have momentous consequences for alleviating the disastrous ecological maelstrom into which our modern premises about property use apparently have plunged us.[6]

The idea of the promised land raises issues about the moral significance of habitat. To possess land (or any other resource of substantial worth) is to face issues concerning stewardship. A promised land has to be cared for. Similarly, a community of people must be governed—even a community of people especially called to covenant fidelity. Just as possessions must somehow be managed—so likewise even the chosen people must be politically directed toward certain ends. The experience of Israel with government by tribal confederation (the amphictyony), and with the institution of kingship that replaced that confederation, prompts us to consider the moral issues that surround governance.

During the period of the Exodus the people's agenda was largely determined by the things that worked against them. Just as their oppression in Egypt constituted a clearly identifiable problem that brought the people together in unified opposition to externally imposed disablements, even their escape provided its own dynamic—one that kept them together through struggle and promise. But once the people moved beyond oppression and beyond wilderness, having escaped their predicament, they could no longer rely on a common revulsion to furnish guidance for their corporate behavior. They had to take control of the affairs within a habitat for which they have come to hold responsibility for governing.

This shift in circumstances is encountered in every experience in which liberation as a social/political experience successfully overcomes the conditions that have cemented people in common opposition to oppression. In Israel's case the change in circumstances is obvious—there can no longer be any question that Egypt is behind and Canaan lies just ahead. Geographical translocations often reconstitute a group's whole situation—everything from the past has been given up; everything in the future has to be created.

However, every achievement of liberation poses the question: How is a group of people to handle itself once the shackles of bondage have been broken, or at least sufficiently removed so as to require it to wrestle with decisions about the governance of its own societal relationships? The first and highly commendable impulse of a liberated group is usually to create a new order that does not have the corruptions and shortcomings of the system that has just been escaped. The Exodus experience and the moral sensitivities engendered by the Mosaic tradition produced a strong momentum for the establishment of such a new social order, what both Paul D. Hanson and Walter Brueggemann call an "alternative community."[7] This term denotes features of Israel's early corporate life that contrast sharply with the social organization of its surrounding neighbors. According to Bruce Birch, "Covenant faithfulness required of Israel the effort to embody justice, righteousness, and steadfast love in systemic social structures and practices."[8] Not only must land be held as a trust and therefore not be exploited, but the poor are to be cared for and justice is to be administered fairly. The corruptions of power are to be avoided by depending on leaders who are to be emulated for their fidelity rather than followed because they occupy some high place in a hierarchical social system or merely possess the clout to make everyone else submit to their rule.

In theory, Israel's *shoparim*, or judges, are leaders who symbolize the liberating experience. In practice they may be a strange collection chosen by God, partially to demonstrate that God can use even unattractive and unlikely oddballs to rule—an alternative to the barren machinations of humanly oriented power politics. Supposedly, the judges exemplify faithful obedience to the covenant ideals, but often they come to leadership roles less because they demonstrate special sensitivity to a theoretical ideal than because they demonstrate military heroism.

This way of bringing order to the life of a people relies more on leadership by personality than on government by policy—which is to say the people tend to respond more to the kind of person the leader is than to the kind of policies the leader advocates. The attractiveness and appeal of the leader are prime considerations in the selection. Judges 5 provides an early story that offers a clue to the kind of personality that often captures the imaginations and the loyalties of the people by being steadfastly loyal to God and staunchly effective in struggling for the cause of the people. Numerous other stories relate how the judges came to positions of leadership by similar demonstrations of prowess: Othniel, by success in battle (Joshua 15:16–17); Ehud, by a daring assassination of the king of Moab (Judges 3:12–30); Shamgar, by harassing the Philistines (Judges 3:31). The story of Gideon, who openly attacks the Canaanite worship of Baal and leads the confederation of tribes in its battle against the Midianites (Judges 6–8), provides a somewhat longer account of one of Israel's best known judges.

Do we not often see a similar tendency at work in contemporary political life? Following dramatic upheavals, the public sometimes turns to persons who have been successful military leaders to govern their societies. Military success is equated with patriotic fidelity and leadership potential. This has occurred in the choice of American presidents as well as of so-called "strong men" in other parts of the world. If fortune telling or literary skill were more honored practices in our time, we might even see persons with skills like Deborah's elected to office. A tendency to choose leaders on charismatic grounds persists in the tendency of many voters to approve candidates on the basis of personality rather than for the policies they advocate and would try enact into law if elected. The selection of leadership on the basis of charismatic factors often rewards individuals who symbolize prowess rather than pensiveness, or persons who are paragons of moral uprightness rather than highly aware of the inevitable ambiguity in all historical possibilities. Most leadership that depends for its warrant on charismatic appeal tends to attract a following in proportion to the degree it can crystallize options into simplified alternatives and can obscure ambiguity by creating slogans that make complex matters seem simple.

Leadership by charisma is often associated with a scheme for social ordering premised on a conviction that the communal life of a faithful people can be directed and sustained by the cohesive power of a true and proper faith commitment. It is such a conviction that prompted Israel at first to govern the relationship between its tribes with a confederation, called the amphictyony. This confederation was born out of the common realization that God had brought the people out of bondage. It was presumed that this same God would lead the people in their new condition of freedom if only they would put their whole confidence in those who demonstrated unquestioned loyalty to the covenant. The pursuit of adequate governance under such assumptions involves reiterating the covenant foundation for cooperation rather than making hard decisions about specific policies.

An account of the covenant renewal service reported in Joshua 24 indicates how Israel initially relied on this way of governing. In confronting the tribes who had not yet joined the religious confederation, Joshua rehearses all the mighty acts of God in the Exodus, and then asks each tribe to choose which God it will serve. The solicitation of allegiance is considered the crucial factor for bringing order to Israel's life—though, interestingly, such allegiance is not coerced (because a coerced allegiance can never really be a true commitment). It is believed that if two groups have the same covenantal allegiance, they will cooperate, whereas if they have different commitments and different loyalties, they will be at odds.

As the size and complexity of a group grows, the capacity of faith-engendered loyalty to provide social cohesion often wanes; zeal gets diluted; the awareness of ambiguity rises.[9] The voluntary basis of community proves less and less effective. "Halfway covenants" arise to make it possible to include either subsequent generations, who are no longer responsibly inspired by the liberating event that originated the life of the community, or to include people who have come into the group by birth and do not necessarily share the convictions of their parents. Halfway covenanters are allowed to participate in the life of the group without following its moral expectations as fully as the founding members.[10] As this takes place, the high moral visibility of the intentional community evaporates and pressures build to govern by more compelling means.

The biblical description of the chaotic conditions that occurred in Israel's life as the effectiveness of the covenant league waned is illustrated by an interesting and rather curt comment in Judges 17:6 "In those days there was no king in Israel; all the people did what was right in their own eyes." This phrase describes the centrifugal forces that were evident as the original power of the uniting experience grew too distant, when voluntary fidelity ceased to ensure communal cooperation, and when the charismatic appeal of the leadership was no longer convincing. Recognition of the resulting disorder (maybe even anarchy) led to the rise of powerful forces intent on establishing schemes of law and orderliness that could maintain stability by coercive means.

Many, if not most, of the other nations in the ancient Near East had kings, and those kings could muster military wherewithal to cohere communities with both temporal dispatch and operational might. Israel's pattern of voluntary cooperation between the several tribes apparently was less able to do that. Even if Israel was opposed to having a human king—since God's sovereignty was considered central—as long as the other nations had kings, Israel was seemingly disadvantaged, both in managing its internal affairs and in dealing with threats from its hostile neighbors. Despite its theological scruples Israel was forced to face the problem of political necessity. The movement to anoint a king gained momentum.

As soon as talk about having a king begins to take place, a major controversy arises. Many argue, "You can't be serious! That would be to create a Pharaoh! We have gone through too much in the effort to escape from imposed authority to turn around now and ask for it." One example of the opposition is found in Jotham's fable (Judges 9:7–15). This fable is partly a comment on a particular choice for king—namely the choice of Abimelech, who had murdered rivals in his rise to power. But in the context of the whole situation Jotham's fable may also suggest a critical attitude toward the institution of kingship itself.

> When it was told to Jotham [that the people were asking for a king], he went and stood on the top of Mount Gerizim, and cried aloud and said to them, "Listen to me, you lords of Shechem, that God may listen to you.
> The trees once went out to anoint a king over themselves:
> So they said to the olive tree, 'Reign over us.'
> The olive tree answered them, 'Shall I stop producing my rich oil, by which gods and mortals are honored, and go to sway over the trees?'
> Then the trees said to the fig tree, "You come and reign over us." But the fig tree answered them, "Shall I stop producing my sweetness and my delicious fruit, and go to sway over the trees?"
> Then the trees said to the vine, "You come and reign over us." But the vine said to them, "Shall I stop producing my wine which cheers gods and mortals and go to sway over the trees?"
> So, all the trees said to the bramble, "You come and reign over us." And the bramble said to the trees, "If in good faith you are anointing me king over you, then come and take refuge in my shade; but if not, let fire come out of the bramble and devour the cedars of Lebanon."

A more explicitly critical comment about the proposal to establish a kingship is found in 1 Samuel 8, when Israel asks Samuel to anoint a king. Samuel doesn't feel comfortable with the idea, and so prays to God to guide him in what to say. Samuel is told that the move to kingship is a rejection of the direct divine sovereignty—but, nevertheless, that Samuel should "do what they want and give them a king." Only, Samuel is told to point out to the people what they are asking for: the king is going to put their sons into military service on a scale they do not imagine; he is going to put their daughters into public service; he is going to seize their grain and vineyards—or at least a tenth of their vineyards, mainly for the support of the military. In short, the people are going to be slaves again, this time to a tyrannical ruler of their devising.

The development of kingship—and the realities would not be that different if we said queenship, insofar as that term designates a monarch who rules by the exercise of coercive power—provides an institutionalized continuity that isn't present in governance by charismatic leadership. A monarch comes to power by predefined arrangements for determining succession—not by becoming visible as a talented leader in some contest for acclamation that begins when the former leader has died or been deposed. In most instances, kingly succession is hereditary—which means there is no hiatus between the death of one leader and the selection of a new one.

Then too, whereas a charismatic leader must define the nature of an office by what can be achieved, the king or the ruling queen is the occupant of an office performing a role that is generally defined in advance. This has the important function of providing a common set of expectations as to what the leader is supposed to do, and by what means the leader is to proceed to fulfill such expectations.

Whereas the charismatic leader solicits responses, the monarch commands obedience—and the distinction between engendering response and commanding obedience is a crucial one. In the case of the charismatic pattern, personal qualities are apt to be decisive; but in the case of the official such qualities may indeed even be irrelevant. A member of the police force, for instance, is obeyed because the office has authority. The authority is "objectivized," and is only minimally a function of the personal virtue or appeal of the officer. If you get stopped on the highway you don't start by telling the police officer that she has no moral right to stop you unless she is kind to animals, morally upright, or "moving on to perfection."[11] Similarly, in the realm of religious practice, the sacramental function of the priest illustrates the objectivized function of an office in contrast to charismatic leadership. The benefits of the sacraments performed by the priest are believed to be dispensed irrespective of the moral achievements or personal character of the person who performs them.[12]

The biblical narrative makes it clear that the authority of kings isn't dependent on the virtue of the individuals who occupy the office. Take David as the case in point: There is, of course, the story about the slaying of Goliath with the slingshot—a story that reminds us somewhat of the days when military prowess was one of the ways charismatic leadership was demonstrated. But there is also the story of David and Bathsheba in 2 Samuel 11. That story reveals serious personal immorality in the king. But the suggestion never comes forth that this means that David's official authority is annulled. David is king even if personally disgraced.[13]

Another way of distinguishing between the role of the charismatic leader and the role of a monarch is to suggest that the basis of decision making is significantly reconceived. Whereas the judge or charismatic leader appeals for fidelity to a system of values and ideals, a king tends to be measured in terms of shrewdness in dealing with operational realities. A vignette in 1 Kings 3:16–28 indicates how true this was in the case of King Solomon.

The shrewdness of kings does not depend on any special way of knowing the divine will. Kings can't domesticate soothsaying or prophecy for that purpose. An especially telling way of suggesting this is found in 1 Kings 22:1–37. Here Jehoshaphat the king of Judah comes to Ahab the king of Israel proposing a joint military venture to reconquer Ramoth-Gilead from the hands of Syria. Ahab is uneasy, and so he suggests they ask the prophets (the soothsayers) whether it will succeed—and at first they get a positive answer. But because Ahab is still uneasy, they ask Micaiah—an individual prophet who is not a member of that band of prophets—what he thinks, and he also at first gives a positive answer until Ahab bristles with, "How many times must I make you swear to tell me nothing but the truth in the name of the LORD?" (v. 16) Then Micaiah prophesies the defeat of the venture—but the kings undertake it anyway and are defeated. The story suggests that prophetic functions are not to be domesticated for the purposes of ensuring the political success of kings. Indeed, the political role of the king and the prophetic role are in perpetual tension—the contemporary evidence of which is the ongoing tension between public officials and the free press, a tension that exists regardless of the party in power.

These stories suggest that none of a monarch's actions and decisions are preserved from error by some supernatural guidance. There can be prayer rooms in the Capitol building—but every member of Congress, both secular and pious, still has to decide policy on the basis of the issues at stake, the relative claims of justice served by particular legislation, some vision of the overall public good, and duties owed to constituencies.

Finally, a monarch also differs from a charismatic leader in the structural authority and the trappings of the office. The monarch is surrounded by officials who usually operate by "chain of command" lines of authority. A monarch very likely dresses in a special way, is surrounded by ceremonial guards who provide an aura of power and by staff persons who provide an aura of authority. A monarch may even forget entirely the dynamics that go with the solicitation of consent. In some democracies, like Britain's, the ceremonialism has been preserved in a monarchy that has been divorced from political power, but this is a rather rare and special achievement (which has recently been undergoing its own troubles). In such circumstances, political leadership is provided the freedom to grapple with the nitty-gritty of policy conflicts in vigorous and not always genteel ways.

The issue raised by the contrast between the governance of Israel by the voluntary covenant league and by the imposed kingship has, in somewhat variant forms, persisted throughout all subsequent history. It lies in back, however covertly, of the tension between prophets and kings in the Old Testament narrative (see chapter 5). It was evident in the early church in the tension between those who believed devotion to Christ could hold the church together and those who argued that the church must be institutionally structured and disciplined (see chapter 16). In contemporary terms it is present in the tension between those who believe that religious devotion automatically results in community, and those who recognize that churches no less than governments benefit from defining themselves constitutionally.

Communities that try to make common commitments the basis for governance tend to be separatist, meaning that faithfulness to the ideals defining such a community requires it to live a life that sets it apart from the behavior of surrounding communities. In Israel's case this separatism expressed itself as a policy of remaining distinct from the foreign nations— not having a king as the other nations did.

Just as Israel ceased to rely on the covenant league and moved to kingship to obtain internal cohesion as well as to secure itself against the threats from neighboring nations, so also the main body of Christians eventually ceased to rely on nonviolence and the distinctive morality associated with it and accepted the recognition offered by the Roman emperor Constantine as a means of securing the church's fortunes in the then turbulent Greco-Roman world. Saint Augustine gave a strong theological legitimation for this move with the doctrine of two cities, which he elaborated in the classic treatise *The City of God*. Augustine, perhaps to put it overly simply, suggested that Christians are to guide themselves by the Gospel in dealing with heavenly matters, but to be guided by the ways in which worldly rulers (read: kings) act to govern temporal matters. The faithful have to live in two realms at once; in the city of God as respects matters of faith and religious practice; in the city of the world as regards temporal affairs. Although the terminology is quite different, the moral perspective is remarkably similar to that which prompted the move to kingship in Israel: The community of faith feels compelled to adopt the strategies of the world in order to survive.

The issue emerges again with momentous consequences at the time of the Reformation. So-called left-wing groups, such as the Anabaptists, looking to the Gospel as a guide for faith and practice, attempted again to create themselves as "alternative communities." Following the norms enunciated in the New Testament, they eschewed violence and other means of attaining worldly success. In contrast, the classical reformers, particularly Luther, developed a doctrine of "two kingdoms" that called upon Christians to obey secular princes (the form in which the kingly role was then expressed) in matters dealing with public life. Princes, argued Luther, are to be obeyed because they hold an office. Their role is to hold the line against rebellion and political wrongdoing. The state is a "dyke against sin" upon which Christians depend for the maintenance of civil order. Princes are not necessarily faithful or good; they are merely officials designated for a special purpose. Luther commented on the passage in 2 Samuel 11 that portrays David's personal shortcomings, and noted that while David fell into behavior that seriously affected his own moral standing, that did not eliminate his kingly office. Luther offered no grounds on which Christians could find a way to govern public life other than to obey the princes.

The same difference has persisted into the twentieth century in the contrast between liberal Christian thinking that sees the Gospel as a set of guidelines for moving society toward more humane social accomplishments, and the so-called Christian realists, who argue that orderly public life can only be maintained by officials who act decisively to stem errant behavior or insurrectionist threats. For instance, Emil Brunner, writing about such questions in a European context in the 1940s postulates a necessary dichotomy between the public responsibilities of leaders and the requirements of personal morality. The official role requires its own logic. According to Brunner,

> There is one point about which we must be quite clear: the usefulness of the orders depends on the fact that they are *real*. . . . The specific value of the orders consists in the fact that they actually and effectively create *order*. And the fact that they do actually create order is based upon the further fact that, in contradistinction to moral laws, these orders claim no more than legality, but to compensate for this, this legality can be more or less *enforced*. That is why, in this sphere of legality, motives like fear of punishment, utility, honour, respect for conventions, etc. play a great part. But this is not really the point at issue; what does matter is that—by whatever motives—these orders should be effectively maintained. The Christian, too, as a member of his nation, must cooperate in this task of preservation, and the special part assigned to him—through "the Calling" is: the "office." To act in his "office" means to act in

accordance with the legal obligations imposed by the "orders."
. . . If the Christian's "official duty" causes pain and perplexity
to his conscience, it must simply be endured. The Divine Command
is terribly distorted when difficulties of conscience created by the
"official order" are evaded by setting up a double morality [in which
nonbelieving citizens act one way and Christians act another].[14]

Reinhold Niebuhr, writing from the other side of the Atlantic, similarly
argued that Christians must realistically accept the necessity of ordering
public life by strategies that involve the use of coercive techniques that are
embarrassments to religious ideals. Niebuhr criticized as sentimental efforts to create or to sustain civic order by persuasion rather than coercion.
According to Niebuhr,

The demand of religious moralists that nations subject themselves to
the "law of Christ" is an unrealistic demand, and the hope that they
will do so is a sentimental one. . . .
    The religious idealist, confronted with these stubborn obstacles to
the realisation of his ideals, is tempted either to leave the world of
political and economic relations to take the course which natural
impulse prompts, or to assume that his principles are influencing
political life more profoundly than they really are.[15]

Although Reinhold Niebuhr's thought gained enormous influence
during Niebuhr's lifetime and still inspires many Christians to think about
social issues in realistic terms, today a contrasting impulse is strongly apparent and attracts a growing following. John Howard Yoder, writing from
a revisionist Mennonite perspective, argues that the life, death, and Resurrection of Christ have produced a new state of affairs—one in which the
grip of sin has been overcome.[16] Consequently, fidelity to Christ (as fidelity to the covenant ideal in Israel) calls for a new and transforming kind of
behavior that will play havoc with the working assumptions of a sinful
social order by refusing to be a party to its way of doing things. Yoder
argues that Christian faithfulness requires, not a nonresistance to evil, but a
radically revolutionary way of dealing with evil by refusing to accept its
premises concerning political and social process. We shall examine Yoder's
claim more fully in chapter 12.

Among other recent writers in the field of Christian ethics, Stanley
Hauerwas finds Yoder's perspective compelling. If the price of overcoming
the sharp dichotomy between virtue and official action that Brunner states
so baldly is not being an official worldly functionary, pay that price, argues

Hauerwas. Let the church declare what it means to be a follower of Christ, not a political officeholder. But unlike traditional left-wing sectarians, Stanley Hauerwas sees this special peaceable kingdom as serving the larger world rather than withdrawing from it. He substitutes an "in the world, but not of it" for the more radical sectarian stance of "not of the world."[17]

In the instructive dichotomy symbolized by amphictyony and kingship, one polarity assumes we must set up kingly tyrants because such actions alone prevent sin from overrunning the world, and that we must behave like kings whenever called upon to do so in the exercise of official roles; the other polarity suggests that we must not set up kings (or become kings ourselves) because it is impossible to do so without betraying covenantal fidelity. Are these seemingly exclusive opposites the only possibilities, or are they alternative ways to carry out the governance function, and are Christians called to discover the creative possibilities in those different ways and to work for the transformations, however partial, that can be effected by them?

Although it is impossible to turn kings on and off on an *ad hoc* basis, vacillating from issue to issue, it may be possible to devise governance patterns that deliberately and consistently combine elements of the voluntary and the mandatory, the freely associational and the immutably authoritarian. Constitutional democracy seems to fall somewhere between the polar contrasts. Elected officials do come to power much as charismatic leaders do—because people want them as leaders. But they also occupy offices as kings do—and (particularly if those offices are for stated terms) such leaders have at least a part of the authority that comes with designation as a sovereign.

Some Christians believe that politics is capable of being included, at least partially, in the redemptive activity of God. Holding office need not necessarily require totally harsh behavior. Transformations are possible—transformations that help to mitigate the sharp dichotomy between alternative separatism and a harsh version of political order. Calvin offered such a view, one that approaches political reality with the conviction that some transformation (albeit an always incomplete one) is possible in the quality of social institutions. Calvin held that lesser officials—the magistrates and elders—who exercise subordinate roles in the community can criticize (and even revolt against) kings who misuse power. Writings by contemporary Calvinists like Richard Mouw[18] and Nicholas Wolterstorff[19] argue this perspective suggestively and relate it to political life in the twentieth century. But the conditions required for such transformation are complex.

They develop only as the biblical narrative, as it unfolds, offers patterns for moral reflection that are more subtle and more complex than those we have already examined. One of the most important of those patterns is that of the prophetic figure who calls for a more sophisticated level of fidelity—criticizing at one and the same time the immorality and unfaithfulness of the people that seem to create the need for kings and the truculence and misuse of authority that so frequently corrupt those who exercise political power for the purpose of maintaining order. Our continuing reflection on the biblical narrative now turns to the figure of the prophet and its significance for moral decision making.

5

Affluence, Corruption, and Prophetic Response

The Value and Limits of Social Criticism

To an extent impossible for a loosely confederated group held together only by common convictions, Israel grew and prospered under the monarchy. This development may well have reached its apex during the reign of King Solomon, who brought Israel to an unprecedented level of power and influence in the ancient Near Eastern world. Israel became a highly viable, if not indeed a moderately successful, economic/political/social entity. A corresponding religious establishment centered in the Temple made its own contribution to this impressive national achievement. However, the prosperity was not without its difficulties, the seeming success not without its malfunctions. The institutionalization of religion under Solomon involved a major infusion of Canaanite practices and abounded with corrupting misuses. Bruce Birch has succinctly described the development: "Israel under Solomon ceases to live as an alternative community in the world (although some kept this tradition alive) and instead adopts a model of royal ideology and management borrowed from surrounding Canaanite culture."[1]

Indeed, so great were the disagreements and disruptions in its affairs that the Hebrew nation divided into two kingdoms: Israel in the north and Judah in the south. This division, which occurred in 922 B.C.E., came about in no small measure because the heavy burden of maintaining a royal establishment created sufficient discontent to ignite a rebellion, led by Jereboam in the north. There was a theological issue at stake as well. The southern kingdom embraced a royal covenant theology that uncritically attributed divine sanction to the Davidic throne and dynasty, whereas the northern kingdom adhered to a view of the kingship that involved limited sovereignty and was more in keeping with the theological perspective of the Mosaic covenant.[2]

These developments, which entail socio/political/economic differences as well as ethical/theological disagreements, were accompanied by the rise of a small but important group of persons who asked the question whether Israel's life adequately embodied the divine intentions as set forth in the Mosaic covenant. These persons may be characterized in several terms: One possibility would be "divine-human mediators," or "covenant mediators in the tradition of Moses." Another possibility, drawn from modern secular life, would be "social commentators."[3] These figures, whatever term best describes them, reemphasized the significance of covenantal righteousness as a foundation for the life of the nation. Holding Israel's achievements up to the light of that righteousness, they discovered fault lines in Israel's seeming accomplishments. The prophets of the eighth and seventh centuries B.C.E. effectively extended the meaning of covenantal obligation by underscoring its demand for a particularity of obligation and not merely for a particularity of liberation. They were less concerned with proclaiming release from captivity as Israel's destiny than with calling the nation back from apostasy.

The prophetic role is prefigured in the activities of certain individuals who are discussed in the historical accounts of the monarchy. For example, Elijah, Nathan, and Micaiah stood up to political leaders and fearlessly challenged covenantal infidelity and moral wrong wherever they found it. The accounts of these "preliterary" prophets furnish something of a model for the later "literary" prophets, whose careers and whose writings come to us in books bearing their name. Both groups attacked social wrong when they saw it and chastised personal moral transgressions—not least the transgressions of kingly leaders. Both refused to be domesticated into mere predictors of the future or guarantors of good fortune.

The struggle between the Mosaic view of covenant and the royal view of kingly prerogative is vividly illustrated by the story of Elijah's role in the controversy between Naboth and Ahab over the vineyard (1 Kings 21). Ahab, the king, wants Naboth's vineyard, which is situated near the royal palace, so he can enlarge the royal quarters. He offers a fair price to acquire it. Naboth refuses to sell because the vineyard belonged to his family and in Naboth's view is held in trust for the family in keeping with the unique Hebrew premise that all land belongs ultimately to God. Ahab's wife, Jezebel, whose views of property reflect the commercial attitudes of her native Phoenicia, arranges an intrigue through which Naboth will be accused of blasphemy and stoned to death—allowing the property to be acquired by the king. When Ahab goes to possess the vineyard, the prophet Elijah is there to rebuke the king for violating the fundamental premises of the

Hebraic heritage. His challenge brings about Ahab's repentance. According to Bernhard Anderson, in contrast to the attitude toward property and power under Baalism, under the Mosaic covenant,

> The whole community was responsible to the sovereign will of Yahweh as expressed in the absolute laws that had been handed down from the wilderness period and refined by legal usage. And when the justice of a member of the community was downtrodden by the powerful, Yahweh intervened to defend the weak and the defenseless and to restore the order and familial solidarity of the covenant community.[4]

From its earliest beginnings prophetic religion began to recognize that the very economic, political, and religious successes that stem from the achievement of national strength through the institutionalization of public life are likely to be attended by, and even causes of, moral problems. It saw difficulties for faith and fidelity rising at exactly the point where the group brought together by the covenant enjoyed political and material success and even, curiously enough, something of a boom in the practice of religion. Although the prophets stressed the need to worship the right God, they were concerned for much more than merely choosing the right deity. The moral issue is fundamental: the provisions of the Mosaic Law are to be upheld even as the God of Moses is to be honored.

The careers and pronouncements of the literary prophets are reported in books that bear their names—including Amos and Hosea in the northern kingdom and Isaiah and Jeremiah in the south. These books are quite rightly thought of as offering some of the most ethically significant material in the Old Testament. It is almost a commonplace to think of "prophetic religion" as somehow representing a sublime and significant expression of the moral impulse. Even today, when we speak of a person as a "prophetic figure" we imply that such a person possesses an unusual level of moral insight and has the courage to speak truth to power.

It does not matter whether the prophet came (as did Amos) from a rural background or (as did Isaiah) from a city establishment, from the northern kingdom or the southern kingdom, whether the prophet was sympathetic to or suspicious of the cultic aspects of religious practice, relatively sophisticated in matters of theology or possessed of only a simple piety. The common themes of the prophetic message include judgment on those who had willfully broken the covenant ties with God and with each other; a probing call to ethical sensitivity and the reordering of their lives; and (in most cases) an assurance of hope beyond the disaster being announced as punishment.

Although the prophets did not seek to cause upsets from some perverse relish of controversy, neither did they soften the thrust of their declarations nor shrink from the hostility that was created by their preaching. Some of the prophets were more astute than others in couching what they said so as to get across their message to a resistant audience, yet each of them probed deeply into the moral shortcomings of the group to which they were speaking. Most of them were considered troublemakers, particularly by those who held the purse strings and the power. Instead of saying that the nation "never had it so good" (as those in power frequently like to suppose is the case), the prophets suggested that the nation had never been so unfaithful to the covenant—so morally corrupt. They predicted that the nation would face dire consequences—not so much because the economy was sluggish but because the moral fiber of its wheelers and dealers had atrophied. They sided with the homeless against the affluent, with the widows and orphans against the political rulers, and with the humble and the ordinary people against the priests. Doom and gloom artists rather than public relations types, they were often seen by their contemporaries as having no enthusiasm for the nation's success and still less appreciation for the cultic manifestations of religiosity. Needless to say, they were not popular and certainly could not hold a public relations position in a modern corporation, a chamber of commerce, a political organization, or even in many an academic institution.

We need not try to encapsulate here all that might be gleaned about particular aspects of prophetic preaching by offering a detailed summation of the many scholarly writings in which it has been discussed. For our purposes it is sufficient to indicate the basic nature of prophetic preaching and why it is not enthusiastically received by all groups. In any of the literary prophets one can read vivid, explicit, and relentless descriptions of the breaches of covenantal fidelity in whichever of the two kingdoms a particular prophet is preaching. The strictures of the prophets include three points.

1. Condemnations of Injustice. One of the strongest evidences cited by the prophets as a sign of covenantal infidelity is the widespread presence of economic and social injustice. In Amos these conditions are described with intense literary poignancy: The people of Israel (whom Amos addresses as a compatriot)

- sell the righteous for silver and the needy for a pair of sandals (Amos 2:6)

- trample the head of the poor into the dust of the earth, and push the afflicted out of the way (2:7)

- [its rich women (whom Amos calls the cows of Bashan)] oppress the poor, . . . crush the needy, and say to their husbands, "Bring something to drink!" (4:1)

- [all Israel's inhabitants] lie on beds of ivory, and lounge on their couches, and eat lambs from the flock, and calves from the stall; . . . sing idle songs to the sound of the harp, and like David improvise on instruments of music; . . . drink wine from bowls, and anoint themselves with the finest oils, but are not grieved over the ruin of Joseph! (6:4–6)

The people of Judah (whom Isaiah addresses as a compatriot)

- [are] a sinful nation, people laden with iniquity, offspring who do evil, children who deal corruptly! (Isaiah 1:4)

- [Jerusalem once] the faithful city "has become a whore! She that was full of justice, righteousness [once] lodged in her, but now murderers!" (1:21)

- "Everyone loves a bribe, and runs after gifts. They do not defend the orphan, and the widow's cause does not come to them." (1:23)

- drag inequity along with cords of falsehood . . ." [and] say, "Let him make haste, let him speed his work, that we may see it [i.e., the spoils and profits]." (5:18–19b)

- make iniquitous decrees, [and] write oppressive statutes, to turn aside the needy from justice and to rob the poor of their right, that widows may be [their] spoil, and that [they] may make the fatherless their prey!" (10:1f.)

2. Criticism of False Ritualism. A second dimension to the prophetic portrayal of the breakdown of covenantal fidelity is hypocritical ritualism. Hosea, speaking to Israel, puts the matter of authentic religious belief together with moral conduct: "Ephraim is joined to idols (that is the false ritualism), let him alone. When the drinking is ended, they indulge in sexual orgies; they love lewdness more than their glory (that may mean their loss of personal integrity)." (Hosea 4:17f.)

Amos speaks (4:4–5) of the transgressions that Israel so loves to perform at Bethel and Gilgal—involving sacrifices every morning and tithes every three days. All of this is unauthentic because these same people abuse and exploit their neighbors. Their heart isn't right. He also says, on God's behalf,

> I hate, I despise your feasts, and I take no delight in your solemn assemblies. Even though you offer me your burnt offerings and grain offerings, I will not accept them, and the offerings of well-being of your fatted animals I will not look upon. Take away from me the noise of your songs; I will not listen to the melody of your harps. But let justice roll down like waters, and righteousness like an ever flowing stream. (5:21–24)

A careful look at the prophetic materials reveals a slight difference between the way in which social wrongdoing is treated and false ritualism is treated. Whereas the social wrongs are condemned in and of themselves—they would not be acceptable under any circumstances—the religious ceremonies are criticized because they are not matched by a corresponding fidelity and moral uprightness. This may leave a chance for genuine and authentic ritual—which can have its place if the conditions of covenant loyalty are right, but it leaves no place for social injustice.

The prophets also condemn religious syncretism, a particularly blatant form of which involves flirtation with the Baal fertility cults of the Canaanites. This may lead to false ritualism—but it is not exactly the same as false ritualism. It is possible to be religiously syncretistic without being ritualistically inclined at all, and it is possible to worship in ritual ways without being syncretistic. The prophets criticize religious apostasy as a fundamental misplacing of allegiance (i.e., idolatry) and they suggest how it leads to moral infidelity. Each is a different manifestation of a common drift away from the covenantal convictions in which the society is supposedly rooted.

3. Complaints about Personal Immorality. The prophets also criticize what today might be called "personal sins." This fact should be not be overlooked any more than the prophetic condemnation of social injustice should be downplayed. Conservatives tend to minimize the implications of the prophetic condemnation of injustice, presumably because it sounds too radical. Theological liberals tend to overlook the prophetic condemnation of personal vice, presumably because it sounds too moralistic. The prophets do not presume a dichotomy between social injustice and personal wrongdoing, and can be cited neither in defense of those who feel that social wrongs should be the main target of moral criticism nor of those who think that private vices are the proper object of religious criticism.

We have already indicated some examples of prophetic criticism of social injustice. Consider the following criticisms of personal wrongdoing:

- prostitution, sacred prostitution, is condemned (Amos 2:7bf.)

- so is excessive drunkenness (Isaiah 5:22)

- "These also reel with wine and stagger with strong drink; the priest and the prophet reel with strong drink; they are confused with wine, and stagger with strong drink; they err in giving vision." (Isaiah 28:7)

There is naught here for the comfort of those, like the double kingdom theologians of the Reformation or the Christian realists of more recent times, who would suggest that holders of offices need not be accountable for their personal behavior! It is difficult to imagine one of the Hebrew prophets arguing that Israel needs to suspend the moral requirements of the covenant law in order to maintain its position of power among the nations. Indeed, prophetic religion is seldom interested in procedural success; the prophets are deaf to complaints that social criticism undermines the nation's security. But if the prophets would be disturbed by an effort to bracket out personal morality from the qualifications of political leadership, they would be equally disturbed by any practice in which politicians who discover some personal flaw or indiscretion in their opponents seize upon it as a means to discredit them in the eyes of the public. They would be just as critical of moralism used as a means of advancing political power as of the idea of office used to eliminate considerations of moral integrity. The prophets enunciate a holistic concept of covenantal fidelity that keeps personal and social moral concerns together—a unity all too frequently torn asunder. That is the uniqueness of their integrity, and also the possible focus of their inability to function strategically in the rough and tumble of the nation's political and economic endeavors. Prophets are not strategists or managers; they accept little responsibility for the outcome of temporal affairs. Although they may get a lot said; they may not get much done.

The prophets foresee that these moral and religious shortcomings will produce a common destiny—namely, a punishment consisting either of a total destruction or a temporary banishment of the selected group from the promised land. Moreover, as understood by the eighth-century prophets, the destiny is essentially corporate—though before too long the idea emerges even in prophetic literature itself that a remnant will be singled out to be preserved.

This message of impending punishment is preached by prophets in both the north and the south—precluding one branch of the divided covenantal nation from feeling itself superior to the other branch. The people in each part of the divided kingdom understand clearly why those in the other part need the prophetic warnings, but they are deeply resentful of having those warnings addressed to themselves. In contrast, each prophet directs the most stringent condemnations toward the immediate group.

Because these warnings are couched in terms of future predictions, many people commonly think of prophecy as something much like foretelling. But looking to the future is only an incidental feature of the prophetic enterprise. The main weight is upon judging the shortcomings of the present. Prophets are social critics and social commentators rather than fortune-tellers. The nearest contemporary manifestation of this function is probably found in the editorial writers and columnists who work for the media. The prophetic enterprise has almost nothing in common with preaching that is intended to help people cope with the pressures and difficulties of living so as to enjoy a kind of spiritual contentment amidst unjust conditions they do not seek to change.

The prophets argue that moral wrong stems from a misdirection of fidelity as much or more than from deliberate malice. Hosea's method for portraying this is to marry a harlot, suggesting an analogy to God, who had made a covenant with Israel but then discovered that Israel is (or has become) unfaithful. Harlotry is not merely the violation of a specific moral law, but a holistic condition of infidelity.

The prophets, like the lawgivers in the Book of Exodus, do not separate fidelity from morality, nor morality from fidelity. They offer no warrant for believing a society can have an adequate morality without being attentive to its religious loyalties. In this perspective morality is but a subordinate aspect of religious commitment. To paraphrase a later biblical text: "Where the heart is, there will the behavior (or the misbehavior) be also." According to the prophets, the people of Israel would simply not have allowed social injustice to run rampant, religious rituals to be substitutes for social duty, or personal immorality to flourish had they remained faithful to their God and to the covenant. If the fidelity is true, the morality is assured. If the fidelity is compromised, the morality is endangered.

There is little in the prophetic literature to sustain the idea of an autonomous position for moral action, as though people are able to choose between being morally right and morally wrong without regard for the fundamental location of their commitments. The prophets would resonate with this observation by Fr. Bernard Häring about the attitudinal gestalt to which he gives the name "fundamental option":

> We can be responsible and creative only to the extent of our wholeness, our inner integrity, the integration of all our energies. This means that our leitmotif and our fundamental option take flesh and blood in our life and so transform our desires, our institutions, our imagination, that fundamental intentions become also fundamental attitudes.[5]

The prophets tend to act as individual agents, in some cases as amateurs, and frequently as "loners." They are not to be thought of as officials. They easily "get into the hair" of both kingly types and priestly types—the literature is well interspersed with fascinating anecdotes to this effect.

The prophets don't get into their role by heredity (in this they are like charismatic leaders and different from kings), yet neither do they rise to prominence by securing public support though appealing demonstrations of outstanding leadership ability (and here they are like kings and not like charismatic leaders). They might well be considered subject to deep psychic dislocations and even (as in the case of Jeremiah) suicidal melancholy. Sometimes, as in the case of Isaiah, they are persons at home in the affairs of the city yet not hostage to its culture. Perhaps a copy of Norman Vincent Peale's *Guide to Confident Living* or Robert Schuller's *The Be-happytudes* would have helped one or more of them out of these self-isolating syndromes, but taking the advice in such books might also have meant that the whole middle section of the biblical drama would have been derailed at its most decisive juncture.

Although some qualities of personal selfhood may be functional for doing their work, the prophets don't gain their effectiveness by virtue of being moral paragons of righteousness or stunning examples of leadership potential. They undoubtedly never went to a session of EST. Once when I was lecturing on Amos a student asked, "Professor, was Amos a psychotic?" I had to answer, "He might have been, but even if the clinical diagnosis is yes, would that invalidate the role model or its contributions to the biblical account?" On the other hand, had the prophets been economically affluent, religiously syncretistic, lived on the cultural "fast track," or engaged in flagrant moral malfeasance, they probably would have invalidated their role.

The stance of the prophets brings a new importance to the concept of "calling," or vocation. The prophets undertake their ministries—often re-luctantly and even under protest—because they feel a divine commission to do a particular thing. The idea of vocation involves certain special quali-ties, as does the role of a charismatic leader, but the commitment and dedication of the prophet involve an intense sense of inward necessity rather than an exhibition of some special power that attracts public atten-tion. The idea of vocation involves the impulse to speak for a special rea-son, as is also true in the case of the priest, but the speech of the prophet is personal rather than merely official. Moreover, although they are public figures the prophets exercise no coercive powers, as do kings. Theirs is a quite distinctive role that cannot be subsumed under these other models of leadership. This idea of calling, or vocation, has subsequently appeared in Christian thinking about duty and obligation, perhaps most notably in the time of the Reformation. It is used to denote the sense of moral obli-gation that prompts all Christians (and not only clergy) to see their entire life work as a service to God.

The prophetic stance is both radical and conservative at the same time. Prophets are conservatives rather that merely change-directed social activ-ists. They complain that something crucial from the past has been compro-mised or lost. They see the past as a time of moral authenticity, and look to a future marked by social transformation only to the extent that the moral covenant of the past is recaptured and obeyed. But they are radical in the sense that they refuse to accept the status quo as satisfactory. They see the root causes and not merely the superficial inconveniences of present diffi-culties. They oppose patch-up therapy.

The prophets have as much to say about love as the relational base of the divine-human encounter as about judgment—perhaps even more so. Granted they speak about judgment (and justice) but their understanding of God's relationship to Israel is built on the model of loving fidelity. Rec-ognition of this fact should permanently scratch the notion—which is so prevalent in sentimentalized mainstream Christianity—that the Old Testa-ment is all about justice and judgment, and the New Testament alone conveys the message of love.

The eleventh chapter of Hosea should have put that misconception to rest before it ever got started, but it hasn't:

When Israel was a child, I loved him, and out of Egypt I called my son.
The more I called them, the more they went from me;
they kept sacrificice to the Baals, and offering incense to idols.

Yet, it was I who taught Ephraim to walk,
I took them up in my arms;
but they did not know that I healed them.
I led them with cords of human kindness, with bands of love.
I was to them like those who lift infants to their cheeks.
I bent down to them and fed them. (vv. 1–4)

Then, suggesting that they shall return to captivity and oppression in Egypt as punishment for their waywardness, but that they will not be destroyed, God says:

How can I give you up, Ephraim!
How can I hand you over, O Israel!
How can I make you like Admah!
How can I treat you like Zeboiim!
My heart recoils within me, my compassion grows warm
    and tender.
I will not execute my fierce anger,
I will not again destroy Ephraim;
    for I am God and no mortal,
    the Holy One in your midst,
    and I will not come in wrath. (vv. 8–9)

The prophets are not unaware that Israel's neighbors are guilty of the same kind of actions and false allegiances as Israel manifests. But that is a matter of secondary interest to them, and they stoutly resist letting the sins of the other nations become a means of excusing Israel from condemnation or punishment merely because, comparatively speaking, the other nations are worse.

The "oracles against the other nations" that open the Book of Amos are thought by scholars to be one of the first instances of monotheism in the Old Testament[6]—monotheism that develops out of the very premises of the prophetic stance. In Amos and Hosea monotheism is implicit rather than explicit because the oracles portray God as judging all the nations by the same demands for justice and integrity. The sermon that opens the Book of Amos employs a clever preaching strategy because it prompted the people of Israel to whip up interest and enthusiasm about the punishment of their neighbors' transgressions (which they believed well-deserved) before turning the judgment most severely on the "home group."

The prophetic perspective constitutes a momentous reinterpretation of the covenantal relationship between God and the people. The "scandal of particularity" is changed from one that involves special benefit to one that involves special obligation. The passage that probably states this most vividly is found in Amos 3:1–2:

> Hear this word that the LORD has spoken against you, O people of Israel, against the whole family which I brought up out of the land of Egypt:
>   You only have I known of all the families of the earth;
>   therefore I will punish you for your iniquities."

To understand the momentous thrust of this passage we might consider an analogy with a parent whose child has gotten involved in some mischief with a group of other children on the block. As the matter is discussed in the family setting, the child who has been involved may say, "I may have been involved, but I didn't do nearly as much mischief as the others." What can the parent say other than, "You only do I know of all the children on the street, therefore I will punish you for your iniquities."

In the Chicago edition of the Old Testament, which has headings for different important passages in scripture, the heading on this passage is "The Categorical Imperative." But what a contrast there is between this passage and the categorical imperative as understood by Kant. Kant stated the categorical imperative as, "So act that you might wish your action to be universal." That way of thinking about moral obligation can undercut the very particularity that is at the heart of the prophetic perspective, which says, in effect, "So act as to be faithful to the special relationship that you have with God."

The scandal of particularity isn't nearly as popular when it is set forth as a unique obligation as when it is connected with liberation. Being enabled to escape from difficulties is always a more attractive possibility than being singled out for obligation. There is nothing about the prophetic message that abrogates the contention that liberation is the first dimension of the drama—but by suggesting that liberation leads to special levels of obligation, the prophets create a unique dimension of morality understood in relationship to covenant. Morality under such circumstances is not a flatly applicable requirement that everyone must fulfill to the same extent and in the same way—but a relational particularity that may impose different levels of demand, even more rigorous kinds of demand upon the people who have experienced liberation and have been called into covenantal relationship than upon those who have not.

Many scholars associate an attempted reform that took place in 622 B.C.E. under the leadership of King Josiah with the prophetic impulse.[7] The basis of this reform is another telling of the narrative of Moses that is found in much of what now constitutes the Book of Deuteronomy. If, as the prophets declare, Israel is both unfaithful and morally corrupt, why not seek to rekindle the devotion and to give the Mosaic Law a renewed emphasis? In Deuteronomy, which was written as a basis for this reform, the Ten Commandments are restated (in chapter 5:1–21) but with a different implication. The implication is that they should be followed "that it may go well with thee," rather than as a response to a liberation gratefully experienced. The reforms also restate many provisions of the covenant code. The crisis that the prophets have recognized is admitted, and a remedy proposed. The narrator invokes the figure of Moses to give weight to the call for a moral renewal that is portrayed as a precondition for survival.

In our times, when the momentous threat posed by the nuclear arms race was felt with special urgency, a number of Christians found in Deuteronomy a passage of particular pertinence to back up their call for the nuclear powers to reverse their rush to possible annihilation. In a sense these opponents of nuclear armament stood very much in the prophetic tradition—clearly able to describe the danger and the probability of doom if the arms race was not overcome, but not necessarily focusing on practical strategies such as diplomats and public officials wrestle with. This is the passage that was used so forcefully (often in condensed form) in the call for nuclear disarmament:

> See, I have set before you today life and prosperity, death and adversity. If you obey the commandments of the LORD your God, that I am commanding you this day, by loving the LORD your God, walking in his ways, and observing his commandments, decrees, and ordinances, then you shall live and become numerous, and the LORD your God will bless you in the land which you are entering to possess. But if your heart turns away and you will not hear, but are led astray to bow down to other gods and serve them, I declare to you this day, that you shall perish; you shall not live long in the land which you are going over the Jordan to enter and possess. I call heaven and earth to witness against you this day, that I have set before you life and death, blessings and curses; therefore choose life, that you and your descendants may live. (Deuteronomy 30:15–19)

In the Exodus account liberation is followed by covenant, and covenant is followed in turn by the particularity of higher demand and even specially directed punishment. "You only have I known . . ." Could it be that if Israel had known what the prophets would say, it might have stayed in Egypt? Perhaps, but nobody can stay in Egypt and become a child of covenant. You can, as the prophets sometimes put it, "return to Egypt!" But that is a terrible fate, especially when "Egypt" is now a new and not even a familiar place of bondage like Assyria.

How truly awful a fate will be examined as we look at the implications of the Exile, which the prophets predicted would come, and the ways Israel responded to it. But, first, in the next two chapters we shall examine the biblical materials that deal with the cosmic setting of the moral enterprise. These materials, which come in the first eleven chapters of Genesis, were beginning to be brought together from oral tradition into written form somewhere near the time when the prophets were preaching—and this is an appropriate time to examine them for their possible bearing on our understanding of morality.

6

The Creation Stories

Stewardship, Embodiment, Moral Order, and Natural Law

The stories of the Creation are often the first thing people read when they turn to the Bible. Even though these stories were not the earliest materials to develop, they are placed in their logical place, at the beginning. These stories often prove to be stumbling blocks to modern readers because if taken literally they seem to be descriptions of specific occurrences that are difficult to reconcile with a number of concepts offered by modern science to explain how the world came to be. They portray a series of events that are believed to have taken place even before the patriarchal narratives—even before the memory of any persons who were participants in the biblical narrative. Hence, the stories of the Creation cannot be considered accounts or redactions of events through which the Hebrews or their immediate forebears lived. These materials are products of reflective and inspired imaginations.

But reflections about protohistorical origins are valuable for an epic account of life's meaning, even for an epic account of a history of a particular people. It will not do, as some theologians have attempted, to separate nature from history and to suggest that primary religious meaning is derived from historical narrative rather than from assertions about nature. Stories about cosmic origins are important for thinking about the human enterprise, and they help to affirm the significance of that enterprise in an overall conceptualization of reality. Moreover, just as many of the issues we have already encountered (such as whether or not kingship is legitimate for a covenant group) have been long debated and are still not resolved, so theological understandings about the significance of the Creation are very much in contemporary dispute, with resulting consequences for doing ethics. Some of the most valuable and most potentially fruitful ideas in the

Western religious understanding of the human condition are associated with the concept of a divinely instituted creation, but some of the most troublesome aspects of that same heritage have stemmed from false contentions associated with this idea.

The Creation stories build to a considerable extent—the exact extent is something about which Old Testament scholars constantly unearth new data and will possibly debate for as long as they practice their profession—on mytho-poetic materials found in other traditions in the ancient Near East. The biblical accounts do not provide either specific details or a general picture of cosmic origins that is altogether different from ideas about these same matters found in the religious traditions of neighboring societies, but that is no drawback to their significance. The biblical writers borrowed language and models for thinking about the Creation from stories current in the surrounding cultures and reinterpreted them in light of Hebraic convictions about the cosmic meaning of the human situation. Such reinterpretation has profound implications.

Strange as it turns out to be, to look upon these stories as historical facts—which contemporary movements like creationism are wont to do—often seems to preclude the study of this material for deeper meanings. Those who become obsessed with the question of whether or not the Creation actually took place as described in the Genesis stories often fail to inquire into the significance of the Creation as a symbolic set of categories for helping to understand the human situation. The fundamental issues for morality concern, not how the Creation took place, but what implications the idea of the Creation has for dealing with the meaning and significance of human life.

The materials concerning the Creation provide a matrix in which moral behavior and ethical understandings can be examined. Just as the concept of land offers important clues to habitat as an aspect of human experience, the concept of a created order extends the range of moral concern and offers an even broader framework with which to reflect on what life in relationship to the whole cosmos means. After all, the created order is the habitat for all creatures, not simply for humans or for a particular group of humans.

The earliest chapters of Genesis contain two stories spliced together at 2:4a. The first of these stories originated later than the second; the second is a composite of two accounts woven together by a redactor who did not completely hide the evidence of what was done. The technicalities involved in dealing with such textual issues are not pivotal for our inquiry and can be explored with the aid of any biblical commentary or critical introduction to the Old Testament. But one question is pivotal for us: What light do the stories in Genesis shed on moral responsibility?

The idea of the Creation suggests that the physical and material world is a fit context for the life of human beings. Ethics cannot be fully loyal to the purposes of God if it deals only with "spiritual" (as counterdistinctive to earthly/worldly/material) dimensions of experience. The Hebraic worldview is essentially world-affirming and remains that way with minor exceptions for its entire history. Some asceticism crept into minority movements in postexilic Judaism and was present in small Jewish sects at the time of Jesus, and some mystical asceticism appeared in later Judaism—but little mysticism or asceticism is present in the Hebrew heritage as compared with a number of other religions in the world.

Although a somewhat greater amount of asceticism has been present in some forms of Christianity, that asceticism has more often taken the form of a communal discipline for dealing with the created "stuff" of this world rather than an intention to completely detach from it. Monasticism, for instance, as it became institutionalized in the Western church, has been, except for its attitude toward sexuality, remarkably affirmative in its view of the created world. Thus, monks have planted gardens, done manual labor, cared for the material wants of the dispossessed, coupled prayer with labor, and developed institutional habitats. Western monasticism might have been very different if the whole created order had been regarded as a great calamitous mistake—something to be escaped from as quickly and as completely as possible.

Speaking in technical theological terms we can suggest that the presence of the Creation as God's initiating act within the cosmic drama holds together theological ideas of transcendence with theological concerns about immanence. The reality and significance of God cannot be understood except in relation to the reality and significance of the world. This overcomes tendencies both toward a mysticism that is otherworldly and a materialism that is entirely this-worldly. In the first, God remains aloof in spiritualized isolation while the Creation is relegated to a realm of secondary or incidental importance; in the second God is relegated to the margins (or repudiated altogether) and creation is regarded as self-explaining and self-sustaining. Neither alternative is consistent with the biblical idea of a meaningful creation, which implies that both the spiritual realm and the material world are concerns of God and hence proper objects of moral attention.

The question has often been raised as to whether or not this view of the world—which regards the sphere of nature as a proper object of human concern, inquiry, and stewardship—accounts for the rise of science in those cultures influenced by the three traditions rooted in the biblical perspective (Judaism, Christianity, and Islam). A belief in the significance of the Creation opens nature to transformation through the exercise of a cocreative role by human beings. The idea of the Creation means that there is a place in a biblically oriented scheme of things for being a scientist—that, as some scientists have put it (more so in the eighteenth and nineteenth centuries than in the twentieth), "science involves thinking God's thoughts after Him." Being a scientist and utilizing technology might also be said to involve "continuing to do God's creating work." This claim, although substantial, nevertheless has tremendous problems associated with it. Lynn White Jr., in an essay entitled "The Historical Roots of Our Ecological Crisis," has pointed out that the exercise of codominion with God may well account for the development in the West of an exploitative relationship to nature—and that the raping of creation so prevalent in Western countries is partly a consequence of thinking that the human realm is superior to the natural order.

White's essay has been enormously influential among the ecologically concerned,[1] but it can be misread. The problem stems from a misuse of a proper relationship, not the premise on which that relationship is based. Others have nuanced the issues more adroitly. Rosemary Ruether claims that the classical interpretations of the idea of creation in Western Christianity have been falsely framed in terms of domination—domination of a male monotheistic God over the world. This has "reinforced symbolically the relations of domination of men over women, masters over slaves, and (male ruling-class) humans over animals and over the earth."[2] If this is true, then it is the idea of domination and even the androcentric understanding of domination, not the idea of creation as such, that is the root of the trouble.

If by "dominion" we mean the way kings behave coercively over their subjects, then indeed the idea that humans have dominion over nature is likely to produce the consequences White and Ruether decry. But if "dominion" is imagined as the way in which God acts toward the Hebrew people, as a solicitous enabler of liberation rather than as a controlling master, then human responsibility in the created order could entail the liberation rather than the subjugation of the natural world and its surrounding space. Instead of the conquering of nature, we would speak of interacting with nature in a creative manner, or of seeking to nurture nature. The difference between these two ways of understanding how humans are to act in relation to the created order does not rest in how the biblical story is written nearly as much as in how the story is read and interpreted. It is entirely plausible to interpret the stories of the Creation as well as other biblical materials in the latter rather than the former sense.[3]

If we take a clue from how Israel's religion guided its relationship to the land, we have ample warrant for holding that the stories of the Creation should be interpreted as prompting a sensitive use of creation in ways that liberate and enrich the natural order rather than as prompting a dominion that subjugates it. The utilization of the natural world for the good of human beings does not necessarily have to result in its exploitation. Even though the term "subdue" appears in one of the stories (1:28) this need not be read as saying God dubbed everything else in creation subservient to the human and thus invited humankind to rape the earth. The divine mandate to "have dominion" does not necessarily license the exploitation of the natural world by human beings. Humans may be mandated to exercise a cocreative function in relationship to the natural order—but only insofar as they can respect all orders of being. All aspects of creation are good, and neither human beings nor natural phenomena are entitled to their being at the expense of the other.

White may well be right about the fact that human beings have treated nature very thoughtlessly throughout Western history, but it is not necessarily the case that such a calamity stems inevitably from the biblical idea of creation. The biblical idea of creation, which involves both the natural and the human aspects of God's work, can serve as well for an ecological ethic as for exploitation. In the work of the World Council of Churches dealing with faith, science, and technology, Eastern Orthodox theologians (who sense nature in more sacramental terms than most thinkers in the West), have insisted that the idea of the Creation means we stand within the same order of being as nature, and not merely above it. E. F. Schumacher turned to Buddhism to declare *Small Is Beautiful*.[4] His reasons for doing so are quite understandable, but the same consequences could be developed through an interpretation of the meaning of creation that acknowledges the commonality and interdependence of all levels of created beings.

The inclusion of the Creation in the biblical narrative and the interpretation of the Creation as something valuable and important, i.e., as "good," means that God is concerned for the achievement of God's purposes in the natural world as much as in the human heart. Justice, for instance, involves how bread is made and distributed—not merely how some theory about equality and fairness is conceptually spun or how an attitude of fairness is spiritually espoused. Justice has to do with how wheat is grown, what happens to farmland, what kinds of pesticides are used and in what ways, and whether or not care is taken to prevent the development of dust bowls. Concerns about material consequences, about the elimination of hunger, about bodily comfort, about agricultural sustainability, about the beauty of landscaping and architecture, and about other technological and aesthetic achievements are not relegated to some secondary level of importance exempt from moral scrutiny. The purposes of God are worked out with the instrumentalities of material substance and within the dynamics of historical process. To believe in the Creation is to hold that the earth, natural resources, the sustainability and integrity of creation, and a host of other vital ecological concerns are of momentous spiritual importance.

The concept of the human stewardship of nature just described is a warranted interpretation of the biblical stories of the Creation. Although this concept has, admittedly, been a model that has lent itself to misuse, if properly understood it does offer grounds for dealing responsibly with the created order. There have been variant models used to portray the relationship between the natural world and the human enterprise. Some of these models are being presented in certain contemporary theological reflection as contrasts to interpretations employing the idea of stewardship.

One model that is attracting considerable attention is suggested by Matthew Fox under the general rubric of "creation spirituality." In this model, the cosmic order rather than the divine being is the primary ground of being. As Fox states it,

> Creation is the source, the matrix, and the goal of all things—the beginning and the end, the alpha and the omega. Creation is our common parent, when "our" stands for all things. Creation is the mother of all beings and the father of all beings, the birther and the begetter. It is all-holy; it is awe filled, from the tiniest onion seed to the towering redwood tree. It is all powerful; it resurrects. If just one person has ever been resurrected from the dead, then we all have, and creation is the inheritor of still more divine surprises. Creation is never finished, never satisfied, never bored, never passive. Creation is always newly born, always making new. It entices us as a lover does to a secret place where it alone will play with us until we lose all sense of past, present, and future, and we become at last and in spite of ourselves fully present to all space and time.[5]

Fox argues that this view is found, not only in the native spiritualities of many religions, but in the Bible and within the Christian tradition.

He reads the second chapter of Genesis as consistent with this perspective (though without explicitly indicating how this is the case); he argues that this view is found in the prophetic books and in the Wisdom literature, as well as in New Testament materials like the prologue to John's Gospel. He finds this view present in the Christian tradition, in church fathers such as Basil of Caesarea and Gregory of Nazianzus, and more explicitly in Hildegard of Bingen and Francis of Assisi (even Thomas Aquinas) during the twelfth century. It is especially evident in Meister Eckhart, as well as in Mechthild of Magdeburg, Julian of Norwich, and Nicholas of Cusa.[6] "Creation spirituality," Fox writes, "re-envisions the Bible and asks new, but very ancient questions of it, honoring as it does the Wisdom literature and the ancient tradition of the Cosmic Christ."[7] Fox contends that this understanding allows us to see ourselves as part of the creation story,[8] and encourages the "deep ecumenism" of solidarity with all religions.[9] It encourages an aesthetic rather than an ascetic direction to spirituality.

Nor is Fox's creation spirituality the only variant for thinking about the significance of creation that contrasts with the more God-centered and even human-centered views that seem to have been most evident in traditional interpretations. Other models have been developed by feminist thinkers. Elizabeth Dodson Gray suggests that it is more fruitful to think of creation as having occurred, not as an artifact that is manufactured by a man's hands, but as a living organism that emerges from a woman's womb.[10] A worker may believe he has utter control over the making of an artifact (though that may not actually be true), but a mother recognizes herself as an instrument of grace in relationship to emerging life. Indeed, according to Gray, the whole of creation itself may be thought of as a womb that gives life to new being. The change in metaphor has important implications, though it does not move entirely beyond a creationist premise. It pushes a theological ethic to take the Creation seriously as a symbol of nurture.

Sallie McFague understands the idea of the Creation as stressing the similarities between the divine and the human, between the human and the natural. According to McFague, however, too much of the traditional thinking about the Creation, which pictures God as external to the world and human beings as sharply differentiated from the natural order, has robbed us of "the sense of belonging in our world and to the God who creates, nurtures, and redeems this world and all its creatures, [so that] we have lost the sense that we are part of a living, changing, dynamic cosmos that has its being in and through God."[11] The inadequate consciousness that has resulted from this way of thinking can be changed, argues McFague, if we think (not descriptively, but analogically and metaphorically) of the world as God's body. In such a view, not only is the dualism between spirit and matter transcended, but a planetary perspective emerges "that calls for all religions, nations, professions, and people to reconstruct their lives and their work to help our earth survive and prosper."[12]

Though McFague does not use the actual terms, she seems to be suggesting that the idea of creation expands the meaning of the idea of land (which is important as habitat) from particular to universal implications. Creation is the habitat of the entire human race, not the private possession of one group within it. But interestingly enough, the implications of this organic, planetary, holistic view also move from the universal to the particular. Individuals can find the ground from which to respect and honor their own created nature—their individual bodies. These become, not things to be disparaged or subdued (as has been done in too much of Western thinking), but in a special sense, "habitats" to be respected, nurtured, and even enjoyed. Human bodies are aspects of creation, the very creation that in the biblical stories is deemed "good."

McFague does not develop her theology from the biblical stories explicitly, but from what she calls "a common creation story" that is woven out of religious and cosmological as well as scientific ingredients. This represents a yearning for a unified view of reality, not a bifurcated one that draws one set of understandings from religious materials and other understandings from philosophy, from the arts, or from science.[13] Although McFague does not build her arguments with explicit use of the biblical materials, there may be something essentially biblical about her approach. It is biblical to speak of human beings as "made in the image and likeness of God." One of the deepest possible implications of the creation stories of the Bible is that all reality has a common origin and an ultimate meaning. Although our efforts at conceptual understanding do not enable us to grasp completely what that unity is, or to describe it in fully satisfactory ways, it stands at the foundation of a creationist perspective.

The ways in which Fox, Gray, and McFague deal with the possible meanings of creation prompt us to consider more imaginatively what it means to be created beings. An interest in what is sometimes called "embodied theology" has probably not been as fully represented in Christian history as the idea of stewardship, and we are hearing it stated with conceptual seriousness as part of the major rethinking that is going on in theology today under the impact of liberationist and feminist reflection.

Nor do we yet know where this will lead. Some will want to repudiate these variants right at the start, judging them to be too different from traditional understandings; others will hail them as important and much needed breakthroughs to a new perspective. Still others will cautiously wait to see whether or not they prove as fruitful or as transforming as their contemporary advocates claim.

We must now turn to a quite different issue that inheres in the significance of the idea of creation for moral reasoning. This issue may be of even greater and more direct importance for ethical reflection than the foregoing one. It can be posed in the form of a question: Does the idea of creation imply that the cosmos has been so arranged and its operation so mandated as to make certain kinds of behavior and certain actions functionally possible but other kinds of behavior and other kinds of action self-defeating? Does certain behavior face inherent difficulties and/or inevitable downfall? Do we live in a world open to any kind of manipulation—moral or immoral as the case may be—or do we live in a world where order operates and where wrongdoing is sooner or later curtailed by a disposition to moral value in the very structure of creation itself?

It is quite clear that it is possible to do only certain things in the realm we call nature. We speak of certain "laws" that govern the workings of that realm. They are the proper object of scientific study. For instance, in hydraulic engineering we know that unconfined liquids will flow according to gravity along the path of least resistance. Unless otherwise contained, liquids always flow downhill. That principle, for instance, governs the design of sewer lines—which are not made to go up and down as does the grade of the street. If the sewage has to be lifted from one section of the city to another in order to continue flowing to the disposal station, it first has to be confined in the chambers of a pump. This is because, in contrast to freely flowing liquids, confined liquids can be forced upward by the application of pressure. That principle governs the design of water lines—in which the confined liquid will go uphill and downhill to arrive where it is to be utilized. We speak of principles such as this as "laws of nature." All the king's edicts and all the president's rhetoric won't make liquids behave differently from this; an act of Congress can't change such laws. Marvelous accomplishments are possible because there is regularity and dependability in such laws, which can be thought of as inherent aspects of creation. Moreover, the accomplishments of engineers are possible only in conformity to such laws and not in defiance of them. Such laws of nature belong—as theologians might put it—to the order of creation.

We must realize, however, as any historian of science can point out, that our perceptions of these laws of nature vary from time to time, sometimes in details, sometimes in the basic paradigm. The laws are not mere facts—because they extrapolate generalities from the observation of discrete phenomena. Particular instances of the flow of water in streams, gutters, or sewer pipes on the one hand, or in closed-in aqueducts and water mains on the other, are describable as facts—but the laws that generalize about the patterns that govern the behavior of liquids belong to another level of knowledge, a product of what is often called induction. Theories about more complex physical processes change more than theories about the more everyday occurrences, and theories that attempt to explain how nature works change more than descriptions of the phenomena with which they deal.

The biblical stories of creation do not, as such, offer much specific content about laws of nature. There are, to be sure, some observations in the biblical stories about how some things occur regularly in the natural world—for instance, about the regularity of the sunshine of the day and the moonlight of the night. The biblical account also observes that a man leaves his father and his mother and cleaves to his wife—though this observation may be considered to be stated descriptively rather than as a prescription. Likewise, the idea that woman is to help[14] man (not necessarily vice versa) probably reflects the social and economic practices of an androcentric culture rather than an immutable natural requirement. It certainly does not have to be treated as a law of nature.

But the relationship of an ordered creation to moral responsibility cannot be comprehensively understood by looking only at so-called laws of nature. The matter becomes more complicated. What goes on in the case of hydraulic engineering may be examined in contrast with what goes on in the development of legal rules governing water rights. Water rights are largely governed by so-called common law; that is, by laws that have been brought into being by the adjudication of cases whose outcomes establish precedents. If you live on a stream, for instance, and build a dam so large that it impedes all of the flow—and someone living downstream depends on that water to drink and to give to his cattle to drink—the courts will tell you that you have to let some of the water escape even while you are filling your pond. A person who violates this common law does not suffer the same immediate consequences as a person going against the laws of physics. In law, the "cannot" of physical laws becomes the "may not" of legal proscription, but that also opens the door for the "should not" of morality to enter into the considerations. Whereas it doesn't really make sense to say you should not try to make unconfined water flow uphill—such an effort might be described as merely frustrating and nonsensical—it does make sense to describe the withholding or polluting of water in a stream as illegitimate (i.e., as illegal or immoral). Legality and morality, therefore, would initially seem to deal with matters where transgressing law is not so much impossible as it is contrary to moral considerations.

The ethicist can ask whether those legal and moral factors that enter into the creation of water rights are rooted in some way or other in the created order just as are the laws of physics that govern water flow. About this ethicists disagree sharply. Some argue that these two kinds of phenomena are similarly governed by the structured workings of creation itself, and that it is just as contrary to the intentions of the natural order to withhold water flow from a downstream neighbor as to try to make unconfined water go upward.

While on the surface it is hard to prove the functional significance of a moral order, there may be some counter evidence in one of our most pressing modern predicaments. Although we have long insisted that a person may not completely withhold the water flow of a stream—we have not insisted with equal intensity that people may not dump pollutants, such as PVCs—into rivers. But maybe the dumping of pollutants violates an ecological law, and we are now paying the price for doing so. This suggestion cannot be proven conclusively, but it cannot be dismissed as nonsense.

But let us examine the question of moral order by looking at arguments and claims that have been made about another issue. In the mid-nineteenth century there were a number of theologians who saw the laws requiring rest on the Sabbath to be based fully as much in the created order of things as the laws of physics. That was the argument my father used on me when I wanted to work in my shop or the yard on Sunday! He carefully explained that human beings were so created as to need one day of rest in every seven calendar days—not one in six or one in eight—and he told me about the unsuccessful attempt of the French Revolution to alter this pattern to one day in every ten.

I don't think my father, who was a Methodist, knew that the conservative Presbyterian theologian Charles Hodge had made a similar argument in defending the Fourth Commandment. Hodge put his contentions this way:

> It is important for all men to know that God created the world, and therefore is an extramundane personal being, infinite in all his perfections. All men need to be arrested in their worldly career, and

called upon to pause and turn their thoughts Godward. It is of incalculable importance that men should have time and opportunity for religious instruction and worship. It is necessary for all men and servile animals to have time to rest and recuperate their strength. The daily nocturnal rest is not sufficient for that purpose, as physiologists assure us, and as experience has demonstrated. Such is obviously the judgment of God.[15]

Two assertions are woven together in this statement of Hodge. One clearly refers to the will or judgment of God, but the other appeals to a sense of how human beings have been created and the limitations they consequently must observe. If Hodge is right, it violates a natural order of things and not merely a divinely enunciated Sabbath law to keep on working and working without taking off one day in seven.

Many ethicists are bound to have questions about such reasoning, and probably emerge with genuine differences about the extent to which it is convincing. The merchants at the shopping mall seem quite able to violate the law of the Sabbath with less immediate consequences than the architects and engineers who build the malls can violate the laws of nature. And, many people in our culture now do something different from their sustenance-earning work two days out of seven. Nobody seems to have been struck down because the pattern has become two out of seven rather than one out of seven days. But even these judgments are not necessarily airtight. Would it not be possible to suggest, with warranted plausibility, that we have all been affected by changes in the social patterns of work in ways that are either too obscure or too subtle to be recognized? For example, is an increase in hypertension a possible consequence of disregard of Sabbath rest? Is the disruptive harshness of contemporary life in modern technological societies a result of the incessant economic scramble that does not pause to rest periodically as it should?

Rabbi Abraham Heschel, in his discussion of the Sabbath does not argue in terms of the created order, but he does speak convincingly of the importance of Sabbath rest and how it constitutes an affirmation of labor, not a means of depreciating its significance, he says,

To set apart one day a week for freedom, a day in which we would not use the instruments which have been so easily turned into weapons of destruction, a day for being with ourselves, a day of detachment from the vulgar, of independence of external obligations, a day on which we stop worshipping the idols of technical civilization, a day on which we use no money, a day of armistice in the economic struggle with our fellow men and the forces of nature—is there any institution that holds out a greater hope for man's progress than the sabbath?[16]

Hodge and Heschel both enunciate the value the Sabbath, but on slightly different premises. Those premises are important to how we think of morality.

An even more general sense of the possible connection between a created order and moral obligation has figured significantly in the preaching and thinking of a number of theologians—though the idea was expressed more frequently in the 1940s and 1950s than it has been recently. I remember that Harry Emerson Fosdick once preached about the terror of Hitler by asking, "Where is Nero now?" He suggested some principle is at work in history that assures the downfall of tyrannies, the demise of dictatorships. He held up the influence of Jesus Christ as a continuing reality to show that Christ's way will triumph over that of tyrannical political power such as Hitler represented—and argued that we must bet our loyalties on Christ, not on the possible triumph of the dictator. He also argued, in several sermons, that one of the things one can see in war is the fact that the people who are victorious frequently adopt the very habits and characteristics of those they conquer. Perhaps he was right. It is quite possible to suggest that America has become as militarized (though probably not as demonic) as the nations it conquered in the World War II.

A similar, perhaps more generalized, expression of this same perspective is found in an early work of the theologian John C. Bennett, who declared "that there is a moral structure in the world which can be discovered, and that this structure can be known apart from any religious authority." Bennett continued, "There is an order of consequences in life that neither individuals nor social groups can long defy without bringing obvious punishment upon themselves. This morality, based upon our general human experience, is not in itself the whole Christian ethic but it is the substructure on which that ethic is based."[17]

In another place, Bennett made the same point at greater length:
Whatever we may think of the ultimate origin of the characteristics of the created world there can be no doubt but that the world has a definite character and when once created it imposes further limitations upon God. For one thing, it is a world of time. Events are

successive. Results follow preparations. Growth and progress mean lowly origins. Also, it is a moral order in which men reap what they sow and God cannot intervene to prevent the harvest, even when it is red with the blood of the innocent, without turning moral order into moral chaos.[18]

Georgia Harkness, the theologian/ethicist who taught for so many years at Pacific School of Religion, was a little more circumspect in declaring belief in a moral order. Nevertheless she was able to go this far in arguing its reality:

Looking around us also to get a cross-section of time, we find a mixture of divine and demonic forces operative in human nature which in their out-working give evidence of God. The negative evidence of God's power, long submerged under a too optimistic view of the world, is reasserting itself in a day of chaos, and preachers are again proclaiming that "whatsoever a man soweth, that shall he also reap." One of the most clear-cut notes in modern (not modernist) theology is that "God is not mocked," that God is a God of wrath and justice as unmistakably as God is a God of love and tender mercy. We see fresh evidence that no society or culture can endure that persistently thwarts the moral ways of the universe, for the forces of aggrandizement by which it climbs to power are the very forces which eventually destroy it. It is written in "the signs of the times," more clearly than in any signs of the heavens by which our forefathers thought to read destiny in the stars, that there are eternal moral laws in the structure of things.[19]

Such professions of belief in a moral ordering of the created universe can be powerful sources of confidence for those who wish to pursue a moral life, particularly in the face of human opposition. Belief in moral order suggests that the whole weight of transcendence lies behind certain kinds of behavior and catches up with violations of the proper doing of things. Perhaps people who believe in a divine order are more likely to pursue the moral path in the face of adversity than those who believe that only chance and coercion affect the course of events. If a person believes that a created order reinforces moral action and undoes (or thwarts) immoral behavior, that conviction can provide an incentive for doing what is right.

But these assertions about moral order are conjectures and stem more from faith than from the observation of human affairs. If such patterns and mandates exist, perhaps they are less immediately operative and observable than the laws of nature. It may be wrong to pollute the environment, but it takes decades for the consequences to come home to roost. Putting PVCs in a river may violate the moral order—but the consequences don't show up immediately and say, "This can't be done!" But even some consequences that we might assign to the laws of nature—such as the laws of nutrition—are a bit like that as well. We don't get zapped for the first violation. Judge Lois Rohr of the federal bench in Philadelphia once told a conference I attended that even though the Bible says that a person who bears false testimony will be struck down—she only saw one fatal heart attack in the witness chair and she is sure that more than one witness gave false testimony.

But some moral obligations do have fairly immediate consequences if they are violated; e.g., in the matter of being honest and maintaining trust. It takes a long period of scrupulous integrity to build up a relationship of trust—but one falsehood can destroy a whole edifice of trust with an immediacy that is almost as certain as anything operating in the case of the laws of nature. Just one discovered betrayal or admitted falsehood casts doubt on all of a person's subsequent behavior.

While we do tend to use the quasi moral language "it shouldn't be done" in cases where the consequences are slower to be felt, the time factor alone isn't a sufficient way to distinguish between the laws of nature and the laws of the moral order. Perhaps language that distinguishes between "laws of nature" and "laws of history" might be helpful—though that hasn't ever been consistently employed on any widespread basis.

One of the factors that the analysis of moral behavior has to reckon with, while laws of nature do not, is human freedom. If wrongful behavior were to have immediate automatic retributive consequences, the moral agency of human beings would be abrogated. While it is risky business to have a created historical order in which malfeasance may proceed with apparent immunity from devastating consequences, that risk is the corollary of having human beings function as fully coparticipants with God in the creative venture of living rather than as pawns in an automated destiny.

When I went to college the tentmate whom I was assigned for orientation camp left and enrolled at Wheaton College in Illinois. We corresponded for a while, and in one of his letters he said, "Japan bombed Pearl Harbor because the Navy was drunk on Saturday night." I do not think he was merely explaining the choice of early Sunday morning, when the sailors were having hangovers in their hammocks—which would have made that observation merely a conjecture about the shrewd logistics of the enemy in choosing a time when its opponents were off guard. Rather, knowing him and the content of his letter, I took him to be saying the attack was a retributive consequence for the moral transgression of a group of people whose behavior was not exemplary.

What do we do with that kind of analysis? It is possible, of course, to regard it as so absurd as to deserve only to be dismissed by laughter. But some of the preaching of the prophets isn't all that different, is it? Furthermore, if you heard something like that in a sermon, on what grounds would you be able to refute it? Those who would merely laugh it off would only betray the fact that their controlling understanding of reality is different, not that they have a clearly demonstrable ground for refuting the idea of a moral ordering of experience.

An experience with a sharply contrasting mind-set has forced me to realize the momentous implications of this issue. I clearly remember a sermon given in a seminary chapel on the Creation story that likened moral judgments to the "naming of the animals." The argument went as follows: Animals can be given any names that can be spoken clearly—the choice reflects no necessary conformity to order, and punishment for choosing particular names is entirely inappropriate, since none of the names are either right or wrong. To be sure, once names are chosen, there does evolve a presumption in favor of using them consistently. (Anthropological relativism has become more prevalent even in seminaries than it was when Fosdick, Bennett, and Harkness were mentors.) If, as the person was arguing, morality is more like the process of picking the names of the animals than like the requirement of consistency in using the names once they are selected, then very little warrant for a particular ethical outlook or standard is incipient in creation. Under such a view no historical calamity is conceivable and no judgment or retribution can be expected against wrongdoing because no created structure exists by which a particular morality is so established in the nature of things as to be counterfunctional to certain kinds of behavior.

Both of these stories deal with the same problem, but portray an entirely different judgment about it. The college orientation tentmate was probably simplistic on one side; the anthropology professor in the chapel talk probably erred on the other. If a moral order exists, it is discerned only dimly through the eyes of a faith conviction and cannot be proven with a merely rational outlook or as a simple backing for a moralistic standard. If we can give any moral behavior approval as readily as we can give names to animals, creation is of doubtful significance for morality. If that is the case, there isn't anything like a created moral order, but merely privatized valuational worlds attracting the loyalties of differing groups, who can only tell their stories to each other without ever arriving at any agreement as to which of the stories is most compelling. This outlook may well describe the wide range of moral behavior that can be observed in human societies, but it is probably not entirely consistent with biblical faith.

This leads to yet another way of thinking about these matters—one that has historically been known as "natural law." A book dealing with the concept of natural law sets forth the definition succinctly:

Natural law: This term does not refer to the laws used in science, such as the laws of gravity or thermodynamics, or chemical formulas. In the field of theology and ethics, natural law really means almost literally "rational law." This theory is derived from the belief that there are rational structures embedded in the process of life; there are realities "out there" in the natural structure of life that can be observed or discovered by man's rational mind. A rational structure in nature is seen by men's reason. An example of such a reality would be the principle of social order, i.e., the need for some kind of minimal state or government. The particular type of state may vary, but the need for a state is a natural-rational condition. Similarly, "Thou shalt not murder within the tribe," is a natural-rational universal principle. This is not an artificial rule "devised by priests to keep the masses down," it is a rather obvious "natural" principle that helps provide survival or protection. Natural law, then, refers to general ethical principles that can be rationally derived from natural structures in life.[20]

There are distinct differences between what is described here as natural law and the ideas that were described in the previous discussion as moral order. Natural law doctrines do not generally contend (there are exceptions) that goodness and consequences relationships operate in the created order in a rewarding/retributive way, but rather that the content of—or at least some content of—the moral obligation can be known apart from any special religious position. Natural law assigns a content to morality that is dependent on reason alone and not on narrative and particularized experience. That content is thought to specify the way in which human affairs must be conducted if they are to be morally satisfying and humanly productive. The provisions of natural law are usually thought of as belonging to the order of creation rather than to historically entered covenants defining the obligations of special groups. Natural law represents that portion of morality that can be acknowledged by all persons regardless of their basic worldview. Hence the ideas embodied under the term "natural law" might also be called "rational law"—and stand in contrast to laws of nature and events of history. Appeal to natural law has frequently been used to warrant an authoritarian imposition of certain requirements upon an entire society, since such requirements are deemed rationally grounded, not the special dictates of a religious tradition.

Those who believe in the concept of natural law—and the idea may stem historically more from Stoic thinking than from biblical experience—hold that all rational beings can know the content of natural law and pattern their behavior accordingly. There are no preconditions of faith or covenantal experiences required to know natural law. Moreover, the requirements of natural law can be made obligatory on all persons, whether or not they are members of any faith-defined group having a special set of standards and commitments. Moral truth in the natural law tradition is often claimed to be independent of any specific narrative or moral response that changes from epoch to epoch or from one set of circumstances to another.

But does creation offer us that kind of assured formulation—a formulation that can be demonstrated conclusively from commonly available experience? Does the idea of creation imply such assured formulations about a special range of so-called natural knowledge—even though it does not necessarily offer the whole scope of moral obligation that is necessary for a person of a particular faith commitment? Those who say that it does will argue that the very nature of creation, including the rationality found in the human mind as a part of the created order, suggests that God created a world in which:

- it is impossible to have a society unless stealing is proscribed
- social order will disintegrate if violent murder is allowed
- telling falsehoods (especially under oath) will undermine the trust necessary for human community
- parents must be respected if families are to thrive

But natural law has also been used to declare that:

- it would be wrong to lie even to save a life
- it is wrong to do anything that might hasten or contribute to death, even to relieve suffering
- it is wrong to perform abortions
- it is wrong to use mechanical (i.e., artificial or "unnatural") means of birth control

These and other moral stipulations have been proposed as based on reason and applicable to all persons in all circumstances, but they remain very much matters of genuine and legitimate debate.

Needless to say, the validity of belief in natural law is a matter of intense disagreement. A large group of Christians believe that to postulate the existence of natural law is to rob God of the freedom to determine what is morally required, the holy providence to set forth commandments by virtue of a transcendent rule, or even to reveal to persons in the particular contexts of their ongoing experiences what is required of them in unique circumstances. Such believers in the ethics of divine commands and situationally located guidance hold that the idea of natural law must be repudiated lest God's freedom to guide moral decision be abrogated by the imposition of inflexible law.

But the advocates of natural law are impressed with the dependabilities that are rooted in the idea of a created order, and they prefer to hazard making God's will inflexible in order to render it trustworthy rather than to relate God's command to particular contexts in order to render it relevant. The stories of creation probably warrant some of the affirmations that inhere in thinking about moral order and natural law, but it is doubtful that they can be used to substantiate a wide-ranging and inflexible use of the doctrine to bolster a set of positions that one particular group has arrived at through historically contingent judgments and feels warranted in forcefully imposing on all others.

But the stories of the Creation are not the only parts of the Bible to be considered in thinking about moral issues. Some interpretations of the Wisdom literature are consistent with the idea of natural law; other aspects of the narrative, some of which we have already examined, support the contentions of those who emphasize God's total freedom in giving shape to moral obligation on a changing and ongoing basis. If the stories of the Creation were the only parts of the Bible, natural law might be affirmed with considerable plausibility. If there were no stories of the Creation, contextual situationalism could probably bear most, if not all, of the weight of Christian morality. Although difficult, the task of working out an appreciation of how history and nature, flux and structure, context and law, specific happenings and ongoing patterns, contribute in complementary ways to a sense of how God works through the lives of persons and communities is one of the most challenging tasks of theological ethics. The Bible helps us to do this but it does not relieve us of the burdens that go with doing so and it does not eliminate the complexities involved.

7

From Garden to Tower

Perceiving a Disruption of the Original State

In his socioliterary introduction to the Hebrew Bible, Norman K. Gottwald observes that the religious significance of the Creation, particularly as found in the first chapter of Genesis, may be captured by the following rubric: "Everything in its Place; A Stable Cult in a Stable Cosmos."[1] Although Gottwald probably has in mind the account (Genesis 1:1–2:4a) that was composed by a priestly writer concerned with stabilizing Jewish life liturgically in a time of disorienting circumstances, Gottwald notes how the idea of the Creation contributes to a worldview "in which every object, person, and activity has its meaningful place and its proper/improper function."[2] As we have seen in the last chapter, this understanding of the Creation supports the idea of moral order and is generally consistent with such ethical categories as natural law. By deeming creation "good" the Creation stories render plausible the belief that there is cosmic reinforcement for doing what is right.

However, chapters 3 to 11 of Genesis contain several stories that involve a quite different sense of the human condition. These stories portray in various ways a deep sense of disruption, and most particularly a sense of how wrenched the relationship between God and human beings has become. These stories include:the account of the Garden and the violation of the prohibition against eating the forbidden fruit (Genesis 3); an account of how human wickedness has become so great that God regrets having created human beings and even makes an effort to start over again (6–7); and finally a story about a human effort to escape the limitations that distinguish human from divine prerogatives (11:1–9).

These stories of the Garden, the Flood, and the Tower of Babel can be read as mythological explanations for such ongoing phenomena as the toil necessary for productivity, the pain involved in giving birth to children, the reason people wear clothes, the reason there are so many languages in the world. Such etiological explanations are interesting enough but are incidental in comparison with the deeper moral implications of this material. The moral thrust stems from the way in which these stories suggest a view of the human condition that stands in dialectical contrast with the ideas of harmony and order implied by the Creation stories.

Although these stories come to us in mythological form, they are significant for moral reflection for several reasons. First, they evidence a deep-seated realization that there is something profoundly amiss with the human condition; second, they warn against human presumption, particularly against a presumption that amounts to a denial of dependence upon divine sovereignty; third, they have been cited by many theologians—particularly those in so-called "realist" camps[3]—as warnings against relying too naively on the good intentions of others; fourth, they portray a divine forbearance with which God remains determined to achieve God's ultimate purposes without giving up on the human enterprise despite the problems presented by human behavior. The stories also tend to reflect a pattern of male domination that is under intense contemporary scrutiny.

At least three apparent explanations for the disruptions that afflict the human situation are identified in these several stories. One suggests that the disruption stems from disobedience; human beings are seen as very early refusing to abide by specific injunctions laid upon them by their Creator. A second suggests that the disruption stems from presumption: human beings are described as seeking to transcend their role, to go beyond their appointed place in creation. A third indicates that personal disintegration is responsible, a disintegration stemming from the internalization of disruptive forces and leading to a loss of integrity and the breakdown of all relationships. One or another of these explanations may be more evident in some of the accounts than in others, but all of them are implicitly present in each of the stories.

In the story of the Garden one of the most interesting passages is the one where Adam and Eve are told, "You may freely eat of every tree of the garden; but of the tree of the knowledge of good and evil you shall not eat!" (2:16–17) Adam and Eve disobey this restriction—though it is difficult to see how they could disobey without in at least one sense knowing right from wrong. But the restriction itself is a curious one. It is not so much a prohibition of moral wrongdoing as it is a limitation on moral capability. To rephrase it rather freely into the terms that we have been using—the first human beings were told they were not to come to know the natural law—that they were to understand morality as a matter of obedience and not as autonomous decisions about what is right and wrong. This implies, perhaps, that they would be allowed to enjoy the Garden contentedly so long as they didn't try to think ethically! Admittedly, there may be a strange similarity between the Fall and doing theological ethics; both of them do play havoc with bliss. But the meaning of the story goes deeper. The disobedience that is the root cause of the problem is not some transgression of a moral command, but a presumption that is discontented with a divinely imposed limitation on human beings. Another reading of this story would emphasize that a call to ethical awareness and responsibility cannot be divorced from the necessity of choice, and that the necessity of choice cannot be exempted from the possibility of choosing wrongly.

Similarly, in the story of the Tower there is nothing that implies the people in the city were doing anything contrary to a rationally established measure of good versus evil. They were not punished for organized crime, or for personal vice, but were stopped in their ascent for a presumptive use of elementary engineering skills. Neither this account, nor the story of the Fall, portrays the action that leads to the punishment as a violation of a moral obligation in the natural law sense of that term. Similarly, in explaining the probable cause for the Flood no list is given of specific transgressions that had been committed by the people. Instead, the writer merely says, "The LORD saw that the wickedness of humankind was great in the earth, and that every imagination of the thoughts of their hearts was only evil continually" (6:5). This is to say that these stories suggest that evil has become internalized in the human creature and is not merely a form of external malbehavior that an innocent or neutral agent gets caught doing.

It is, of course, impossible to read these stories without realizing that they have to do with sin. The average person-in-the-street thinks of sin as something involving moral transgression or rule breaking—frequently of an individualized nature. Sinful actions include such things as stealing an apple from the grocery store; cheating on the tax return; using some deleted expletives on the tapes of office conversations. (Even sophisticated leaders fall into this tendency. For instance, Billy Graham was convinced that the Watergate episode revealed a serious corruption in the Nixon administration only when he heard that the unedited tapes had contained language unacceptable in polite society.)

In many respects the common person's understanding of sin seems to make far more sense than do these biblical stories. The stories may even seem to imply that God is a jealous tyrant who demands to be obeyed even when the commands that are issued arearbitrary, or else that God gets afraid when skillful activity among the people promises to get them too close to an exclusive domain that is jealously guarded as a divine prerogative. While these stories from the Bible talk seriously about the human condition, they don't use the word "sin" as such and certainly not the term "original sin." Yet, these narratives suggest that whatever it is that is wrong in the human condition is much deeper than the intentional doing of moral evil. That aspect of the experience is something present in the human condition even when no moral wrong (at least moral wrong as understood as the deliberate and malicious violation of a rational set of ethical standards) is involved. It is no wonder, then, the Bernard Ramm, in a small but probing discussion of the doctrine of sin, employs the phrase "offense to reason."[4] Referring to Pascal, Ramm says, "[He rightly] said that the doctrine of the Fall and Original Sin is folly to the human mind. It insults it; threatens to undermine it; it challenges its autonomy; it makes a magisterial accusation."[5] It might be somewhat more precise to say, not that these stories assault reason, but that they run counter to a use of reason that regards autonomous moral choice as possible and legitimate for human beings.

This biblical view of the human condition is particularly offensive to the heirs of the Enlightenment because it flies in the face of deep assumptions about the human condition. There is a very real sense in which the mood of the Enlightenment (which is the controlling mood of much contemporary thinking) finds these stories either puzzling or difficult to accept. Preferring to think positively and to concentrate on what human beings can do if allowed to pursue their good senses rationally, the intellectual heirs of the Enlightenment utilize concepts like the infinite worth of each individual to portray a created order that will be purged of malfeasance by morally earnest goodwill. They find the idea of remaining in the role of the creature—and more particularly the idea that such a role will be happy and fruitful only if enjoyed in a premoral condition—particularly unacceptable.

But the sense of deep disruption implied in these stories is also troublesome (and hence unacceptable) to certain religious perspectives. The stories seem to deny that human beings can be inspired and guided to live out the possibilities of the Creation (with its assertions about the goodness of things) by proper upbringing and spiritually guided moral formation. Instead, the stories seem to assert that human rebellion against the divine ordering of things is deep-seated and has apparently been intertwined with the nature of things from almost the very beginning. Pushed logically, this develops into a doctrine of original sin. This term does not appear in

Hebraic thought, but those Christian theologians who embrace it find the story in Genesis 3 one of the chief sources for the idea. Typical of later Christian thinking is an observation made by Blaise Pascal: "Yet if [the idea of original sin is] not granted nothing can be explained; [whereas] if granted, all can be explained.[6]

One way of determining whether or not the idea of original sin is a plausible interpretation of the story of the Garden would be to ask whether anything in contemporary experience provides a similar awareness of a radical disjunction between the harmony intended for creation and the experiences common to people. To examine that question it is possible to start with a story that describes an event that could happen in almost any of our lives.

> Mary and John were proceeding along a busy street at much slower than the posted speed limit. Their car was in top mechanical condition—and had been carefully checked for safety just the day before. John, who was driving, was as alert as it is humanly possible to be, and Mary also was watching the road.
>
> First, the ball: Then the child ran out between the cars parked on the side. John applied the brakes with all deliberate speed, but to no avail. The child was fatally hit.
>
> The investigating police refused to charge John in any way. He had committed no crime, they said, because he had broken no traffic laws and had exercised every precaution that could be expected of any prudent person. The insurance company settled with the child's parents, but marked a special notation on the driving record—claim paid but accident not the driver's fault! The child's parents came to see John and Mary to express their sense of solidarity in suffering, knowing that John (and even Mary, who wasn't driving) felt terrible. A professor of philosophy, who knew the couple, explained that no direct or intentional culpability was involved.
>
> But John and Mary felt awful. Their feeling can be described as closer to guilt than to any other experience they knew. They were troubled in a bone-deep way—in a way that went even deeper than the sense of remorse that one feels when one realizes that one deliberately has done something quite wrong. An identifiable wrong for which one is clearly responsible is often relatively easy to "fess up to," but this sense of having been caught in a historical situation by an entanglement with circumstances that cannot be lightly shrugged off is another matter. John and Mary's nights were restless, and they were not at peace with themselves.

In some bone-deep sense, but not in a highly cogent and rational-ized way, they felt guilty, even though the police said they weren't culpable, the insurance company didn't hold the event against them, and the dead child's parents were trying their best to indicate they harbored no anger. Mary and John were experiencing life as dis-rupted.

It is no more possible to understand this story on a moralistic level than it is to understand the biblical story of the Garden with a moralistic idea of sin. These stories pose issues about a disruption that is still deeper and more fundamental.

We can also imagine that Mary and John would be troubled by their feelings. Perhaps they shared their sense of psychic dislocation (or dis-ease) with a local minister. In this time of such diverse theological perspectives, there is no way of predicting what the minister might have said to them. The minister might have some Freudian perspectives picked up in a psy-chology or counseling course, and have suggested that the sense of guilt they were experiencing was irrationally founded on earlier childhood trau-mas. Moreover, he or she might have indicated that the guilt could be therapeutically expunged by recalling those traumas so as to relive them without attaching guilt complexes to them.

The minister might, God forbid, have suggested that John and Mary might be undergoing a punishment for some transgression they personally had committed even if they had already forgotten about it. Far too many ministers suggest to persons who are sick that something like this is the case! The minister might have indicated that this whole problem could be solved if only they would "pray about it a little harder"—perhaps even thinking of that prayer as a way of confessing the wrongs they had done.

John and Mary might even have gone to church seeking some way to deal with their experience. They might have been to a service offering absolution and reconciliation. But they might have been in the chapel service at a well-known seminary chapel on February 19, 1987, where in place of the peace offered as forgiveness and reconciliation flowing from God's work in the drama of redemption, they would have been asked to join in this affirmation:

I dare to say, I AM; to believe in who I am; to look at foe imprisoning me, to open my eyes and fin'ly see that I'm the one who chooses what I'll be. I dare to say, I AM, to believe in who I am, to thank the friends who stand by me and lovingly have set me free to say, I AM, to say I'll always be.

But the minister might also have indicated that John and Mary were feeling one aspect of what it means to live after the Fall—that is, to be part of a human enterprise as it is experienced outside the garden of bliss. The minister might have pointed out that John and Mary are now in a position to realize why sin cannot be understood merely as private culpable wrong-doing but must be seen as a characteristic quality of historical existence itself in a disrupted world.

We now can move from parable and narrative to the discursive genre of scholarship by quoting a passage from an encyclopedia—one with short entries almost like a dictionary. In it we might find this description of the term *sin:*

> Sin, as distinguished from crime (violation of the civil law) and [sin as distinguished] from vice (immorality resulting from the disregard of the social and ethical standards of society) is an act or attitude by which the reality of God is denied or violated. The conception of sin is therefore meaningful only in the context of religion.[7]

The key phrase here is "an act or attitude by which the reality of God is denied or violated." That phrase may be quite meaningful in shedding light an the several stories in Genesis. Adam and Eve did not violate an ethical principle or standard that could be warranted independently of God's command. The injunction, "Thou shalt not eat of the tree of the knowledge of good and evil" is a divinely given command, not a rationally defensible categorical imperative having a legitimacy of its own. Breaking it involves denying the reality of God.

Similarly, the action of God in breaking down the Tower of Babel implies that any effort to get into heaven by humanly devised strategies is doomed—doomed, we might say, because it would be "an act or attitude by which the reality of God is denied or violated."

When the concept of denying or violating the reality of God is further abstracted and made into a category, it is called "hubris," or pride. That is, a penchant on the part of the creature to declare an independence of the Creator. If the Garden is a place of utopian bliss, who needs anything from the Creator? Who needs to acknowledge the sovereignty of the God who made the Garden as long as the Garden's benefits can be completely and perfectly enjoyed on the basis of doing well within it? Human beings can name the animals, cultivate the trees, enjoy their own company, be fruitful and multiply—all without deference to deity. Adam and Eve might well be said to have seized the initiative, but the message of the story is that they did so in such a way as to imply they could do without God—and that was their undoing.

But the phrase, "an act of attitude by which the reality of God is denied or violated," does not fit the Mary and John of our contemporary story as clearly as it fits Adam and Eve's behavior. John and Mary weren't deliberately trying to deny or violate the reality of God. They weren't rebelling at all— just going about a normal and legitimate way of living. But something per- ilously close to hubris comes into play in all the different scenarios with which various persons with whom they spoke tried to deal with that inci- dent. These bear closer scrutiny: If there isn't any culpability, the whole thing might supposedly be easy to assign to oblivion. "No crime," said the police. But why does the insurance company pay instead of simply telling the child's parents—"Tough luck!" If the feeling of guilt is merely the evidence of a maladjusted psyche, and can be expunged by therapy, then wouldn't it be appropriate for John and Mary to celebrate by having a grand fling to revel in their newfound sense of well-being and to rejoice because their counsel- ing had enabled them to put behind them all those religious hang-ups? But wouldn't that be a way of denying the majesty and existence of God? If Mary and John tried to discover some hidden wrong their moralistic minis- ter says they must have committed, and if that had propelled them into a form of works/repentance, could that not have easily become a means for manipulating God rather than relying on God's grace?

The possibilities for denying or violating the providence of God are not present only in the initial event, but become significantly magnified in all of the possible ways people can respond to the initial event. Such a pattern can be seen in the Story of the Fall—where Adam passes the blame to Eve, and Eve passes it to the Serpent. Even if eating of the tree of the knowl- edge of good and evil isn't an immoral act as judged by an autonomous measure of right and wrong, the dumping of guilt on somebody else after the event clearly is!

The element of presumption as embodied in the condition of human sinfulness not only undermines human dependence on God, but poisons human interactions as well. Those who attempt to make theological ideas understandable to the general public do not find it easy to counteract the prevalent perception of sin as merely moral wrongdoing. Nor is it easy to demonstrate how behavior that does not involve moral malfeasance can nevertheless be presumptive and even socially disruptive. However, per- haps this can be done, even with a children's sermon:

Billy was very proud of the new bike that had just been given to him for his birthday. It had red fenders with mud flaps and white trim on the frame. It had a big red reflector on the back and a shiny chrome light on the front. What more could any boy want for a birthday than a big shinybicycle like this? Billy started out to show it to his friends on the street.

Billy's heart was pounding faster, it seems, than it had ever pounded before. "Now I'll show them," Billy said secretly to himself. "Nobody else on this whole street has a bicycle as new and as 'keen looking' as mine. When the other kids see it they will just have to treat me as the 'big wheel' around here."

Billy spotted Arthur down the street, just coming out to play. Around his waist he had tied his nearly worn-out cowboy gun and leather holster. "See my new bike?," said Billy, as he ground to a sudden stop near Arthur's driveway. "Yes," said Arthur, "it sure is new, but one pop from my old cowboy gun would fix your tire for good. A gun is better than a bike—who ever heard of cowboys who ride bikes?"[8]

Billy was taken aback by Arthur's attitude. Arthur was not impressed by his bike, and he did have a point about the cowboys. "Arthur must still think he's the 'big shot' around here," said Billy to himself.

Just them Billy saw Johnny coming out of his house, and quickly rode up to show Johnny his shiny new bicycle. Johnny looked it all over very carefully, and finally said, "But where's the horn?" My bike has old dull paint, but at least it has a horn. How are you going to warn people you are riding near unless your bike has a horn?"

Now Billy had never given the matter of a horn attention, since he was so pleased with the rest of the new bike. But now that Johnny mentioned it, he began to be very unhappy inside. "Nobody can have the most important bicycle on the street if it doesn't have a horn on it," Billy thought to himself. "It doesn't matter how big or how shiny the bicycle is, it has got to have a horn!" Billy asked Johnny, "How much do horns cost?" "I think they cost about $7.00," Johnny replied. Billy did some quick arithmetic (and wished now he had learned his school lessons better). "My allowance," he figured, "is fifty cents a week. It will take fourteen weeks to save up that amount. Gee, that's a long time to wait."

Billy did not know what to do next. Nobody, he mused, would be impressed with his bicycle as long as it had no horn. Suddenly he got an idea and turning to Johnny said, "But my bike has a shiny new headlamp and yours doesn't. Isn't a headlamp as good as a horn?"

"Oh no," said Johnny, "our mothers don't let us ride after dark anyway. You will never use your headlamp."

Billy turned to go home. His heart was heavy and he walked alongside his bike rather than riding it. "Why aren't you riding your bike, Billy?" said a friendly voice from behind the bushes in front of one of the houses Billy passed. It was the voice of Mrs. Jones, who was out in the yard digging up the soil under her evergreen trees. (Three days earlier her neighbor had dug up the soil under her trees and had remarked that everybody else on the street had sloppy tree beds!) But despite the rush to get finished before dark, Mrs. Jones walked out to have a look at Billy's new bicycle. "That's some bicycle," she said admiringly. "But the other boys don't think so," said Billy. "Arthur thinks his cowboy gun is better and Johnny says a bike is no good without a horn. He has a horn on his old battered bike, you know."

Billy began to cry a little. Somehow you could cry in front of Mrs. Jones when you could never cry in front of the other boys. Mrs. Jones understood. Finally, Billy sobbed, "Mrs. Jones, why don't the other boys like my bicycle as well as you do?"

Now boys and girls, our time has run out. What do you suppose Mrs. Jones said to Billy? Talk this over with your parents and see if you can bring some answer when you come to church next Sunday.[9]

The stories that portray the human condition as disrupted may provide a possible restraint on presumption, whether that presumption takes the form of a human claim against God or the form of a human pretension against other humans. But these same stories can also be used to argue for the necessity of behaving, not as human beings in their essential nature might have been created to behave in an ideal world, but as human beings who live in a fallen world seemingly have to behave in order to survive in a world deeply affected by the Fall. Moreover, as the story of Billy and his bike suggests, the condition of human beings is disrupted when they base their sense of importance on the possession of things.

Think back to the movement that arose to establish a king in Israel and its counterparts in subsequent Christian history. These have all been premised on the belief that in a fallen world it is necessary to employ coercive measures to establish internal order and to ward off external threats. These movements gain plausibility whenever it is believed that human beings are so disposed to sin that they can be made to observe minimal standards of decency only by facing the prospects of punitive action and even the threat of destruction. The relationship between original sin and coercive politics is not put in quite such stark terms in the biblical accounts of the rise of kingship, but it is set forth in unmistakable form in the thinking of Christian figures like Augustine and Luther. To use phraseology derived from Augustine: If we live in a fallen city of this world, even as strangers and pilgrims, we must make peace and sustain order by the methods that function in the city of this world. These methods are determined by the fact of sin—the sin that shapes human responses in a real world, including those responses that Christians can (and must) make to stem political and social malfeasance by the use of coercive power. In such thinking the idea of a moral order that supports and sustains faithfulness to what has been created good and right is seriously qualified (not necessarily explicitly) as irresponsibly sentimental or irrelevant.

Although such political "realism" enjoyed widespread acceptance in many circles during and right after the World War II, and is still influential in some quarters today, it is currently being questioned, protested, and rejected from a variety of alternative outlooks. These outlooks include creation spirituality; anthropological exploration into the possibility that human social structures were once more egalitarian and peaceful because they were matriarchal in form; several views that hold that the primal wilderness was essentially harmonious; ecofeminism; and radical post-Christian feminism.[10] According to Rosemary Ruether, the traditional interpretation (which combines Hebrew, Platonic-Gnostic, and Pauline-Augustinian ways of thinking) has caused major social problems in the Western cultural tradition because it depends on creating a polarity between good and evil, which prompts those who identify themselves as good (primarily males) to dominate others. This perspective "creates ideologies that justify the doing of evil to others as a means of overcoming evil!"[11]

Ruether's argument certainly forces a radical reexamination of the traditional view. It contends that instead of serving as an antidote to presumption, the stories actually serve to engender a number of presumptions—the presumption of males that they are destined to have dominant roles, the presumption that human beings are destined to conquer and subdue nature, and the presumption of persons who consider themselves so righteous that they are commissioned to perform the necessary task of attempting to stem evil by coercive means.

It may be necessary, as the exponents of creation spirituality and kindred positions argue, to eliminate the idea of a Fall and to repudiate the theologies of redemption that have arisen to deal with the subsequent human condition. If that is the case, further probing along the biblical narrative will presumably point us in that direction and provide collaborating considerations. If, in contrast, the possible use of these stories as an antidote for presumption has more to commend it than their use to warrant harsh moralism and political realism, that judgment will be substantiated by further reading of, and reflection on, the biblical narrative.

This chapter should not end without one further set of observations about the stories that have been the focus of all the foregoing reflections. While each of the stories indicates that the harmony of the created order has been lost, each of the stories also indicates that the effect of that loss does not abrogate the possibility of continued human life nor cancel the intention of God to work through human beings to consummate the purposes that are implicit in creation. In brief compass and with modest suggestiveness, each of these stories portray a divine grace profoundly tendered even as they each portray a loss of original innocence.

Adam and Eve are given clothes to cover their nakedness (Genesis 3:21), and although they are expelled from the Garden they are allowed to live together in mutual support and companionship. They are permitted to have offspring and to populate the earth with their own kind (4:1). After the Flood, God assures Noah that no matter how evil the imagination of human hearts may become, human beings will not ever again be destroyed, and that the regular patterns of nature so essential to human life will not be disrupted (8:21f.). Moreover, Noah is to be blessed with offspring. Although the builders of the Tower are scattered and confounded with a multitude of languages, they are not destroyed, nor is their capacity for making artifacts taken away. As this is written many states are enacting "three strikes and you are out" laws to put those who commit three felonies in prison for life without parole. In this part of Genesis the pattern can be described as "three strikes and human beings are still in."

We now have another dialectic. This is the dialectic between sin and salvation. Indeed, there is a symbiotic relationship between the acceptance of a radically "pessimistic" view of the human condition and acceptance of the view that God takes an ever increasing initiative in proffering salvation. The more a person considers salvation to be a gift from God, the more likely that person is apt (or able) to stress the depth—and, as measured by human powers, the hopelessness—of the human predicament. Severe views of sin, which can even employ terminology like "total depravity," are acceptable only when held in relationship to promising views of salvation, views that may even employ terminology like "irresistible grace." Without the dialectical tension, such terms (and even all the lesser descriptions of human nature and human destiny that point to its very complex and ambiguous quality) make little sense. We will see this more clearly as the biblical narrative unfolds for us deeper understandings of the idea of salvation.

8

Exile as a Crisis of Faith

Contrasting Reconfigurations of the Moral Stance

We left the narrative of Israel's history with the preaching of the eighth-century prophets. Figures like Amos and Hosea were convinced that Israel had been unfaithful to her covenantal obligations, and they anticipated that the chosen people would be punished because of that infidelity. The eighth-century prophets anticipated that the foreign nations would overrun (if not, indeed, destroy) Israel and Judah. In that prophetic perspective God's special concern for Israel produces this form of the categorical imperative: "You only have I known of all the families of the earth; therefore I will punish you for your iniquities" (Amos 3:2).

The doom oracles of the eighth-century prophets were reinforced in the judgment of the seventh-century prophets and became all too true. Babylon, under a ruthless leader, Nebuchadnezzar, attacked Jerusalem and carried some of its inhabitants into exile in 597 B.C.E. Eleven years later a far more devastating siege occurred in which the city and the Temple were destroyed, the Davidic kingship was cut off, and a large number of the remaining population were taken to Babylon to live. The term "the Exile" is used to speak of the events that crescendoed in this decade of tragedies. Not all members of the covenant group were carried into Babylon, however. Others were scattered into different places, including Egypt.[1] Nevertheless, the serious scattering and attendant disruptions created a crisis of faith. How could the people understand God's continued concern for Israel under such circumstances?

The moral implications of the Exile differ from the moral implications of the bondage in Egypt. Egypt represents a situation of oppression for which the victims have no responsibility; the preaching of the prophets forces the conclusion that the Exile is a condition of captivity brought about by Israel's infidelity, for which the Israelites therefore bear responsibility. Being oppressed by the accidents of history and being made captive as a punishment for infidelity have very different moral meanings. The experiences may not differ radically in terms of suffering and/or disruption, but the understanding of the experience differs sharply. In relationship to Egypt the blame for the difficulties can be laid entirely at the feet of others; in relationship to the Exile much of the blame has to be taken upon the self. In the situation of Egypt the experience is one of being wronged; in the Exile, prophetic preaching presupposed, the experience is one of having done wrong. In the case of oppression the potential solution can be escape; in the case of wrongdoing the potential solution must be a turning around, or metamorphosis. Bruce C. Birch is quite right in suggesting "that exile offers not a new setting for Exodus theology but its own models of exile theology which speak to radically different alternatives for understanding God and God's people than does Exodus."[2] Even though Exodus and the Exile are both parts of the overall biblical narrative, theological ethics responding to the Exile will differ from theological ethics responding to Exodus.

Efforts to explore the moral meaning of the Exile take diverse forms in the writings of the prophetic figures whose careers span the time period when these momentous events took place—most notably the writings of Jeremiah, Ezekiel, and the author (or authors) of the latter part of the Book of Isaiah (chapters 40–66). The efforts of these several figures to make theological sense out of the Exile not only deal with the crisis at hand but also become the basis on which persistent wrestling with similar issues continues throughout most of the remaining biblical narrative. In the writings of these figures a new dialectic emerges, a dialectic involving a tension between punishment and hope, between a sense of having proven profoundly unfaithful and a belief in the possibility of being renewed.

The dialectical tension between punishment and hope is especially vivid in Jeremiah. He castigates the unfaithfulness of the people with as much fury as did any of the eighth-century prophets. He admonishes the people to accept their punishment as just dues for their waywardness. For his efforts he suffers the arrows of hostility that are aimed at those who preach judgment against their own group, and he reacts with intensive melancholy and dejection. But he also foresees an eventual renewal—a time when the punishment will be lifted and the faithfulness of the people restored. Boldly he declares:

The days are surely coming, says the LORD, when I will make a new
covenant with the house of Israel and the house of Judah. It will not
be like the covenant which I made with their ancestors when I took
them by the hand to bring them out of the land of Egypt, a covenant
which they broke, though I was their husband, says the LORD. But
this is the covenant which I will make with the house of Israel after
those days, says the LORD: I will put my law within them, and I will
write it on their hearts; and I will be their God, and they shall be my
people. No longer shall they teach one another or say to each other,
"Know the LORD," for they shall all know me, from the least of them
to the greatest, says the LORD; for I will forgive their iniquity, and I
will remember their sin no more. (Jeremiah 31:31–34)

Throughout his book Jeremiah places a good deal of confidence in the
new covenant—a covenant built more on the experience of forgiveness
than on the experience of liberation.

In speaking about forgiveness Jeremiah implies that the experience of
having been unfaithful differs from the experience of having been oppressed. It involves self-blame rather than resentment of what others do. It
involves a sense of having betrayed a trust rather than of having had one's
rights or person violated. We can understand this difference when we realize that Judas hanged himself because he was crushed by a sense of guilt
after he betrayed Jesus. Had Judas experienced only oppression, going to
prison as a witness to Jesus as Paul and Silas did, he might even have joined
them in singing in jail at a midnight hour. Perhaps the experience of guilt
is even more devastating than the experience of oppression. But such a
suggestion is apt to be unconvincing, even offensive, to those experiencing
oppression. Suggesting that the feeling of guilt is psychologically, at least
(and perhaps even spiritually), even more devastating than the experience
of oppression is likely to prompt controversy. When I once made this suggestion in class it provoked a vocal and insistent complaint, primarily from
minorities, that only a white male tenured professor would suggest that
guilt produces a greater despair than oppression! After all, a person in the
shoes of privilege has everything to be guilty about but cannot have any
idea what oppression is like. Perhaps a concern about guilt is an affluent
middle-class hang-up.

It is probably fruitless to push for an answer to the question: "Which is
more devastating to the moral self—the condition of oppression or the
experience of guilt?" Moreover, moral reflection on the experience of the
Exile does not depend on demonstrating that a Babylonian captivity is
worse than an Egyptian slavery. The biblical materials don't argue whether
Egypt or the Exile is the more devastating disablement. Both are present in

the overall account; each raises a particular kind of problem for faith. It is no more faithful to the biblicalnarrative to emphasize the Exile and ignore Egypt than to emphasize Exodus and ignore the Exile.

It may be true that there have been (and continue to be) forms of Christianity that construe biblical faith as almost entirely concerned with the problem of guilt—if fact, such forms of Christianity are probably most characteristic of Western orthodoxies. They need to be corrected by theologies that are concerned about the problem of oppression. But if the preoccupation with oppression eliminates concern about guilt and moral shortcomings in the covenant group, the consequences can be just as unbiblical as have been the preoccupations with guilt that have rendered so many versions of Christian theology seemingly oblivious to oppression.

The career of the prophet Ezekiel spans the period of the early Exile, and his writing reveals a profound effort to come to terms with its meaning—sometimes in similar and sometimes in different ways than does the outlook of Jeremiah. The renewal of fidelity holds great promise for both prophets. But whereas Jeremiah does not portray renewal has having any particular structural or institutional forms, Ezekiel gives an elaborate vision of social and cultic restoration.

The first part of the Book of Ezekiel (chapters 1–24), written before 587 B.C.E., criticizes the rupture of the covenant relationship between the people and God. Although the imagery is different (consisting of weird symbolism and highly imaginative allegories), the message is much the same as that of Amos, Isaiah, Hosea, and Jeremiah. Ezekiel was probably even more radical in his criticisms than any of the other prophets, for he saw the rebellion and apostasy at work in Israel's life from the very beginning. There had never been a golden age of fidelity: Not in Egypt, not in the wilderness, not under the Law (Ezekiel 20:8–13). The fall of Jerusalem is foreseen as the inevitable consequence of this long history of infidelity.

A central section of the book (chapters 25–32) contains oracles against the foreign nations, particularly those nations who seem to gloat over the fall of God's chosen nation. These chapters are consistent with an important element in a prophetic message, in contrast to an external critic's perspective. The prophet is loyal to the very group whose shortcomings are criticized. For all the inadequacies and the infidelities of the prophet's own group, the prophet never argues that another group is doing any better. The prophets want their own covenantal group reformed—even if punishment is a necessary aspect of getting that to happen—but they don't support the victory of an outside group or push for the triumph of an alien covenant.

A third section of Ezekiel (chapters 33–48) offers a program for the restoration of Israel—a restoration that requires a clear and unmistakable break with the structures of the past that have never been satisfactory. It might be said that Ezekiel's proposals are directions for Israel "to go back and do it right." He suggests the need to go very far back indeedbecause there had never been a time when Israel really "did it right."

In chapters 33–39 this anticipated restoration is presented as a new achievement. According to one scholar's summary of Ezekiel's vision, "The homeland will once again be free from foreign control; it will be redistributed and refreshed. Political structures will take on new shape; cult and temple will be reestablished; Israel and Judah will be reunited; and over all shall rule a king of the Davidic line."[3] This restoration will be possible because the nation will have a new heart—a heart of flesh to replace the heart of stone (36:26). But the most central feature of the restoration, one described in painstaking detail in chapters 40–48, is a restored Temple. This gives concrete form to the high hopes of renewal and envisions a religious center for it. There will be both new princes (45:8b) and a new priesthood (44:15). The new leaders will no longer oppress or transgress. They will use just and fair balances and measures, will see that each tribe fully and precisely respects assigned boundary lines, and will govern with fairness and in full obedience to the law of God. In short, this is a vision of a pure theocracy—one in which there is no group apostasy. And Ezekiel uses a vision of the valley of dry bones in chapter 37 to suggest that no matter how remote this prospect seems to the people, it is sure to come about because it is clearly in the mind of God himself—God can make dry bones live even if that seems impossible for humans.

Ezekiel isn't so foolish as to suppose there will be no wrongdoing or backsliding in the restored community. There will be mistakes and rebellion. The rationale for dealing with this problem is implicit all through the book, but is very explicit in chapters 14 and 18. Again, in the narrative terminology so typical of the Bible, Ezekiel puts the message this way:

> The word of the LORD came to me: What do you mean by repeating this proverb concerning the land of Israel, "The parents have eaten sour grapes and the children's teeth are set on edge?" As I live, says the Lord GOD, this proverb shall no more be used by you in Israel. Know that all lives are mine: the life of the parent as well as the life of the child is mine; it is only the person who sins that shall die. (18:1–4)

This is spelled out with great precision and clarity! The righteous person shall live (vv. 5–9), the unrighteous person shall die (vv. 10–13). The son of an unrighteous parent who turns righteous shall live (vv. 14–18), he will not be punished for the sins of the parent. (By implication, an unrighteous child of a righteous parent will not live.) Moreover, the last action of any individual makes the decisive determination of that individual's fate. It doesn't matter how long an individual has been doing evil—if that individual turns and does what is right—even at the last minute, the individual will live. Conversely, if an individual has done the right for a whole lifetime, and trusts in that righteousness, and turns and does just one evildeed at the last, that individual will die (see 33:10–17). And, moreover, guilt and innocence are individually ascribed and are not transferable.

> The word of the LORD came to me:"Mortal, when a land sins against me by acting faithlessly, and I stretch out my hand against it, and break its staff of bread and send famine upon it, and cut off from it human beings and animals, even if Noah, Daniel, and Job, these three, were in it, they would save only their own lives by their righteousness, says the Lord GOD. (14:12–14)

That assertion is repeated four times in various ways! (This reverses the thinking set forth in Genesis 18:22–33, where the city of Sodom is saved because Abraham intercedes and finally winnows the number of righteous to a minimum of ten—their righteousness being sufficient to save the whole group.)

Ezekiel's outlook portrays a highly calculative and rationalistic fairness that allows complete control of a personal or group destiny by the quality of the moral life of the person or group. We find this same highly rationalistic calculus of moral responsibility expressed in Ezekiel's sense of his own calling.

> The word of the LORD came to me. O Mortal, speak to your people and say to them, If I bring the sword upon a land, and the people of the land take one of their number as their sentinel, and if the sentinel sees the sword coming upon the land and blows the trumpet and warns the people;then if any who hears the sound of the trumpet do not take warning, and the sword comes and takes them away, their blood shall be upon their own heads. They heard the sound of the trumpet and did not take warning; their blood shall be upon themselves. But if they had taken warning, they would have saved their lives. But if the sentinel sees the sword coming and does not blow the trumpet, so that the people are not warned, and the sword comes, and takes any of them, they are taken away in their iniquity, but their blood I will require at the sentinel's hand. (33:1–6)

Who, thinking in terms of rational good sense, would want to be made a watchman on any other conditions?

The tension in Ezekiel between what has been taken to be apparent individualism and the idea of a group restoration has proven to be a vexing one for scholars to interpret. Both Ezekiel and Jeremiah repudiate the proverb "The parents have eaten sour grapes, and the children's teeth are set on edge" (Ezekiel 18:1–4 and Jeremiah 31:29–30), but the implications of this idea are carried much further in Ezekiel than in Jeremiah. Many of us can remember hearing this phrase cited as an example of commendable development in the moral thinking in the Old Testament. Under the influence of Enlightenment and Kantian views of moral responsibility, this shift was considered a high point of Old Testament morality because it does away with group solidarity in evil and treats each person according to that person's own moral achievements.

Many of the commentators who have attributed moral individualism to Ezekiel have been intent on fostering a theological rationalism in Enlightenment terms. Those who have applauded Ezekiel's individualism and also fought against the idea of original sin are basically consistent. After all, it does not stretch the meaning of the story of the Garden to construe it in this parallel terminology. "Our progenitors have eaten the forbidden fruit and their children have experienced a sense of disjuncture with their original condition." Theological liberals who no longer want that said in Christendom can claim to be followers of Ezekiel and cite him as having contributed greatly to making religious morality compatible with moral responsibility.

The use of the category of individualism to understand this passage from Ezekiel has been undergoing strong challenge.[4] We have already noted that Ezekiel feels that the renewal or restoration will need to have communal and structural features, so it is not plausible to think that he simply individualizes religious destiny. Many contemporary commentators interpret the passage about the sour grapes as Ezekiel's attempt to keep the people of Israel from blaming the past for their predicament and hence failing to rise to the possibilities and demands of the present. In a situation in which many of Ezekiel's compatriots are feeling that their condition of exile is a result of what their ancestors did, and feeling that it cannot be reversed or overcome, this passage in Ezekiel comes as a startling challenge:"Not so. The condition is not hopeless; the future can be changed. Do not say the sour grapes eaten by the fathers prevent the present generation from doing what it should to turn things around."

The passage about the responsibility of the watchman seems to reveal even more about the thinking of Ezekiel than does the repudiation of the ancient proverb. That passage specifies conditions that make it quite reasonable to undertake something like a prophetic or a pastoral responsibility. No frustrating agony or heartbreak need be involved. Agree to blow the trumpet by all means, but don't accept any responsibility for how the people respond. Moreover, the passages that follow shortly thereafter (33:10–16) also portray moral responsibility in highly manageable terms. The individual can be totally assured that the last decisive action is controlling. Although I do not recall having seen this aspect of Ezekiel's message utilized as the rationale for revivalism, it would easily lend itself to that purpose because such revivalism presents a "decision for Christ" as a single decisive and controlling eradication of all past behavior. And, strange as the connection may seem when first noticed, late-nineteenth-century types of revivalism—in which the act of becoming a believer makes a person able to wipe away all of his or her past in one stroke—may be influenced by the same impulse toward moral management that appears in rationalistic repudiations of the idea of original sin. Both tend to look upon religion as a means of making one's standing certain and secure.

It is not individualism that dominates Ezekiel's outlook, but the effort to make morality a dependable means of assuring a secure destiny. Every relationship is so described as to render its consequences clear. The watchman has a strictly prescribed duty; he is not charged with wrongdoing as long as he blows the whistle even if others refuse to hear it. The lifelong sinner can repent in one decisive action and be confident that all is forgiven. (Conversely, the righteous person is warned that one act of betrayal will mean all is lost.) Ezekiel's vision of a restoration is clear, cogent, decisive, and detailed. He provides a vision for redoing the odyssey of Israel, this time avoiding the mistakes and infidelities that sidetracked the first attempt and landed the people in exile.

Chapters 40 to 66 in the Book of Isaiah provide another way of dealing with the moral meaning of the Exile. The pattern here is quite different, as is the historical situation itself. Persia has begun to threaten Babylon, which signals a possible end to the Exile. The new situation generates new words, oracles, and themes. The suffering through which the people are going is interpreted as an opportunity to enlighten all the nations with a knowledge of God and his purposes. The Exile takes the chosen people away from old familiar haunts and carries them to new places. By doing this the exiles allow their story to become known as they witness to the actions of God in their odyssey.

The Book of Isaiah contains declarations of hope and comfort, acknowledging the reality and severity of the punishment, but declaring that something new is about to unfold. This is a different picture of renewal, not one marked by consistent obedience to a new covenant in which the resolves of the people achieve a new level of righteousness, but one that gains meaning from the extent to which the exiles become instruments of revelation and beacons of hope to those who see their remarkable fidelity while under duress.

In this pattern the extent to which the people preserve their purity by keeping their lives set apart from all others is less important than the extent to which the people and their trials are seen by others as clues to new truths. Nor is this renewal reserved exclusively for the covenantal group—set apart from all outsiders. It is something to be shared with all the nations.

This vision is set forth most clearly in four poems, called the Four Servant Poems. Whoever this servant is in the mind of the writer, the model is clear. A chosen one who undergoes public suffering and humiliation becomes a benefit to others. Exile becomes the opportunity for God to become more widely and more deeply understood, in a process of freely offered and even sacrificially tendered pedagogy by those who suffer rather than by those who triumph.

The first of these poems (42:1–4) suggests that the servant will bring forth justice in the nations—not by theimposition of authority nor by the use of force, but by patience and fidelity even under stressful circumstances. The second poem, speaks explicitly of Israel as follows:

> Listen to me, O coastlands, pay attention you peoples from far away!
> The LORD called me before I was born, while I was in my mother's womb he named me.
> He made my mouth like a sharp sword, in the shadow of his hand he hid me;
> he made me a polished arrow, in his quiver he hid me away.
> And he said to me, "You are my servant, Israel, in whom I will be glorified."
> But I said, "I have labored in vain, I have spent my strength for nothing and vanity;
> yet surely my cause is with the LORD, and my reward with my God.
> And now the LORD says, who formed me from the womb to be his servant,
> to bring Jacob back to him, and that Israel might be gathered to him,
> for I am honored in the sight of the LORD, and my God has become my strength—

he says,

"Is it too light a thing that you should be my servant to raise up the
    tribes of Jacob and to restore the survivors Israel;
I will give you as a light to the nations, that my salvation may reach
    to the end of the earth." (49:1–6)

The third poem (50:4–9) describes the benefits that are possible from
the patient acceptance of suffering—being perhaps the least explicit or
powerful of the four passages. The fourth (52:13–53:12), the longest,
cannot be read by Christians without thinking of the person and work
of Christ—though when originally written it possibly was a eulogy to
the life and work of the author of the other three poems upon his (or
her?) martyrdom. While the exact identity of the servant is not clear, the
paradigm is decisively instructive. Even the difficult suffering involved in
the Exile can be utilized as a means making God's purpose known to
others.

This vision of Isaiah gives a quite new perspective on the problem of
particularity. It overcomes punishment/discipline/exile by moving on to
redemption for others rather than seeking to hoard the reward for the self
by redoing the experience without moral slippage. In Isaiah's scheme, innocence, humility, and the acceptance of adversity are more valuable than
morally impeccable achievement. Even Exodus becomes meaningful, not
because it affords an opportunity to secure a promised land possessed only
by the chosen people, but because it leads to the eventual inclusion of all
the nations in the knowledge of God's saving purposes. Exile is significant,
not because it can lead to a new and more successful management of
consequences through the pursuit of goodness, but because it can be a
pedagogical opportunity to extend word of God's healing mercy to an
ever wider circle.

Ezekiel's vision becomes the foundation for a priestly and legalistic solution to the problem of the Exile. That is to say, it furnishes a program for
thinking about how to do the whole covenantal odyssey over again in
such a way as to make it work. It prompts strict obedience to the Law as a
means of warding off historical calamity. This is a paradigm for every religio-
ethical scheme in which salvation is to be achieved by dint of effort and
resolve (that is, a scheme of works/righteousness). That strategy leads to
legalism because it creates the necessity of knowing with ever increasing
certainty and precision exactly what must be done in order to be righteous. It promises "life" (salvation) in exchange for achievement and lo-
cates destiny in that which can be morally attained.

Isaiah's vision becomes the foundation for a messianic religion in which redemption is offered by vicarious suffering, as a movement of grace. In this pattern the forgiveness of sin becomes more decisive than the elimination of sin. Divine forbearance is more crucial than moral fidelity. An outward-directed movement to make God's loving concern known to all peoples becomes more important than an inward-directed effort at attaining purity. Isaiah's vision was woven into the meaning of messiahship as it was later developed in Christian theology.

The contrasting conceptions of fidelity and the institutional outgrowths of religion that stem from thesealternative understandings are enormous. The contrast between these two visions accounts for tremendous differences in how traditions grow and develop. While it accounts in some measure for differences between traditions, it accounts even more for differences within traditions. Every tradition can develop a managed religiosity in which the attainment of goodness is the prevailing thrust and graceless moralism takes over.[5] Every tradition, in contrast, can understand the significance of so acting as to enlighten and redeem others. Even a messianic faith can imagine the potential Messiah as a source of control over unrighteousness, as a figure of power able to put all evildoing in its place. But a messianic religion can also understand a Messiah as one who vicariously lives for others and thus brings healing through the experience of exile. That model furnishes the paradigm for a theology in which the idea of redemption becomes central for understanding how God continues to act in the lives of the people with whom there is a covenant relationship of ultimate promise. Each of these options can be traced in the continuing narrative of Israel's life, even in the continuing story of the life of the church as the new Israel.

Nevertheless, each of these ways of understanding the relationship of divine intention and human responsiveness is subject to possible distortion, particularly if it is made into a self-contained and morally self-confident agenda for patterning faith and action. The contrast between Ezekiel and Isaiah should not be construed as a simple alternative that gives validity to a moral scheme that is built on one without tension with the other. The Old Testament contains additional materials—many of them designated Wisdom literature—that help us to realize this, and the New Testament writings exhibit a variety of perspectives that keep either side of this contrast from becoming triumphal. In the following chapters the perplexities and profundities that develop as the complex nature of the moral situation comes to be recognized in the continuing experience of God's people will require us to consider at great length the implications of the different reconfigurations of the moral responsibility prompted by the experience of exile.

9

Attempts at Restoration

The People and the Nations; Morality and Wisdom

The imagery of the suffering servant is so compelling that it tempts Christians to move quickly from the poetic imagery of Isaiah to the meaning of the Christ event without paying attention to what happened in the long historical interval that separated the period of the Exile from the birth and ministry of Jesus of Nazareth. While this is an understandable impulse it overlooks a number of important parts of the Old Testament story that deserve attention. It is well to take the following warning to heart:

> As important as is the image of the Suffering Servant for the church's self-understanding, the common practice of skipping over the entire period between Second Isaiah and the birth of the Christian church in tracing the history of the biblical notion of the community of faith is a serious mistake.[1]

Although the vision of the suffering servant eventually becomes pivotal for Christians in giving meaning to a momentous scenario of redemption, the significance of that imagery was not suddenly realized merely on the basis of Isaiah's visionary concept. The people of Israel had various possibilities for responding to the Exile and expended enormous energy asking how to understand their identity as a community attempting to be faithful to God's expectations in new circumstances. The thinking of the Hebrew people about the restoration period is reflected in several writings, both old and new, that wrestle with the best way to overcome the situation created by the Exile. Most of these writings—which include retold history, additional prophetic utterances, imaginative stories, moral admonitions, and even devotional materials—form a significant portion of the canon. The differences between them offer important insights into the complexity of moral choices in the life of a religious community finding itself having to live in new, trying, and difficult circumstances.

Two issues having moral import that emerge in this period will be the focus of our attention. The first of them involves the problem of Israel's relationship to other nations, and particularly whether the aim of a restoration should be to reestablish the purity of Israel's own moral life without regard for the practices of other groups or whether the restoration should somehow be a channel for extending the benefits of covenantal religion to a wider circle. The other issue, perhaps less immediately obvious, is whether morality must continue to be derived from a narrative of saving history or whether there are sources of moral insight that stand by themselves as reliable indicators of worthy human behavior. In this chapter we will look at each of these issues in turn.

The books of Ezra and Nehemiah help us to understand the enormous problems that confronted those who wished to restore Israel's life after the Exile in Babylon. To be sure, a number of factors enabled the people to undertake what they believed to be a restoration. The power of Babylonia was curtailed by the extension of Persian influence under Cyrus, and with the breaking of Babylonia's power a more friendly environment for Israel emerged. An edict by Cyrus issued in 538 B.C.E. permitted the exiles to return and to rebuild the Temple in Jerusalem (Ezra 1:1–4). Similar support came periodically from subsequent Persian rulers. Despite this support, however, the task of restoring life in Jerusalem proved to be fraught with difficulties. The Hebrews who returned to restore Jerusalem were but a small minority several generations removed from those who were originally exiled to Babylon. They were an even smaller band as measured against the number of Hebrews dispersed throughout other places in the ancient world. Their endeavor depended as much on the sufferance of the foreign rulers as upon the strength they could muster by themselves. Moreover, neighboring peoples (and even some Judeans who had remained in Jerusalem and its environs because they had not been subject to deportation to Babylon) were less than enthusiastic about the return of the exiled group. They did little to help and sometimes even seemed to thwart the restoration being attempted by the returning exiles. When, centuries before, the Hebrews had left Egypt for the promised land, they faced wilderness; when the exiles left Babylon for the return to Jerusalem, they faced hostility—at times even from some of their own kin. Although the returning exiles did not need to deal with the problem of governing a whole new geographical region (whether by means of charismatic leadership or hereditary kingship), they did face the problem of structuring their own life in a responsible manner amidst another culture and under conditions they had little power to control. To do this they utilized a pattern of social organization that had taken shape in the time of the Exile and was transported for use in the new set of circumstances. According to Bruce Birch, the importance of the family unit was replaced with "father's houses" (the NRSV translates this as "ancestral houses"). "They are as large as three thousand individuals, more akin to the size of the preexilic clan. It is clear that there can no longer be a biological familial base for this social unit, but genealogical lineages, sometimes clearly fictive, have been preserved for each "father's house."[2]

There may have been some distinguishing behavior unique to each of the "ancestral houses," but there certainly was a major difference between the returning exiles as a group and the culture of the land to which they returned. This created a pressure on the exiles to maintain distinguishing behavior over and against the dominant society within which they were a legitimate (but not necessarily welcomed) minority.

Distinct and identifiable patterns of religious behavior often emerge from a condition in which a small minority that is religiously identified seeks to live within a larger society. The special community often proceeds to preserve its identity by actions that distinguish it from the surrounding world. One means of maintaining distinctiveness is to be careful about membership. In the case of the returning exiles, genealogy (whether real or fictional) becomes important for this purpose and is reinforced by opposition to marriages outside the religious community. This opposition is expressed several times in the book of Ezra, though it is found in the book of Nehemiah as well. It is one aspect of a religious/ethnic separatism that develops at the time.

However, blood kinship is not the only possible way by which a social policy of strict separatism can be maintained. The returned exiles find a center of identity in a decision to reconstruct the Temple at Jerusalem. Both Haggai and Zechariah envision a renewed life for the people centered in a house of worship dedicated to Israel's God, much as Ezekiel had offered a detailed vision for such a development. It is, of course, one thing to anticipate the prospects of a rebuilt Temple; it is another to bring it to concrete reality. Moreover, as anyone who ever served on a church building committee knows, building "temples" is not always a process of wallowing in friendly consensus! Among the returned exiles in Jerusalem a struggle occurred over who would take the lead in developing temple and cult, a struggle in which the Zadokite priests took the commanding role with a strategy that put power in the hands of a priestly class, that emphasized domestic (i.e., particularistic) solidarity at the expense of universal impulses, and that pursued cooperation with the Persian authorities in exchange for protection of the process.[3] The contrast between the strategy advocated by the Zadokites and that being followed by the Levites, the original priestly group, is not one between those avowing group purity versus those favoring amalgamation with the larger society—both groups favor group purity—but one favors a strategy that holds to the separatism with an urgent zeal that will have as little to do with others as possible, and the other is willing to make strategic concessions that gain opportunities for the separatist group to enjoy its own identity practices. Every group that seeks to define its identity over and against that of the world in general has to choose between these alternatives. Does the separatist group completely withdraw to itself or does it accept benefits from the wider society, providing those benefits are given without threatening its efforts to maintain uniqueness in limited and nonthreatening ways?

Another important means of defining membership in the special community is moral rather than ethnic or cultic in its expression. Obedience to the Torah becomes a consuming passion because such obedience is seen as a means of preserving the community's identity. The observance of the Sabbath is made increasingly rigorous and the importance of the tithe is emphasized.[4] Such measures are motivated by the desire to maintain the uniqueness of Israel's heritage, and (quite possibly) also by a presumption that religious fidelity is somehow a means of ensuring temporal well-being. After all, if the prophets had been right in suggesting that punishment and exile follow as a result of infidelity, is it not reasonable to think that well-being is possible if the group is faithful and careful in observing the Law?

Groups can find themselves in a minority situation as a result of several kinds of historical fortune. In some instances, as seems to be the situation in the case of the returning exiles, groups find themselves moving into an environment that is alien to their identity and perhaps even hostile to their values. In other instances, as in the case of the early church, groups come into being in the midst of an already hostile world and never have even a memory of a previous situation that was different. In still others, the world that once surrounded a religious community with a supportive and congenial ethos (indeed, a cultural milieu that their religious forebears might even have dominated and controlled) changes even as they continue to live in it. Whatever the manner in which the religious group comes to find itself a minority within its cultural setting, the thrust to maintain a distinctive separatism is a very understandable response.

The contrast between the Zadokites and the Levites over how much cooperation with the surrounding world is legitimate raises fundamental moral issues and results in different versions of separatism. An even more stringent separatism is possible, one that insists the religious group must withdraw into a protected and self-contained environment of its own making and its own control in order to be faithful. Such groups eventually arise in Judaism as the difficulties of remaining faithful in an alien culture intensify. This withdrawing separatism seeks to avoid the compromises that may face those who have to live as a minority in a cultural situation dominated by different values. Within its own enclave it can establish the norms of acceptable behavior, but it is still dependent to some extent on the toleration of its enclave by the external world.

Moral judgments about the wisdom and validity of such separatism differ widely. Some contend that authentic allegiance to the heritage requires the people to take great care not to conform to the mores of the surrounding culture. Surely they are right in pointing out how easy it is for a religious group to be assimilated and hence to lose its moral distinctiveness without even recognizing that such a consequence has taken place. Moreover, they are right in pointing out that any of the ways by which a religious community finds itself in a minority position involve serious problems and dilemmas.[5]

Groups that place importance on remaining separatist tend to develop distinguishing marks and strict internal disciplines. Moral conformity is frequently very important, and maintenance of a traditional lifestyle a likely preoccupation. When religions start to move in the direction of separatism, there are seemingly few limits to the extent to which they may go in preserving the identity by remaining exclusivistic.

Even today some Jewish groups maintain a distinctive lifestyle and unique set of moral practices that set them apart from society. Similarly, some Christian groups behave in a comparable way. The lifestyle of the Amish, for instance, is shaped by a pattern of togetherness that consists of identification with something a bit like "ancestral houses." Membership is largely determined by factors of birth, and behavior is governed by distinctive rules and mores that are sharply different from those of the surrounding society. To be sure, the Amish are not trying to reestablish themselves after having been geographically transported from a land they once occupied and to which they have returned. But their attempt to maintain a distinguishing lifestyle that they understand to be a faithful allegiance to their religious heritage offers suggestive analogies to the attitude of some groups in Israel during the return from the Exile.

But religiously motivated separatism is not the only response found in Judaism at the time of the Exile, or evident in the biblical record. Other parts of the Old Testament that were probably written in this same period and even out of this same experience offer a quite different moral thrust— a thrust more in line with Deutero-Isaiah's vision of Israel's role as a light that benefits other nations. Followers of Deutero-Isaiah are among the people who return to Jerusalem to help effect a restoration, although their influence on the way things get done is overshadowed by the developments that were guided by Ezra, Nehemiah, and kindred spirits. Many scholars believe that someone from the group of Deutero-Isaiah's followers composed the third great section of the Book of Isaiah (chapters 56–66), in which the nature and the intention of the restoration are understood in universal rather than particularist ways.[6] This more universal outlook is expressed early in this section of Isaiah:

> Do not let the foreigner joined to the LORD say,
> "The LORD will surely separate me from his people";
> and do not let the eunuch say, "I am just a dry tree."
>
> For thus says the LORD; "To the eunuchs who keep my sabbaths, who choose the things that please me and hold fast to my covenant, I will give in my house and with my walls a monument and a name better than sons and daughters;
>
> I will give them an everlasting name which shall not be cut off.
>
> And the foreigners who join themselves to the LORD, to minister to him, to love the name of the LORD, and to be his servants, all who keep the sabbath, and do not profane it, and hold fast to my covenant—these I will bring to my holy mountain and make them joyful in my house of prayer; their burnt offerings and their sacrifices will be accepted on my altar; for my house shall be called a house of prayer for all peoples.
>
> Thus says the Lord GOD, who gathers the outcasts of Israel, I will gather others to them besides those already gathered. (56:3–8)

According to Paul Hanson, these followers of Deutero-Isaiah rely not so much on a program of restoration that is achieved politically and pragmatically as on a belief in God's eventual return. The consummation for which they yearn is seen in terms of something as momentous as Jubilee—a time of transformation of the ordinary way of doing things and a time when all of the people would be righteous.[7] Yearning for an eventual consummation marked by a more universal outlook can occur in merely a part of the minority group even while the more separatist stance is espoused by most of the others. But that may not be all that is at work. A genuine alternative vision may well have grown out of the inclusive outlook that looked to embrace the destiny of all nations in the unfolding narrative.

There are still other expressions of an alternative vision to the outlook on which the program being carried out by Ezra and Nehemiah depends. Although there is considerable disagreement among scholars as to when the book of Ruth was written, it is generally recognized that the import of the book is to counter exclusivist tendencies. The book itself is written as though set in a much earlier period, in the time of the tribal confederacy (although even if that is the case it would not mean its story was of no significance for how the restoration was being carried out). The book tells how Naomi, a Judean woman, is driven to Moab by famine conditions in Israel and is widowed there. Her two sons marry Moabite women, but in time they die, leaving her responsible for two Moabite daughters-in-law. Naomi decides to return to Bethlehem of Judea. Ruth, one of her daughters-in-law, decides to accompany her. In Bethlehem Ruth marries an influential citizen and eventually becomes the great-grandmother of David. Bernhard Anderson observes:

> Many scholars believe that the story is a subtle piece of "propaganda" against the view that one's position within Israel was dependent upon purity of blood or correctness of genealogy. For God's greatest favor was bestowed upon Israel though a mixed marriage—the very thing that Nehemiah and Ezra frowned upon! Even if the author did not intend a direct attack upon the policy of Ezra and Nehemiah, his delightful story, with its human interest and its spacious view of Yahweh's sovereignty, shows that tendencies other than narrow exclusivism were at work in postexilic Judaism.[8]

A third example of an inclusive thrust is found in the book of Jonah, the date of which is a matter of scholarly uncertainty.[9] The theologically meaningful point of the book is not (at least as I remember what I learned in Sunday school) that a prophet of God is miraculously enabled to survive ingestion by a whale, but that God's message of judgment/hope is to be preached and can be heard in foreign nations as well as in the chosen or covenant nation. The story of Jonah indicates that God will send servants to other nations to preach repentance even if that means including other nations within the orbit of divine salvific purposes. Indeed, the story has an even deeper bite. It is the prophet himself who is portrayed as stubborn and resentful: stubborn in refusing to go to the foreign city of Nineveh and resentful when his preaching there actually does bring about the repentance of the foreign city.[10]

The foregoing biblical materials highlight a contrast between a separatist way of implementing the restoration and an alternative vision that keeps alive the possibility that restoration can involve an extension of God's covenantal purposes to a much wider circle of nations. The contrast between them reveals not only a tension that vies for the loyalties of those who were concerned with the restoration following the Exile, but a tension that similarly affects the life of almost every community that seeks to establish patterns of morality on a religious base. The tension between the thrust to preserve the unique fidelity of a religious group by seeking a special level of purity and the thrust to share the moral traditions of the same religious community with those who do not have such a tradition is a perennial one. Nor is the tension easily resolved. If a group intentionally seeks to achieve a high level of fidelity, it almost inevitably focuses on itself and grows suspicious of interchanges with others; if a group seeks to interact with other groups in order to share its moral impulses and make contributions toward a more inclusive common good, it may very well find the uniqueness of its moral identity eroded.

Yet still another body of literature emerged during this same period that reveals a difference that is somewhat more difficult to set up as a sharp contrast yet may be even more momentous in its potential significance for understanding the moral significance of the biblical narrative. This literature, known as the Wisdom literature, tends to portray morality less in terms of responsiveness to a divine action in history than as a set of insights based on ordinary human experience—that is, on human wisdom.[11] The clearest and most stereotypical expression of this perspective in contained in the Book of Proverbs, which many scholars believe attained its present form in the postexilic period, even though it utilizes some materials that had a secondary role to play very far back in the tradition. The materials in Proverbs are arranged in several subcollections.[12] The subcollections, which arrange the material according to different supposed origins, do not offer identifiably different moral messages. A number of underlying themes carry throughout the different subcollections and give the overall moral stance of the book an identifiable direction.

A casual modern reader might very well think that this book of wise sayings is far more typical of what we mean by ethical guidance than many of the narrative materials found in other parts of the Bible. Taken as a whole the Book of Proverbs portrays the nature of good and proper deportment and those qualities of personal selfhood that are normally associated with being wise and good. The morality is couched less in terms of responsiveness to an experience of some mighty divine act, and less in terms of divinely mandated prescriptions for being obedient to God's will, than in terms of seemingly commonsense ideas about human goodness. Much of this material is believed to have been originally composed for the moral upbringing of leaders by teachers attached to the royal court, but its incorporation into the canon warrants a serious assessment of its significance. Who among us, pious or otherwise, would not resonate approvingly with such sensible admonitions as these?

> Do not plan harm against your neighbor
> who lives trustingly beside you.
> Do not quarrel with anyone without a cause,
> when no harm has been done to you.
> Do not envy the violent
> and do not choose any of their ways. (3:29–31)

> There are six things that the LORD hates,
> seven that are an abomination to him:
> haughty eyes, a lying tongue,
> and hands that shed innocent blood,
> a heart that devises wicked plans,
> feet that hurry to run to evil,
> a lying witness who testifies falsely,
> and one who sows discord in a family. (6:16)

> Whoever loves discipline loves knowledge,
> but those who hate to be rebuked are stupid. (12:1)

> Do not look at wine when it is red,
> when it sparkles in the cup
> and goes down smoothly.
> At the last it bites like a serpent,
> and stings like an adder. (23:31f.)

In the book of Proverbs morality is portrayed as closely linked with wisdom. To be wise is to be good; to be good requires wisdom. Wisdom includes the ability to perceive a moral order (presumed to be divinely established) that determines the nature of right and wrong and rewards those who seek to do what is right. Folly, which does not discern the good or chooses to ignore it, leads to punishment. Reason has an important role to play in the discernment of what is good (and conversely in the discernment of what is evil) and also in the process of making choices that lead to good fortune. There are similarities between the outlook in Proverbs and that in the Deuteronomic historian—both believe in a moral scheme of rewards and punishment—but whereas Deuteronomy's outlook is largely cast in terms of divinely experienced group destiny, that of Proverbs tends to be cast much more in terms of individual fortune. There are also similarities between the Book of Proverbs and the Book of Ezekiel—both tend to make morality a means of managing consequences, of controlling historical destiny, and both suggest that being moral can be done in sensible ways. Proverbs represents an attempt to develop a morality based on reasoned deliberation either alongside (or in place of) a morality based on responses to a narrative of God's mighty actions in history.

There has been, and will continue to be, much debate about the legitimacy of such an undertaking. Theologies of salvation history that were influential in the middle decades of the twentieth century had little sympathy for moral thinking based mainly on wise deliberation, but recent scholarship has come to realize that there are values in the Wisdom literature that cannot be ignored without some truncating of our appreciation of morality and even of biblical faith.[13]

Two other canonical books (Job and Ecclesiastes) are also classified as Wisdom literature. These books offer a counterpoint to the thrusts in the book of Proverbs without necessarily disassociating themselves from the wisdom model. In Job, the premise that goodness leads to prosperity is challenged in a masterfully told story of a righteous man who is afflicted by great troubles. The main part of the book was probably quite old, but emendations that came from the period of the Exile make it pertinent to the process of reflecting on the meaning of those times. Job's understanding of moral righteousness owes much to the wisdom tradition, even though it challenges the version of wisdom that draws too neat a correlation between proper behavior and good fortune. Although moral attitudes that are found in covenant and law are woven into Job's defense of his own righteousness, the overriding pattern is typical of wisdom thinking rather than of a morality based on response to mighty acts of God.[14]

The Book of Ecclesiastes (or, the Preacher) also probes the meaning of human existence with the eyes of human wisdom rather than from the stance of a response to mighty divine actions. But the musings of the Preacher emphasize the limitations and ambiguities of experience rather than moral orderliness. The opening passage of the book contains the shocking observation, "Vanity of vanities all is vanity" (1:2). The chapter goes on to suggest that life revolves endlessly and meaninglessly from one set of events to the next without necessarily moving toward a constructive culmination. This is not the stuff on which a firm belief in a divinely directed moral purpose is founded! Perhaps, as some scholars suggest, this book got into the canon largely because Solomon's name was attached to it. Perhaps it got into the canon because it gives expression to some deep sense that the approach to wisdom in the Book of Proverbs tends to describe the moral condition too neatly.

The overall impact of the Wisdom literature is to suggest that while the impulses behind it are commendable, any version of morality that supposes all that is required for human fulfillment is to define goodness and virtue with clarity, and to live life faithfully in accordance with that definition pays insufficient attention to the enigmas and ambiguities that are part of the human lot. This means that a morality of achievement and accomplishment cannot be made to work even if the engine of religious zeal is used to motivate it. The problem of exile is not overcome merely by the process of restoration, for no restoration is sufficiently complete or satisfying for moral achievement to deal with all of the conditions of life that confound efforts to delineate the meaning of the human enterprise in simple rational terms. The overall consequences of these various treatments of moral wisdom is to suggest that the Bible as a whole is highly doubtful of its adequacy.

10

Estrangement and Resistance

Tolerated Minorities and Persecuted Groups

The conditions enjoyed by the Jews following the return to Judah lasted for almost two centuries. Early in the fourth century, however, Alexander the Great of Macedonia conquered much of the Near East. He overran Persia in 334 B.C.E. and two years later captured Jerusalem. As a result of his conquests, pressure developed on the vanquished countries to conform to Greek culture and use the Greek language—a trend known as Hellenization. In time this resulted in the translation of the Old Testament into Greek (producing the Septuagint). The New Testament was written in Greek because that had become a generally used language in the cultural world outside Palestine (where Aramaic was more common).

This pressure for Hellenization posed new problems for the Jewish community—problems that had not arisen under the less culturally aggressive policies of Persia. (There had never, for example, been a thrust toward "Persianization" corresponding to this thrust for Hellenization.)

Changes in a cultural milieu always pose problems to a religious community whose life is set within that milieu. Should the religious community adapt to the changes, transforming its practices to take into account the new situation and to position itself to enjoy its potential benefits? Or should the religious community maintain strict allegiance to its heritage and to the forms and practices in which that heritage has traditionally been embodied? This issue became increasingly vexing for the Jewish community as it experienced the shift of circumstances from what seemed to be a possibility for restoration of their own group identity to what became an increasingly insistent thrust for acculturation to a new set of cultural values.

Religious communities that face such conditions must deal with the problem of accommodation. They must decide whether the cultural forms in which their heritage has been previously embodied are or are not crucial to its continued integrity. The particular relationship between faith and the cultural forms in which the biblical heritage was carried on had already undergone transition between the time of Elijah's contest on Mount Horeb and the patterning of Judaism around the Temple at Jerusalem. The Hebrews had already adopted some practices from other cultures. Therefore, it is not surprising that some of them felt that accommodating to Hellenism would not necessarily be a flagrant betrayal. Judaism in Hellenistic garb might not necessarily be apostasy and might be a viable strategy for serving Jewish interests. However, while some members of the Jewish community wanted to adapt to the new trends, believing much was to be gained by doing so, others wanted to resist such changes, feeling that much is to be lost by further relinquishing traditional forms and practices.

It was understandably difficult to decide whether or not Hellenization is a temptation to apostasy or whether it is the most promising way for Judaism to survive under a new set of circumstances. The biblical materials indicate that the people responded to the situation in both ways. Many asked, "If Ezra and Nehemiah could accept the beneficence of Persia in order to accomplish a successful return from Babylonia, why is a voluntary acceptance of Hellenistic practices to be shunned, especially if it could lead to a wider influence and even continued existence of the covenant tradition in rapidly changing times?"

Just as this question brought contrasting answers from the fourth-century Jewish community, so it always brings contrasting answers whenever it is posed. For instance, a contemporary form of this problem in American life involves so-called "civic religion." Civic religion consists of an amalgamation of generally popular aspects of the biblical heritage with the mores and commercial activities of American life, such as public celebrations of Christmas—which includes trees, Santa Claus figures, and specially designed postage stamps. Many people find such practices acceptable; others argue that they all but destroy and/or pervert the true meaning of the Christian event, despite the seemingly religious symbolism of things like lightbulb crèches.

The situation that was created by Alexander the Great's conquest of Judah generates one kind of issue, namely the problem of maintaining religious fidelity in a culture that tries to be friendly but threatens to be smothering. In 175 B.C.E. a new ruler, Antiochus Epiphanes, came to power.

His policies were quite different. He aggressively sought to introduce Greek cultural influences into the territories under his rule. Hence benign toleration was replaced by outright pressure for conformity, coupled with hostility toward those who maintained their unique identities. Antiochus found some willing collaborators among the Jews, including a high priest, Jason, who favored Hellenization. Jason helped transform Jerusalem into a Hellenistic city, even building a coliseum (a gymnasium) to the Greek gods Hermes and Hercules. This became a social center in direct competition with the Temple itself. But not all the Jews followed Jason, and Antiochus, determined to enforce a policy of cultural amalgamation, brought a garrison of Syrian troops to Jerusalem. This was not done, at least initially, in an effort to crush Judaism as such, but to create pressure to incorporate it into the mainstream of the culture of the time. Walter Harrelson has probably correctly assessed the dynamics by observing, "Antiochus seemed unable to understand why any people would resent or resist the bestowal of the benefits of enlightened faith and high civilization which he proffered."[1]

However, resistance to these new measures became more pronounced. In response to the resistance, Antiochus besieged and conquered Jerusalem and erected an altar in the Temple to the Greek god Zeus. All Jews were ordered to perform pagan (i.e., Hellenistic) sacrifices. This effrontery is identified in the accounts as "the abomination of desolation." The description of this as found in the apocryphal book 1 Maccabees is terse, but provides a telling account of these actions from the perspective of its opponents:

> Then the king [Antiochus Epiphanes] wrote to his whole kingdom that all should be one people, and that all should give up their particular customs. All the Gentiles accepted the command of the king. Many even from Israel gladly adopted his religion. They sacrificed to idols and profaned the sabbath. And the king sent letters by messengers to Jerusalem and the towns of Judah; he directed them to follow customs strange to the land, to forbid burnt offerings and sacrifices and drink offerings in the sanctuary, to profane sabbaths and festivals, to defile the sanctuary and priests, to build altars and sacred precincts and shrines for idols, to sacrifice swine and other unclean animals, and to leave their sons uncircumcised. They were to make themselves abominable by everything unclean and profane, so they would forget the law and change all the ordinances. He added, "And whoever does not obey the command of the king shall die." (1:41–50)

This action by Antiochus prompted a religiously motivated armed rebellion under the leadership of the priest Mattathias and his son Judas Maccabeus. Using guerilla warfare against the Syrian garrison and those Jews who were cooperating with Antiochus, these resisters succeeded in "liberating" Jerusalem and purifying and rededicating the Temple. This event is now celebrated in the feast of Hanukkah. The group that opposed the policies of Antiochus, though not a party in the strict sense, came to be called "the faithful ones," or *hasidim*. Two books now in the Old Testament canon play interesting roles in dealing with the vexing issues of those times.[2] The Book of Esther offers a fictional exploration of how a religious group can respond in a alien environment; the Book of Daniel examines how and why direct persecution should be resisted without capitulation to oppressive demands.

The Book of Esther is written in the form of a novel that weaves together a series of related stories involving figures from the Persian period. This does not necessarily date its writing, for just as American folklore can use stories about Benjamin Franklin and George Washington from the eighteenth century to make moral points about the nineteenth and twentieth centuries, so the Book of Esther can use figures from the early fifth century B.C.E. to enunciate some moral guidelines for the middle second century B.C.E. Many scholars believe that the Book of Esther was written in the early Hellenistic period, just prior to the Maccabean period.

In the account in Esther, which does not explicitly mention God as an active agent of the drama, King Ahasuerus holds a feast to celebrate his power and glory. He orders that his queen, Vashti, be brought before the guests to show off her beauty, but Vashti refuses. The raconteur of the story suggests that Vashti's refusal sets a dangerous precedent—the right of wives to refuse orders of their husbands. Modern feminists honor her example. Vashti is consequently deposed and a competition set up to choose her replacement (1:10–22).

The contestants in the resulting "Miss Persia" contest (2:1–4) include a young Jewish orphan named Esther, who is sponsored by Mordecai, a Jew who has adopted her. The king selects her because of her beauty even though she has not undergone the rigorous year of grooming normally expected of contestants (2:15–18). Esther further consolidates the king's appreciation by informing him that two eunuchs were plotting against his life—knowledge she had obtained from Mordecai. This enables the king to thwart an assassination attempt on his life (2:19–23).

Meanwhile, the king appoints a new prime minister by the name of Haman, who expects that all the subjects of the king will do obeisance to him as the king's representative—an expectation not untypical of those who hold authority. Faithful to Jewish scruples, Mordecai refuses to perform the required rituals, infuriating Haman. An edict is prepared, at Haman's suggestion, "giving orders to destroy, to kill, and to annihilate all Jews, young and old, women and children, in one day" (3:13). Obviously distraught, Mordecai puts on sackcloth and ashes and attracts the attention of Esther, who notices her patron's behavior. When Esther inquires why Mordecai is distraught, he implores her to intercede for her people. Skilled as she is, Esther first asks permission to have a banquet, which both the king and Haman agree to attend (5:4–9). Meanwhile, Haman has prepared a gallows on which to have Mordecai hung for his stubbornness.

That night, fretfully awake, the king has the book of records read to him—the book that tells about the role Mordecai had played in thwarting the plot against his life. The next day Haman approaches the king to speak to him about having Mordecai hanged as punishment for his refusal to perform the necessary rituals of obedience (6:4), but the king turns the conversation to a discussion of the preparation that should be made for honoring a person who has served him faithfully. Haman thinks he will be the one so honored, but then the king tells him it will be Mordecai (6:10). Haman is anything but pleased, and considers how to counteract the king's selection. But before he can devise a strategy he is hurried off to the feast Queen Esther has prepared, where his plot against the Jews is recognized as directly in conflict with the king's plan to honor Mordecai (7:5f.). The king is angry and orders Haman executed on the very gallows on which Haman had expected to do away with Mordecai (7:9f.). The next two chapters tell how Mordecai becomes the chief officer of the king and how the Jews avenge their enemies. Mordecai orders that these events be celebrated in all subsequent years, which is the origin of the feast of Purim.

This story provides a complex—and not necessarily very conclusive—set of considerations for understanding possible ways for a religious group to live amidst a hostile society. The telling of this story could very well have the effect of prompting the members of religious groups to remain loyal to their faith, not to compromise essential convictions, and not to turn their back on their spiritual kin. That would have a tendency to reinforce fidelity under persecution and possibly to foster a separatism that ensures the purity of faith.

But the same story might also prompt its hearers to seek office within the dominant culture and to use such office to protect the interests and fortunes of their group. This second way of reading the story would seem to commend an effort to gain controlling influence within the prevailing power structure, not merely urge the maintenance of fidelity under pressures for acculturation. It might even legitimize subtle subversion and overt violence as ways of acting if these are required in order to succeed. This way of reading the story would seem to commend religious fanaticism. Read this way it would engender resistance, not merely separation.

The final two chapters of the book also portray a turn of events similar to other instances—as following the making of the golden calf (Exodus 32:25–29) or the defeat of Jezebel by Elijah (1 Kings 18:40)—in which the group that was once persecuted becomes an avenger. Not only do the "righteous" gain control; they annihilate their enemies. Perhaps religious fanaticism wins out. It presumes that serving the interests of the religious community sanctions whatever strategies need to be employed to advance those interests. Whereas a reading of the story as urging fidelity to a religious heritage within a separatist group is not necessarily incompatible with Deutero-Isaiah's concept of the suffering servant, a reading of the story as legitimizing the thrust for conniving subterfuge provides a possible way to derail the vision of Deutero-Isaiah.

The other canonical book that emerged from the postexilic period is the Book of Daniel. This book is an example of apocalyptic literature, which uses esoteric references and visions of end-times to comment on contemporary conditions. It is designed to prompt continued fidelity under stress. Such literature often appears during times of persecution. As we shall see in chapter 17, the Book of Revelation in the New Testament, which was written when Christians were facing persecution, is another example of this kind of literature.

Consisting of six stories and four dream visions, the Book of Daniel opens with an account of how king Nebuchadnezzar of Babylon seeks young males to be trained as members of the palace court staff. Daniel and three friends are among those selected for this special training. In what is really an early example of conscientious objection, they ask that they not be required to defile themselves by breaking the Jewish dietary law in order to eat at the "training table" (1:8). The master of the guard is sympathetic to this request, though he fears that the king will be displeased if these young men do not acquire as handsome a visage nor become as wise in mind as the others. After ten days their vegetarian diet makes them impressively superior, and they are stationed in the king's court, much to the immediate relief of everyone concerned (1:20f.).

A year later the king has a troubling dream. His Babylonian "magicians, enchanters, and sorcerers" cannot tell him what it means. Daniel, who is given a clue about the dream by the God of his heritage, asks to go before the king, where he tells the king (without being told about the dream's content in advance) what the dream was about and then proceeds to interpret its meaning (2:31–45). Impressed, the king promotes Daniel to chief prefect and appoints his three friends to high positions.

The king—urged by the Babylonian satraps, the prefects, governors, counselors, treasurers, justices, and magistrates to cement his authority— sets up a golden statue and commands that the people of the land bow down to it. This, of course, requires an action that violates the religious scruples of Daniel and his friends, Shadrach, Meshach, and Abednego. They are hauled before the king, to whom they try to explain their scruples, but are ordered hurled into a fiery furnace (3:13–23). When they are not burned, even by a fire seven times as hot as normal, the king is impressed and orders the whole land to worship the God of Daniel and his friends.

Then the king has a second dream, which as before cannot be interpreted by the magicians and enchanters of Babylon, but is interpreted by Daniel (now named Belteshazzar). This dream had frightened Nebuchadnezzar, because (as Daniel pointed out) it predicted that proud boasting would bring about his downfall (4:4). The king undergoes seven years of insanity, which cuts him off from human society, but at the end of that time both his reason and his kingdom are returned to him (4:28–37). Nebuchadnezzar's son, King Belshazzar, then comes to power and throws a big feast of celebration, during which he performs a great sacrilege by using the vessels from the Temple for the praise of other gods (5:4). Belshazzar sees writing on the wall—writing that he and his Babylonian interpreters cannot decipher (5:5–12). Daniel, however, can do so, and indicates that the king has been weighed and found wanting. Consequently, the days of his reign are numbered. However, in appreciation for his skill at telling what the dream means, the king makes Daniel third in rank. But that same night the king is killed (5:29) and the power moves to a new monarch, Darius, a Mede. The new monarch restores the power of the satraps, leaving Daniel as one of the presidents among them (6:2). Daniel distinguishes himself in the service of Darius, incurs the jealousy of the satraps, and is caught in another problem of conscience. The satraps persuade the king to promulgate an ordinance prohibiting anyone in the kingdom to pray except to the king (6:6–9). Daniel violates the ordinance in the privacy of his own home, but is discovered (6:10–13). Although the king is greatly distressed when this is brought to his attention, under "the laws of the Medes and the Persians" he cannot change a decree that had already been issued. Daniel is thrown into the den of lions, but is not harmed (more Sunday School stuff!). When King Darius sees this, he gladly acknowledges that Daniel's God has special powers, and decrees that Daniel's God is to be worshiped in the whole kingdom (6:19–28).

The message of this much of the Book of Daniel is remarkably similar in form and import to that of the Book of Esther. The stories suggest that moral fidelity to the true God is vindicated even though it has been hazardous and costly. They provide a powerful incentive to fidelity under persecution. In Daniel there is an equally strong vindication of faithfulness under trying circumstances, but there is less of the "turning of the tables" than was present in Esther.

But the Book of Daniel has a second part, starting with chapter 7 and continuing through chapter 12, that consists of four of Daniel's own visions. This is the apocalyptic section, a section that is somewhat more difficult to interpret and that carries moral understandings to new levels of speculative complexity. In these visions the overpowering of the powers of evil by forces of good is portrayed in suprahistorical terms, as consequences of cosmic intervention rather than as a vindication of fidelity within historical events. This material clearly has the potential to reinforce the steadfastness of people enduring repression.

This section of Daniel also greatly extends the symbolism of the term "son of man." This term had been used in Ezekiel to address the prophet. In Daniel it is used to speak of a human being who comes from the clouds of heaven (7:13). While it is easy to extrapolate this terminology into a messianic category (just as it is easy to interpret Deutero-Isaiah's category of the suffering servant in messianic terms), verses 27 and 28 of the chapter suggests it applies to the "people of the saints of the most high" rather than merely to an individual. It is enough to suggest that this imaginary figure is used to affirm a belief that powerful forces from outside the historical/political process are at work to ensure that fidelity amidst persecution is warranted.

The movement of Israel's experience from the events that took place under Ezra and Nehemiah, through the pressures for Hellenization under Alexander the Great, to the repression under Antiochus Epiphanes is momentous. It provides a broad spectrum of conditions under which religious groups can find themselves having to live. Benign toleration yields to pressured acculturation, then to outright repression. These conditions prompt moral reflection. What should the covenanted community do under such circumstances? And where, indeed, do faithful believers find themselves today?

Many subsequent groups professing loyalty to the biblical heritage have experienced similar conditions again and again across the years: life as a tolerated group in a culture largely dominated by other values and loyalties; life under conditions in which religion is expected to reinforce prevailing cultural values; life under repression and persecution. Reflections on this part of the biblical narrative, therefore, may be especially significant for thinking about religious obligation in relationship to the surrounding world.

As we noted in the last chapter, the protective beneficence of the Persians had allowed the Jewish community to build a new life in which observance of the Torah was possible as a symbol of group identity. Significant cultic and moral achievements resulted. Within the covenant community the plight of the poor was given attention, tithing was reformed, Sabbath observance enforced, and foreign marriages frowned upon. Not much literature from the period between the return of the exiles and the pressures to Hellenize (515–334 B.C.E.) has made its way into the biblical canon, so we do not have extensive insight about all the moral issues that emerged. It may be that the life of the Jewish community was marked by a moral conformity to the Torah unmatched in any previous period in Israel's history. Except for Joel, who lived in the early part of the fourth century, few voices were raised to suggest that there were problems of widespread injustice and infidelity. It is reasonable to assume there was a fairly functional fidelity to the covenant within the Jewish community under these conditions. After all, like any coherently identified religious group living within a larger society, it could exclude from its life those who were not uniquely devoted to the covenant heritage. Such individuals could drift back into the larger culture and no longer be problems to the group seeking to live a life of special fidelity.

In many ways this is a situation conducive to the flourishing of voluntary associations. Under such circumstances members of religious organizations belong because they wish to do so, those who belong support the group out of heartfelt commitment to its purposes, and those who chafe have a place to go if their behavior does not conform to the expectations of the group. To be sure, this same set of conditions has drawbacks. The moral influence of the group may be limited largely to its own life and membership. Difficulties can arise, particularly if individuals fail to conform to the expectations of the special group yet refuse to withdraw voluntarily, or if quarrels within the group have to be settled by appeal to the outside sovereignty. Perhaps some, if not all, of these dynamics were present in Israel's life during the fifth and fourth centuries B.C.E. The picture of the situation offered by the Book of Joel probably comes out of the very early years of this period and therefore does not deal extensively with the developments that took place as the new situation unfolded in all its complexities. Moreover, the prophetic model of judgment that dominates the Book of Joel overshadows any more complex inquiry into the relationship between faith and culture.

But, as we have already seen, the challenges posed by the pressures to Hellenize and the conditions of repression imposed by Antiochus gave rise to much more vexing problems. The tension between those who accept and those who reject accommodation became very great. Pressures to move from separatism to complete withdrawal also developed. These are evidenced in the rise of the Essenes, who set up a community at Qumran that was so separatist that it involved completely different lifestyles, including community ownership of property and celibacy. Indeed, the intensity of moral rigor in the withdrawn community sets it at odds even with other groups in its own tradition, which it criticizes as making too many accommodations. Every religious community faces problems relating to the culture in which it finds itself, since no religion can exist totally free of some cultural embodiment. Judging what is, and is not, an acceptable level of accommodation is often difficult and a source of great contention.

Contemporary examples of similar quandaries are numerous and instructive. For instance, something happened a few years ago with respect to the celebration of Thanksgiving as a national holiday in the United States that illustrates problems that religion can have, even with a generally tolerant culture. This holiday observance is probably one of the most readily accepted aspects of American civic religion—a counterpart to Hellenization. This conjunction of religious and civic concerns is readily honored by the great majority of people. Each year, sometime in the fall, the president of the United States issues a proclamation setting aside the last Thursday in November as a national holiday. These proclamations are pseudo-theological documents that are seldom studied or taken very seriously other than for the fact they set a day aside for the celebration of a national feast and create travel congestion on the airlines. One year, however, in addition to setting aside the day with a proclamation, the White House sent a suggested prayer for the occasion to clergy all over America—presumably thinking that such a prayer would give a unifying quality to the celebration (much as it was presumed Hellenism would provide a unifying quality to the ancient world). The gesture was met with deep suspicion. To respond to a proclamation by celebrating a national holiday that it sets up is one thing; that involves no creedal commitments to theological affirmations and can be lightly dismissed, even if (as often happens) it is compounded with potentially pseudo-idolatries. But saying a prayer in a liturgical context is another, and the White House quickly learned that. Not only did a great many clergy refuse to use the "canned" prayer; they let it be known that the whole proposal was out of place. I am not aware that the discussion was cast in terms of postexilic biblical history, but it might have been. Benign toleration, even substantive aid that did not seek to dictate the manner in which a religious program could be carried out, was acceptable; official interference from secular authorities in the forming and shaping of a liturgical act was not. The White House could do a "Cyrus" thing; it ran into trouble when it tried to do an "Alexander" thing.

A far more momentous and vexing illustration relates to an event with dimensions analogous to those of the Antiochian period. This occurred in Germany under the rise of Nazism. With ever increasing political pressure, the Nazi Party sought to incorporate the churches into its program. It sought to use religion as a source of unity for its agenda of National Socialism. The Nazis probably began somewhat as the Hellenizers began, seeking to accomplish this voluntarily. But they soon escalated the pressure for conformity in much the same way (and, in a curious sense, for many of the same reasons) as Antiochus Epiphanes had done. Many German Christians, both lay and clerical, raised no protest. They probably believed that by cooperating with the National Socialists they could help to shape and influence the party's agenda and thus keep it from excesses. They were the counterpart of Jason. But another group—the modern versions of "the faithful ones"—resisted. They formed themselves into a "confessing church," whose opposition eventually played a pivotal role in bringing down one of the most demonic political movements modern times have witnessed. The historical perspective that we enjoy makes it easy to know these "neo-hasidim" were right in their response, but for many people at the time there was doubt as to what was called for in the circumstances. It is probably easier in hindsight to know for sure what course of action is true and faithful, but nobody who reads Esther and Daniel will take the matter lightly. The biblical materials we have examined in this chapter put the burden of proof on those who feel that "civic piety" can be faithful to covenant obligation.

11

Messianic Categories and the Christological Narrative

Continuities and Discontinuities Between the Testaments

Our attention now shifts from the experiences of the Hebrew/Jewish community as recounted in the Old Testament to the experiences of a community formed in response to the life, teachings, death, and Resurrection of Jesus of Nazareth. A complex set of events forming the Christological narrative is believed by members of this new community to be the fulfillment of hopes and expectations engendered by the Old Testament. There is no doubt that the life, death, and Resurrection of Jesus furnish the central framework for understanding the New Testament.

The New Testament poses a similar problem for constructing a narrative as the one we encountered in the Old Testament, namely, the fact that the materials as they appear in the canon were not written in the same order as the historical events those materials purport to cover. For instance, the Gospels, which are the main source of our knowledge about Jesus and his ministry, were written over a period of several years, many of them later, for example, than the letters that came from the pen of Paul. Yet, even the letters of Paul deal with aspects of the narrative that come after the life and ministry of Jesus. Moreover, all of the writings involve understandings and interpretations that are related to the role that the writer played in the drama. Such understandings undergo growth and transformation with time. This affects the way the narrative of the new covenant community is reported.

Then, too, we are likely to read the materials according to our own understandings even when seeking to be faithful to them. There is no way to avoid these consequences, though this does not make the task of interpretation impossible. Our understandings are most likely to be warranted if we are aware of the difficulties encountered by all interpreters and the problems that must be acknowledged as attending the reading of an ancient text. It is particularly difficult to construct a narrative. To follow the canonical order entails dealing with events in an order that differs from the sequence in which they took place; to examine these materials according to the dates of their writing (as far as those can be known) is little better, since there is no simple correlation between the dates of the writings and the events being reported. We need to be aware of this, not because it should inhibit our inquiry, but because it requires us to be circumspect about our methodology. In a succinct overview of the problem of interpreting the New Testament, Howard Clark Kee has examined the bearing of contemporary understandings of knowledge on the interpretation of the New Testament and the difficulty of arriving at conclusions that escape these limitations. He warns, "We must abandon the effort to force evidence into timeless categories, to weigh it against our own intellectual notions, to seek to discover an external essence behind the supposedly useless or outmoded externals of the evidence as it comes to us."[1] But, as Kee goes on to demonstrate, this does not mean that meaningful and significant interpretation is impossible.

It is possible to view the New Testament narrative as providing a momentous change in theological premises and moral import of biblical faith. The discontinuities between the Old and New Testaments have prompted some scholars to underscore the degree to which Jesus broke from expectations that had built up in the Jewish community.[2] But the continuities between the Old and New Testaments also make it possible to think of the two parts of the Bible as related aspects of the same narrative, with the New Testament constituting what might be called a "transforming extension" of the Old.

The New Testament would not have developed as it has without the categories that developed in the Old Testament. The term "in the fullness of time" bears witness to years of faithful reflection upon Israel's fidelity and waywardness, her covenanted loyalty and morally complex responses. The narrative of the Christ event and its consequences is not, therefore, a new and completely different set of events that emerged in pristine novelty, but a gestalt of related experiences and cherished meanings with a significant relationship to the past. The issues posed and resources offered for moral reflection by the New Testament are not unrelated to those posed in the Old Testament. They transvalue certain aspects of the ancient categories (and sometimes modify conceptions that are drawn from those categories), but they remain dependent upon, indebted to, and understandable only in continuity with them.

For example, many of the terms used in the New Testament to speak about Christ are taken directly from the Old Testament. Indeed, much of the language used for speaking about Christ comes primarily from the Old Testament.

- There is a sense in which Christ is spoken of as a liberator—a new Moses who will overcome all the ways (both old and new) in which the condition of oppression has been or is being experienced. Many New Testament passages underscore the sense in which Christ sets people free, not merely from oppression in a geographically and politically confining bondage, but from a much broader set of limitations and restrictions that hamper human life.

- There is also a sense in which Christ is understood as a special kind of leader—both in charismatic terms and in the categories of political institutions. He enables his followers to become a functioning community. Unlike ordinary kings, however, Christ is seen as leading with such persuasive skill and compassionate concern for his followers that political and institutional realities are subordinated to a richer kind of empowerment. This does not eliminate the place of politics and institutions, but it can transform them through the uniquely empowering skill and wisdom of the appointed one.

- It is also biblical to think of the Christ as a prophet—as the figure who so reveals God's will, judgment, and promise as to push every contingent historical accomplishment beyond the compromise and malfeasance that mar ordinary human undertakings to an ever deeper and more adequate achievement of covenantal fidelity.

- Thinking about Christ also involves the concept of a priest—the great high priest who assures the proper exercise of religion and becomes the very embodiment of the sacrificial process through which God and the people are brought together in completed covenant. Yet the priestly role of Christ is remarkably free of manipulation and coercion, of the creation of subservience and the imposition of control.

- Finally (and perhaps most evidently), Christ is thought of in terms of the suffering servant. This may be the most prevalent and powerful of the terms by which he is interpreted. Through Christ's suffering and victory over death, he both reconciles persons to one another and to God and ensures the meaningfulness of the moral order.

The foregoing terms provide many of the conceptual tools with which to look at the place of Jesus Christ in the moral life of Christians. Everyone who does ethics from a Christian perspective thinks that Jesus Christ (both who he was and what he did) has a significant role to play in the way Christians arrive at moral decisions—but they see that role in many different ways. Many of the most crucial differences in Christian ethics stem from contrasting ways of understanding the role of Jesus Christ in relation to the moral life.

The exposition that follows is dependent on five categories (or models) set forth by James Gustafson in a book entitled *Christ and the Moral Life*.[3] This discussion adopts the models offered by Gustafson and uses some of· Gustafson's rich illustrations, but it arranges the models in a different order for reasons that will shortly be explained. Gustafson is wise enough to know, as we will also suggest, that there is no one model by which to understand the role of Jesus Christ for the doing of Christian ethics. Gustafson is also sophisticated enough to know that these different models tend to make different questions central to the doing of ethics. As these different questions are posed, different understandings of the human condition come to the fore, and ethics finds itself intertwined with philosophy and theology, dependent on issues of metaphysics and ontology as well as questions of value and behavior.

Model One: Christ the Pattern

I put this first because it is the model many people embrace initially, or which they teach children to embrace. In this way of thinking Jesus is seen as the example to follow, the prototype to emulate.

Some years ago, when the countercultural (or hippy) movement was sweeping the collegiate scene, I was visiting a parish in which I had once served as minister to students. Standing on a downtown corner near the local campus, one of the ruling elders in the church with which I used to be associated said to me, as a young man with long beautiful flowing hair and beard walked by, "Ed, what do you make of that?" I gave a flip answer designed to avoid either castigating the youth or confirming the middle-class attitudes of the former church officer. "That's easy. We put Warner Sallman's painting of Christ's head on the front pages of our Sunday school materials for years, and then told the children to be like Jesus. Alas, they have finally taken us seriously!"

That suggests one way in which it might be possible to utilize the Christ as pattern model—albeit a possibly facetious one. In seeking to answer the question, "What ought I to do as a Christian?" it replies, "Be as nearly like Jesus as you can be." To do this requires that we study the life and ministry of Jesus for clues to guide our actions, seeking answers to the question "What would Jesus do?" The moral imperative for shaping our actions may be discernible in any one of the following, or a combination of them:

1. The exemplary behavior of Christ during his lifetime;

2. His revelation of God's will through his actions, such as his acceptance of persons of all conditions of life and moral achievement, including persons rejected and despised by the culture of his day;

3. His perfect obedience on the cross;

4. His self-mortification, not only in the ultimate sacrifice he made on the cross, but in his life of poverty, etc.

The idea of the *imitatio Christi* threads itself through the New Testament and through all subsequent Christian history. The idea of "following the Master," "doing what Christ did," "being imitators of him," "letting Jesus be the example," and "living out a life of conformity to that of the Master," all utilize the idea of Christ as the pattern.

This doesn't necessarily mean merely slavish obedience—as my joking response to the church officer's question ironically implied. Differences in the cultural setting must get taken into account and weighed in deliberating what should be done as persons seek to follow Christ in their time. Nevertheless, asking "What would Jesus do were he in our situation?" becomes a possible model for making moral and ethical choices. John's Gospel puts this as an admonition of Christ himself to his disciples, "For I have set you an example, that you also should do as I have done to you" (John 13:15).

Model Two: Christ the Teacher

In this way of looking at Christ the emphasis in placed on his role as revealing, through teaching and instruction, the will of God.

A teacher can enunciate truths that the teacher does not necessarily embody and possibly cannot even attain. Of course, the good teacher tries to do as much as possible of what that teacher suggests others should do. But in setting forth ideals the teacher can also be expected to hold up a standard that is beyond accomplishment by either teacher or pupil—otherwise there is no "stretching." A teacher can point in certain directions— the directions that behavior should take, even though a particular teacher cannot exemplify and a particular pupil cannot attain such consequences.

Teachers "redact" the tradition—as did the rabbis; they sometimes go beyond the tradition to new and novel insights. They may elicit several responses from those who sit at their feet, and the variety of responses may be both acceptable and salutary. Teaching does not necessarily demand a single stifling response that is uniform in everybody.

It is clear that the New Testament writers saw Jesus as occupying, among other roles, that of a teacher. As Matthew put it at the end of the Sermon on the Mount, "Now when Jesus had finished saying these things, the crowds were astonished at his teaching, for he taught them as one who had authority, and not as their scribes" (7:28–29). John recounts, "[Nicodemus] came to Jesus by night and said to him, 'Rabbi, we know that you are a teacher come from God.'" (3:2)

The concept of Jesus as a teacher threads its way through all of Christian history, and has been particularly powerful in so-called "liberal" theology. For example, Thomas Jefferson, who looked on the teachings of Jesus as the "nub" or "kernel" of what can be believed about Jesus, wrote, in a letter to John Adams explaining his criteria of selection for the "Jefferson Bible,"

> We must reduce our volume to the simple evangelists; select, even from them, the very words only of Jesus, paring off the Amphibologisms into which they have been led by forgetting often, or not understanding, what had fallen from him, by giving their own misconceptions as his dicta, and expressing unintelligibly for others what they had not understood themselves. There will be found remaining the most sublime and benevolent code of morals which has ever been offered to man.[4]

Jefferson's use of the teaching model tends to be reductionistic. He seems to believe that the moral teaching of Jesus can be embraced without requiring particular doctrinal or metaphysical overbeliefs about Jesus as a divine being. In much the same spirit, Harry Emerson Fosdick, whom we quoted in the Introduction, made the teachings of Jesus the culminating outcome of the spiritual development that is recorded in the Bible.[5]

Clearly, the teaching model has widespread appeal, and can be embraced within a variety of theological perspectives. But even those who find greater significance in the supernatural being of Christ than a Jefferson (thinkers who have been sharply critical of the kind of Christianity that has made the example and teaching of Jesus the main foundation for Christian morality) acknowledge the importance of the teaching model. They do not ignore the role of Jesus as a moral teacher, as the following quotations demonstrate.

The ethic of Jesus is the perfect fruit of prophetic religion. Its ideal of love has the same relation to the facts and necessities of human experience as the God of prophetic faith has to the world. It is drawn from, and relevant to, every moral experience. It is immanent in life as God is immanent in the world. It transcends the possibilities of human life in its final pinnacle as God transcends the world.[6]

The Sermon on the Mount . . . is primarily and decisively a notification, a proclamation, a description and a program. Its imperatives, too, have primarily and decisively the character of indicating a position and laying a foundation. The position indicated and the foundation laid are the kingdom, Jesus, the new man in Jesus. . . . The Sermon on the Mount proclaims the consummation of the covenant of grace, and therefore the *telos* of the Law and the Ten Commandments.[7]

Model Three: The Sanctifier

In this model attention is focused on the power of Christ to work a change of life in the believer. The power of Christ is one that makes a new person—a person who is now able to abide by the moral commandments and to achieve newness of life. The heart (or will) of the believer is changed, either through belief in Christ as a personal faith commitment or by membership in the community of Christ as embodied in the church.

This way of thinking about Jesus Christ, while not the only emphasis in John Wesley's theology, is a very important one. Wesley believed that Christians are saved in this world from all sin. His idea of perfection includes a belief that Christians are delivered from all unrighteousness. He knew there are objections to believing this is possible, so Wesley asked,

What reason have you to be afraid of, or to entertain any aversion to, the being "renewed in the [whole] image of him that created you?" Is not this more desirable than any thing under heaven? Is it not consummately amiable? What can you wish for in comparison of this, either for your own soul, or for those for whom you entertain the strongest and tenderest affections? And when you enjoy this, what remains but to be "changed from glory to glory, by the Spirit of God."[8]

There are many biblical passages that stress the role of Christ in the sanctification of believers. Paul says, "But you are not in the flesh, you are in the Spirit, since the Spirit of God dwells in you. . . . But if Christ is in you, though the body is dead because of sin the Spirit is life because of righteousness" (Romans 8:9–10). The Gospel suggests that Christ expected newness of life in his followers: "Be perfect, therefore, as your heavenly Father is perfect" (Matthew 5:48). 1 John emphasizes that religious fidelity is attended by newness of life. "Those who have been born of God do not sin; because God's seed abides in then; they cannot sin because they have been born of God" (3:9).

Sanctificationist thinking stresses the actual newness that is possible by the empowering activity of God in the life of the believer—not merely the acceptance of the sinner as though righteous. We can find sanctificationist overtones in Augustine, in Thomas Aquinas, and in many other figures in Christian history—even those figures primarily associated with a theological emphasis on justification (the next model). There are strong affirmations of the reality of sanctification in Calvin's theology. Sanctificationist thinking appears in the left-wing figures of the Reformation as well as in Anglican moral theology. All of these thinkers have appropriated this outlook from an important strand in the New Testament.

Model Four: The Justifier

In this pattern, or model, the question shifts from "What ought the believer to do?" to "How is the believer to be treated (or regarded) as affected by the work of Christ?" In other words, there is a decisive shift in the ethical question from "How can I do what is right?" to "What is my destiny in light of the fact I cannot do what is right—or, enough of what is right ever to qualify as good?"

The setting forth of moral requirements to be met (i.e., "the law") becomes less important, and the declaration of the reality of grace becomes a new focus. Indeed, in radical justificationist perspectives the "law" (as a set of specific moral prescriptions) becomes secondary and has even been said to be "abolished." The ethical task is portrayed less as learning what is right and doing it than finding the faith that enables one to respond appropriately to the fact that one is accepted by the graceful embrace of God irrespective of moral achievement. The locus of attention in on a bestowed emancipation rather than on achieving a status, on acceptance rather than on attainment.

This way of looking at Christ's significance for the moral life is especially clear in Paul. Paul wrote, "But now, apart from law, the righteousness of God has been disclosed, and is attested by the law and the prophets, the righteousness of God through faith in Jesus Christ for all who believe. For there is no distinction; since all have sinned and fall short of the glory of god, they are justified by his grace as a gift, through the redemption which is in Christ Jesus, whom God put forward as a sacrifice of atonement by his blood, effective through faith" (Romans 3:21–25a).

As understood in this perspective, the chief benefit from the work of Christ for the believer is not the promise of perfection (as empowerment for obedience), but the assurance of acceptance and a consequent freedom from the law that makes creative moral responsiveness possible. Mark's Gospel reports Christ as suggesting, "The Sabbath was made for human-kind, not humankind for the Sabbath" (2:27). In 1 Corinthians Paul ob-serves, "All things are lawful, but not all things are beneficial" (10:23). When the law is replaced by the response of gratitude, spontaneity and freedom replace obligation and anxiety.

Luther, who took this perspective directly from Paul and made it the central focus of his theology, said, "I saw the light of heaven." Although Luther is one of the most completely justificationist thinkers in the history of Christian reflection, he helps us to see that justification does not abro-gate moral obligation (as some critics charge), but puts morality on a dif-ferent foundation:

> Our faith in Christ does not free us from works but from false opin-ions concerning works, that is, from the foolish presumption that justification is acquired by works. Faith redeems, corrects, and pre-serves our consciences so that we know that righteousness does not consist in works, although works neither can nor ought to be want-ing; just as we cannot be without food and drink and all the works of this mortal body, yet our righteousness in not in them, but in faith; and yet, those works of the body are not to be despised or neglected on that account.[9]

A careful and explicit statement of the justificationist position is found in the writing of Reinhold Niebuhr. (Remember that a citation from Niebuhr was also included under the teacher model.) Niebuhr's passage here is especially helpful in suggesting the way in which a new kind of behavior does indeed flow from the experience of justification.

> To understand that the Christ in us is not a possession but a hope, that perfection is not a reality but an intention; that such peace as we know in this life is never purely the peace of achievement but the serenity of being "completely known and all forgiven"; all of this does not destroy moral ardour or responsibility. On the contrary it is the only way of preventing premature completions of life, or arrest-ing the new and more terrible pride which may find its roots in the soil of humility, and saving the Christian life from the intolerable pretension of saints who have forgotten that they are sinners.[10]

Model Five: Creator and Redeemer

This model for describing the significance of Jesus for the moral life asks what consequences Christ has effected in history. It is concerned with Christ as the source, power, and goal of personal life and perhaps even more so as ruler of the structures and vitalities of corporate life. Because (not if!) Christ is victor over sin and over the principalities, we can come to grips with historical destiny in a different way.

James Gustafson expresses this idea in the following way, which warrants quotation at length:

> Jesus Christ is the reality of moral life. He objectively rules, he is the King and Head of every man. He reveals God; in Jesus Christ we know the nature of creation (all things are created in and through him); we know the nature of redemption (for he has brought all things under his feet—principalities, powers, death, and sin); and we know the fact of our new creation. What you ought to do is bear witness in your action to what has been done. Walk in the light. What you can do is express in your moral life the power of Christ who reigns within and without. Actually, really, everything has been done. Evil, sin, death, have been, indeed *are* vanquished. Now you still have some moral conflicts, but finally they are more apparent than real. There is evil in the world, and we must not forget that, but really it has been overcome and is not ultimate threat. You still do what you ought not to do, and do not do what you ought to do. But even though you are not sinless, you are free from the power of sin; you are a new creature, really, even if you seem to be the old one. Christ is Lord. In Christ all is created, in him all is redeemed. This is so; this is *Reality*. Live this reality. (We cannot tell you, live *as if* this is so; this suggests that it is hypothetical, indeed a useful fiction.) Actualize, realize this reality!
>
> What should you do? No one can tell you precisely, but in general—be affirmative, be open to life, be joyous. Surely you will worry about what is required of you; you will see conflicts in your responsibilities and opportunities. But do not let these overcome you. God has said "Yes" to man, to creation. Live in the sense of God's "yes."[11]

Expanding on Gustafson's ideas, and relating them to corporate or social ethics, we can say, "Since Christ has conquered the powers of evil, we do not need to act as though everything is dependent upon our capacity to subdue them—to beat them down by the force of our might (which is frequently just what we do to combat evil—namely adopt its own techniques and strategies)."

The stance of each of these models can be encapsulated in a question that can be asked and understood in the very simplest terms:

Pattern: What would (or did) Jesus do?
Teacher: What does (or did) Jesus tell me/us to do?
Sanctifier: What does (or can) Jesus do through me/us?
Justifier: What does Jesus do (or what has Jesus done) for me/us?
Creator and Redeemer: What did Jesus do in history to make righteousness the controlling reality of life?

The order in which we have presented these five models is closely related to theological affirmations about the nature of Christ! In somewhat technical language, they start with the lowest doctrine of Christ (Christology) and move to the highest. The progression as I have presented it moves from the model that puts the most stress on the humanity of Jesus (pattern) to the model that places the greatest stress on the divinity. If we are seeking to imitate Christ, it is more plausible to believe we can do so if Jesus is ordinarily human rather than supernaturally divine; if, on the other hand, he is Creator and Redeemer, he had better be divine, or else the claim that Christ has conquered the powers of evil is fairly limp. If we want to utilize all five patterns, we will be driven to an orthodox Christology in which the fullness of both natures is asserted—not, however, with ease and glibness—for a truly orthodox Christology is as emphatic about the fullness of the humanity of Christ as it is about Christ's divinity—ideas between which there is inevitable tension. Those who would stress the humanity of Christ but forget the divinity cannot move the idea of messiahship beyond that of charismatic leader or earthly king. Those who would stress the divinity of Jesus without adequately acknowledging his humanity cannot fully relate the idea of Christ's moral significance to the real world in which all of us confront the very problems that a liberating redeemer ought to alleviate. The significance of the Christological event is too big to be reduced to that of a divine being that lacks humanity or to that of a human being that lacks divinity, but that makes the interpretation of the moral meaning of Christ very complex, indeed somewhat paradoxical.

This discussion of the various ways Christ is related to the moral life suggests why the vocabulary with which to understand the saving work of God must be rich and complex. Liberation remains important, but other terms are needed. Salvation takes on a more complex set of dimensions and meanings. Nothing is lost from the concept of liberation that has been the *fons et origo* of Israel's experience. The removal of externally imposed oppression never ceases to be a crucial aspect of God's work. But rich new concepts are overlaid upon that motif. To describe these requires new terminology—terminology that expands and enriches the conceptual frameworks of both theology and ethics.

One of the terms that has to be added to the vocabulary of God's saving work is "reconciliation"—or the re-creation of the broken relationships that arise from human sin. Just as a children's sermon can be written to describe sin in more adequate ways than does a simple moralism, so a children's sermon can also be written to portray experiences that suggest the dynamics of reconciliation as a process of transformation. The following is the promised sequel to the story of Billy's bike.

"Mrs. Jones, why don't the other boys like my bicycle as much as you do?" Billy was deeply upset as he blurted out his question to Mrs. Jones.

Mrs. Jones looked down at Billy and asked him a question in return. "Why does it matter to you," she said, "whether or not the other children like your new bicycle?"

Billy thought for a while. Deep inside he knew it mattered very much, but he was not sure just why. "I guess," he said very slowly, "I guess it is because everybody likes to feel important. Having a shiny new bicycle is one way to feel very important."

"Yes," said Mrs. Jones, "many people try to feel important through the things they own (which other people they know don't own)—or because of the things that they can do (which other people they know can't do as well). Do you think this is a good way to get to feel important?"

"Is there any other way," asked Billy, somewhat puzzled. "Almost everybody tries to feel important by having something or doing something that his friends don't have or can't do. If one of the other boys gets a plastic rocket all of us want to run down to the store and buy a somewhat bigger one right away. You feel uneasy until you have done something like that."

"I know," said Mrs. Jones. "Everybody tries to feel important because of what he or she owns. This is true not only of toy rockets, but of moon rockets. But merely telling me that everybody feels this way doesn't answer my question. Do you think that owning a shiny bicycle is a good way to feel important?"

Billy knew he was on the spot. He wanted Mrs. Jones to tell him why the other boys did not like his new bicycle. Now Mrs. Jones was asking him questions rather than giving him answers: ". . . is owning a bike a good way to feel important?" ". . . is there any other way?" Billy started to think very hard. Finally he said to Mrs. Jones. "I guess that owning a new bike is only a good way to feel important if the other boys admire your bike very much—and the other boys don't admire mine!"

"Did it ever occur to you," said Mrs. Jones, "that if the other boys admit that your bicycle is the newest and shiniest on the street, they must also admit theirs are second best? Only one person can feel important by owning the best bicycle. Everybody wants to be that person. Not everybody can be first."

"Billy," Mrs. Jones asked after thinking awhile, "Isn't there some other way to feel important?"

"Well, it's my birthday," said Billy. "We are going to have a party for my friends and that should be great fun. Next week it's Arthur's birthday, and we are all going to his house for a party."

Mrs. Jones observed that birthdays are something we all have on very much the same terms. Nobody's birthday as such is any grander or longer than anybody else's—unless boys and girls make it so by sending big gifts to some friends and not to others. Each birthday is twenty-four hours in length and comes once a year. "Is there anything else about birthdays that makes you feel important?" Mrs. Jones finally asked Billy.

"I think my birthday reminds me that I am important to my parents," said Billy at last. "I am important because they love me. They gave me that bicycle because they loved me. Yes, that does make me feel important—and it lets all the other kids feel important also. Their parents love them just as my parents love me."

Billy started down the street. "Hi kids," he cried out as several of his friends came out to play, "Let's go ride our bikes together."

Another term to be added to our vocabulary for salvation is "redemption." Whereas reconciliation involves the re-creation of broken relationships, redemption implies an accepting healing of those who experience brokenness and guilt. The idea of redemption comes into the biblical drama with sharpest focus in the thinking that we find in the servant poems in Isaiah. The meaning of redemption is heightened, uniquely embodied, and profoundly enriched by the work of Christ.

Surely he has borne our infirmities and carried our diseases,
yet we accounted him stricken, struck down by God, and afflicted.
But he was wounded for our transgressions, he was crushed for our iniquities;

upon him was the punishment that made us whole, and by his
bruises we are healed. (Isaiah 53:4f.)

There are human paradigms that can help us see the possible significance of this grace. For instance, there has never been a mother in human
history to which those words could not be applied in a significant, even if
sometimes partial way. One of the important reasons why the term "mother"
is helpful in referring to God lies right here. The male—though the roles
should not be rigidly stereotyped—usually exhibits that kind of creativity
that builds material and mechanical "stuff"; the female has the capacity for
the creativity that makes and nurtures life and being. Although neither
kind of creativity comes to its apex without self-giving, there is often a
greater giving of the self to create other selves in the female role than to
create "stuff" in the male role. The nurturing role may possibly have some
transforming power if it can become functional in those places now dominated almost exclusively by the male paradigm.[12]

The transformation that may come from the greater involvement of
women in the wider public spheres, however, may not be operative if the
male model is adopted by women in a grasp of power. It is not merely the
sexual identity that is determinative, but the qualities that are generally
associated with the role and pattern of a particular gender.

But while we may see a glimpse of the redemption that is bestowed
upon us by self-giving love that has made life possible for us, the gap
between the possibilities in human achievement in any of the human
role models and the possibilities of the divine redeemer will never be
entirely closed. The significance of Christ's work transcends all human
role models, even while also embracing what can be beneficial from
each of them. Christ is a liberator—but is misunderstood if looked upon
as only that; Christ is a leader with political significance and office—
though he is miscast if seen only as an official. Like a priest, Christ brings
the holy and the human together—but if Christ is understood only as a
religious functionary something is greatly missing. Surely Christ is like a
prophet—but prophesy alone shall fail because it is more proclamatory
than pedagogical. Christ is one through whom vicarious sacrifice is made
an instrument of grace—but such a role is pathetic if only that of a
victim.

The concept of salvation must be holistic. It involves thrusts and movements that require at least three conceptual frameworks to delineate: that
of liberation, that of reconciliation, and that of redemption. Liberation
without reconciliation and redemption may be but a reductionistic political achievement; reconciliation without liberation and redemption can

create little more than an ersatz chumminess; redemption without liberation and reconciliation runs the danger of being either a private or a corporate selfishness.

The term "justification" also appears in the vocabulary about salvation.
It describes what it means to be regarded as acceptable despite the condition of estrangement and rebellion. We will further explore the meaning
of justification in looking at the contribution of Paul to the biblical story,
although the idea is important to the work of God from the beginning.

Alas, few treatments of the idea of salvation explicitly utilize all of these
concepts. (A study of the literature is instructive [or, sobering!]). One well-
used encyclopedia, for instance, lists entries for "reconciliation" and "redemption," but none under "liberation" or "deliverance." The same is true
of the ideas found in some well-known "North American" types of systematic theologies.

Some other works use the term "reconciliation" heavily, sometimes
exclusively. In some of these, the term refers to the removal of the barrier
between God and persons occasioned by sin—in which case it really has
more to do with what we have called redemption. Some treatments employ the idea of reconciliation to cover the bringing together of alienated
human parties—but the significance of corporate healing is often less evident than the idea of individual acceptance.

The present emphasis on the term "liberation" is an important and
understandable reaction against ways of doing theology that have been
dominated by the terminology of reconciliation and redemption, frequently
interpreted more as God's saving action oriented to a future life for the
believing individual than as a dimension of social existence. Surely the
term "liberation" is to be welcomed as a needed corrective to the long
neglect of the Egypt/Exodus origins of the biblical drama, for which the
term "liberation" (and possibly the term "deliverance") are most appropriate. But the term "liberation" by itself no more adequately covers the range
of necessary thinking about what it means to be saved than do terms like
"redemption" and "reconciliation" that are found in theologies that have
neglected liberation as a social and even political necessity. The momentous import of the Christological event is to offer a transforming extension of the categories by which we think of the healing power of God's
work among us. But, as we shall see, this does not eliminate the moral
issues that we have already explored. It transforms their meaning and alters
their import, but does not shelve them as inconsequential. The following
chapters examine this contention as this becomes evident in the New
Testament portion of the biblical narrative.

12

The Behavior of Jesus

Inclusiveness, Unconventionality, and Alternative Politics

The reflections in this chapter are based on paradigms of moral behavior found in (or ascribed to) the life and ministry of Jesus. We will not, however, assume that the New Testament's portrayal of how Jesus behaved is anything like a videotaped record of what actually took place. This does not mean that the scholarly efforts to affirm what is possible to know about the historical Jesus are unimportant. They have their place, not least in reminding us that moral outlooks based on the use of Jesus as a pattern or example are affected by the same complexities of interpretation and by the same influences from faith understandings of the Christological event as the moral outlooks that depend on the affirmation of Jesus Christ as sovereign over history and the redeemer of humankind. What many of us once used to call the distinction between the religion of Jesus and the religion about Jesus[1] is not a contrast between what can be known with historical certainty and what is affirmed by faith. It is a difference between a portrait of its leader (drawn from both memory and inspired imagination by the early Christian community) and the convictions about the redemptive significance of the being of Christ and the events that he suffers and overcomes (based on the faith commitments of that same community). Both the accounts (and conjectures) about what Jesus does and the theological convictions about who Jesus is have moral significance. John Dominic Crossan is right in declaring:

> Jesus was not just a teacher or a preacher in purely intellectual terms, not just part of the history of ideas. He not only discussed the Kingdom of God; he enacted it, and said others could do so as well. If all he had done was talk about the Kingdom, lower Galilee would probably have greeted him with a great big peasant yawn. . . . It is, unfor-

tunately, one of the abiding temptations of pastors and scholars to reduce Jesus to words alone, to replace a lived life with a preached sermon or an interesting idea. To remove, however, that which is radically subversive, socially revolutionary, and politically dangerous from Jesus' *actions* is to leave his life meaningless and his death inexplicable.[2]

Those who read the New Testament portrayal of the Man from Nazareth[3] focus on any number of striking qualities to his life that are morally suggestive and ethically instructive. Each of the Gospels is more an interpretation of what the behavior of Jesus means than a report of what the behavior actually was. Moreover, subsequent interpretations of the person and ministry of Jesus (which are numerous and highly divergent) reflect, as has often been pointed out, the predilections of the writers—even when those writers are seeking to approach the issues in a scholarly manner. What follows claims no exemption from the tendency of interpreters to read the life of Jesus in terms of their own perspectives and moral inclinations, though it will seek to demonstrate that the interpretations offered here are shared with, or at least compatible with, those of a sufficiently broad scholarly community to give them credibility.

One of the most striking aspects of the life of Jesus is the extent to which he cared for all sorts and conditions of human beings, without regard for distinctions of race, gender, class, mental or physical health, economic standing, group identification, or moral accomplishment. Such distinctions are frequently used to rule people in or out of a circle of acceptance and concern, but not so with Jesus. We will describe this distinguishing feature of the behavior of Jesus with the term "compassionate inclusiveness."

Observers and writers point to this quality of Jesus' behavior in a variety of different ways. For instance, Harry Emerson Fosdick shows how the religious and moral outcasts recognized in Jesus someone who was sympathetic to their condition, who saw the problems they faced.[4]

Moreover, suggests Fosdick, the behavior of Jesus elicited the hostility of the privileged and the contempt of the so-called righteous—attesting by inference to the degree to which it attracted notice and was functionally real. Nor would Jesus have become embroiled in conflict with the civic and religious establishments had he not encountered the hostility that came from those who found his behavior threatening.[5]

Fosdick observes that the stance of Jesus is morally significant because it rules out the blanket condemnation of people by group or class. "To Jesus contempt of a whole class of people was intolerable."[6] But John Dominic Crossan gives the behavior of Jesus a more radical import. Crossan holds that the behavior of Jesus suggests that the social differentiations that make exclusions plausible are to be repudiated. Using the rubric "Open Commensality" to describe the attitude of Jesus—an attitude open to all peoples regardless of social rank or standing—Crossan deems this a "symbol and embodiment of radical egalitarianism, of an absolute equality of people that denies the validity of any discrimination between them and negates the necessity of any hierarchy among them."[7]

Marcus Borg is wrestling with this same aspect of the behavior of Jesus when he underscores the importance of compassion in understanding the historical Jesus. Observing that the prevailing paradigm at the time of Jesus had become holiness, Borg argues that the paradigm of compassion was an alterative vision.

> Indeed, it is only when we appreciate this dimension of Jesus' emphasis upon compassion that we realize how radical his message and vision were. For Jesus, compassion was more than a quality of God or an individual virtue: it was a social paradigm, the core value for life in community. To put it boldly: compassion for Jesus was political. He directly and repeatedly challenged the dominant sociopolitical paradigm of his social world and advocated instead what might be called a *politics of compassion*. This conflict and this social vision continue to have striking implications for the life of the church today.[8]

Borg argues that the most potent of all touchstones of religious and social acceptability is a moral demand for holiness, or purity. Jesus, whose moral outlook might well be summarized, "Be compassionate as God is compassionate,"[9] attacks the purity system which legitimizes the drawing of sharp distinctions between good people and evil people, between the holy and pure, and between the "washed" and unclean.

The implications of the willingness of Jesus to associate with and embrace all sorts and conditions of human beings, overlooking the distinctions that society uses to enforce social stratification or moral purity, are far-reaching. He did this in terms of choosing those with whom he would eat (as the term "commensality" specifically indicates). The selection of people with whom we eat by choice measures willingness to associate with others in a very fundamental way. Although we rub up against a wide variety of persons in public transportation, in major public gatherings such as sports events or even political rallies, and may even eat with them at fast-food establishments, we invite to our tables or to gatherings in which we celebrate friendship only those with whom we feel an approving kinship. The average congregation, for instance, is probably not distinguished by the wide-ranging inclusiveness exemplified by Jesus. Most of us usually recoil from promiscuous togetherness, not least in an effort to uphold patterns of moral decency and civic respectability.

Not only did Jesus befriend religious and social outcasts, he accepted women and children as equals despite a cultural situation in which the condition of women was one of subordination and the treatment of children was often dominated by considerations of utility.[10] In the Egyptian culture at the time of Jesus little girls might even be left to die because they were not wanted.[11] In a culture such as ours, which tends to treat children with special solicitude (unless they are born to welfare mothers or become too boisterous!), it is difficult to sense the radical implications of the way in which Jesus related to them.[12] Even the disciples of Jesus failed to appreciate his free and open acceptance of children (Mark 10:13–16).

The compassionate inclusiveness Jesus acted out is also seen in his relationship with the sick. In an intriguing interpretation of the healing stories, Crossan indicates that these can be understood as examples of radical egalitarianism. Instead of concentrating on the stories as instances of the miraculous elimination of biological disease in single individuals (i.e., as alternatives to medicine) Crossan indicates that the stories suggest that Jesus accepted those who are ill rather than excluding them as unclean. Moreover, he enabled those who were ill to accept themselves. Focusing on the story of the encounter of Jesus with the leper (Mark 1:40–44), Crossan shows how it is possible to distinguish the disease (probably more like what we would call psoriasis or eczema) from the "personal and social stigma of uncleanness, isolation, and rejection" that is associated with it. Drawing an analogy between the way lepers were treated in New Testament times and those who contract AIDS are treated in our time, Crossan shows how important it is to avoid the social contempt and moralistic ostracizing that is so often visited on those with AIDS.[13] This is powerful analogical interpretation! It suggests how far from the behavior of Jesus are the attitudes and actions of some of the very people in modern times who think of themselves as Christian with the greatest self-assurance, yet presume to imply that AIDS is a punishment for moral wrongdoing.

In thinking about this aspect of the behavior of Jesus it is important to realize that inclusiveness is not enough. The quality of life that Jesus exemplifies is marked by sensitivity and concern as well as wide-ranging acceptance. An indiscriminate massacre would be inclusive enough, but it would hardly fit the quality of behavior being examined here. A draft act might be quite inclusive (in fact, such legislation is usually called a provision for *universal* service), but such legislation does not necessarily advance the cause of compassion nor is it geared to recruit persons for activities that serve the well-being of others. The example of Jesus is one in which openness toward all is associated with a deep concern for their welfare and well-being, without regard to the appeal they can make to warrant or merit such concern.

It may not be a major jump to the next rubric for describing the behavior of Jesus. Some of the behavior that illustrates compassionate inclusiveness also illustrates what we will examine as emancipating unconventionality. Other incidents, however, suggest the importance of using a new rubric.

In the Gospel of John we find the well-known story of the woman caught in adultery (8:3–11). The scribes and Pharisees bring her to Jesus and ask whether on not he approves of stoning her (presumably to death), as the Law of Moses prescribes. The scribes are testing Jesus, to be sure, to determine to what extent Jesus will uphold the conventional moral norms of the time. Jesus handles the matter with adroit unconventionality. He asks what group is in a position to pass moral judgment on the woman. Those who bring the women to Jesus in order to judge her (or to trap him) slink away in shame.

There is a sense in which Jesus is showing compassion to a moral outcast (and the story may be so interpreted), but there is a profounder sense in which this is an example of how Jesus used an unconventional response to emancipate persons from the fury of self-righteously propelled moralism. The behavior of the woman is not condoned, but the confident self-righteousness of the Pharisees is annulled—undercutting their harsh judgmentalism. In a profound sense, although the emancipation afforded the woman is clear, the Pharisees were also emancipated from the impulse to allow their moralism to cause them to do a horrible deed. In a time when people have become overwhelmingly preoccupied with defining morally proper sexual lifestyles, this story has momentous implications. Every contemporary person whose moralism about sex is a means of legitimizing hostility and contempt of others needs to take this story with utmost seriousness.

The compassionate inclusiveness of Jesus does not entirely eliminate the need to draw lines and to advocate particular stances. For instance, there is good reason to argue that the behavior of Jesus toward women is more far-reaching than mere acceptance and inclusion. As contemporary feminist scholars have discovered, women had significant leadership roles in the Jesus movement, making it a sharp contrast to the patriarchal and even androcentric social structures of that time. Moreover, as Elisabeth Schüssler Fiorenza points out, this was a decisive factor in developing a theological framework for including pagans in the new community.[14] Although the biblical text has been the same for centuries, only as women have come to read the Bible with fresh eyes has it become understood that the leadership roles in the early church included both sexes on an equal basis.

> Only when we place the Jesus stories about women into the overall story of Jesus and his movement in Palestine are we able to recognize their subversive character. In the discipleship of equals the "role" of women is not peripheral or trivial, but at the center, and thus of utmost importance to the theopraxis of "solidarity from below."[15]

In the Gospel of Luke we have another story that suggests how Jesus reverses the conventional expectations of human relationships. Seeing rich people putting their gifts into the treasury, he chose to commend the poor widow who contributed only a mite (two small copper coins). I write this having just come from the dedication of a truly magnificent new building built with philanthropic gifts. The program listed the contributions to the building by gift-size categories, as do the annual reports of almost all institutions that depend in whole or in part on voluntary donations. According to the conventional pattern, biggest gifts were listed first; others in descending order. Who of us has seen a gift report—even one from a Christian institution—that uses Luke 21:1–4 (cf. Mark 12:41–44) as its controlling principle and mentions the smallest contributions as most important?

Another dimension of the behavior of Jesus that indicates the extent to which he broke with the conventions of his time in order to be about his work is revealed by several stories about his behavior vis-à-vis his family. Aspects of this unconventional behavior started early, at least according to Luke. Every year the parents of Jesus went to Jerusalem to celebrate the Passover. During the Passover visit in the year in which Jesus is twelve years old, he disappears and his parents search for him (apparently without benefit of a 911 system). When they find him among the teachers in the Temple his parents are astonished, and his mother asks him, "Child, why have you treated us like this? Look, your father and I have been searching for you in great anxiety." He says to them, "Why were you searching for me? Did you not know that I must be in my Father's house?" (Luke 2:48b–49) This story is a good one, but would we not be more comfortable if it had told how the young Jesus had been named to the honor roll at the Sabbath school—with his parents applauding with justifiable pride from the sidelines as his name was called?

In the 1940s my parents were dismayed when they realized how I was talking myself into a pacifist position (at a time when such a stance attracted considerable public hostility) at the young people's society of the local parish church. This was not an effort on my part to earn messianic credentials, but it was disconcerting to them because it was unconventional. It was not until years later, after the Vietnam War was over, that, reading the manuscript of *Peacethinking in a Warring World,* my father was able to say to me just before his death, "I have wanted to hear this said by somebody for a long time; now I realize what you have been about all these years." However, to be quite candid, I am not sure I was any more conventional in the latter than in the former stage—though I do think I was less dependent on a hermeneutic of selected texts.

Contemporary scholars are emphasizing that family structure was very important in the time of Jesus.[16] Not only was it associated to some degree with the qualities we attach to a grouping of parents and children, but it was even more the basis of a social system in which kinship lineage provided the foundation of the ability to exert influence. Jesus adopted an itinerant ministry that made continued association with his kin group highly tenuous. This is surely in contrast to all the concern about place and land that figures so heavily (and with good reasons) in the Old Testament narrative. This lack of concern for family is indeed a radical repudiation of highly cherished convention, a matter of which the contemporary religious right seems strangely unaware.

But Crossan is not unaware of the degree to which the behavior of Jesus is unconventional, even threatening. He sees the repudiation of the family as a negation of the patriarchal chauvinism represented by the traditional family structure of the Mediterranean world (which may not have been half as chauvinistic as the Victorian patterns of the late nineteenth and early twentieth centuries). Alluding to those texts that suggest Jesus saw his ministry as a threat to such structures, Crossan indicates Jesus threatened to tear the family structure apart—and for a moral reason.

> The family is society in miniature, the place where we first and most deeply learn how to love and be loved, hate and be hated, help and be helped, abuse and be abused. It is not just a center of domestic

serenity, since it involves power, it invites the abuse of power, and it is at that precise point that Jesus attacks it. His ideal group is, contrary to Mediterranean and indeed most human familial reality, an open one equally accessible to all under God. It is the Kingdom of God, and it negates that terrible abuse of power that is power's dark specter and lethal shadow.[17]

Would not a battered spouse, suffering under the conventional assumptions about the importance of maintaining the family in conventional terms, be entitled to welcome emancipatory unconventionality as Crossan discerns it in the behavior of Jesus toward the family?

We come finally to what may be called "alternative politics," possibly the most radical of the ways in which the behavior of Jesus has been interpreted as having moral significance. John Howard Yoder, in one of the most provocative and challenging treatments of Christ to have appeared in the last twenty-five years, portrays Jesus as a political leader whose understanding of political activity radically challenged that of conventional wisdom.

No contemporary interpretation of the significance of Jesus in the biblical narrative can ignore John Howard Yoder's trenchant argument in *The Politics of Jesus*.[18] Polemical in structure and tone, Yoder's book argues that those interpretations of Jesus that would assign him to the role of a purely spiritual leader who eschewed politics are both historically mistaken and morally misguided. Such an attitude, which appears in any of several variant formulations, argues Yoder, misses entirely the degree to which the idea of the Kingdom of God—the central concept in the ministry of Jesus—denotes a set of political transformations with concrete consequences for the social order. Such consequences—which Jesus quotes (in Luke 4:19) from Isaiah to introduce his purpose and mission—include: the release of captives; giving sight to the blind; and setting at liberty those who are oppressed.[19] Such consequences hardly sound like a proposal to comfort the affluent and powerful with spiritual nostrums.

Yoder's reading of the behavior of Jesus, clearly impelled by an unshakable ethical commitment to nonviolent action, offers a portrait of Jesus as the exemplar of an alternative politics. Yoder uses the Gospel of Luke to trace the life and career of Jesus, which was rightly discerned even in the Magnificat of Mary (Luke 1:46–55) as the doings of "an agent of radical social change."[20] The behavior of Jesus, in Yoder's term, is an "order threatening activity."[21] Its consequences are no less far-reaching than the upheaval that would be caused by an actual coming of the Jubilee, with its attendant equalizing impact upon existing social and political structures of injustice.

Yoder contends that the way of the cross is a strategic political possibility. His view contrasts sharply with that of Reinhold Niebuhr, who argued that ending up on a cross is politically counter-productive. Not so, contends Yoder, the cross is a powerful political strategy, offering "an alternative to both insurrection and quietism."[22] To join and participate in the movement led by Jesus calls for a deep social involvement with a decisively different moral posture. The new order, "though it condemns and displaces the old, . . . does not do so with the arms of the old."[23] Yoder examines the difficulty that Jesus has in convincing the crowds, even the disciples, of the viability of such an alternative, but he suggests that the difficulty centered precisely on the problems that they had in appreciating the decisively different moral stance involved.

> In none of the accounts where this word is reported does Jesus reprimand his disciples for expecting him to establish some new social order, as he would have had to do if the thesis of the only-spiritual kingdom were to prevail. He rather reprimands them for having misunderstood the character of that new social order which he does intend to set up. The novelty of its character is not that it is not social, or not visible, but that it is marked by an alternative to accepted patterns of leadership. The alternative to how kings of the earth rule is not "spirituality" but servanthood.[24]

Nor is Yoder through with this issue when he has commented on the life and ministry of Jesus. He goes on to examine how the uniqueness of this vision was misunderstood and even repudiated in other parts of the New Testament and perhaps even more so in the apostolic tradition.

The foregoing materials raise some of the most vexing and troublesome issues for thinking about Christian moral responsibility. They raise issues that are not dissimilar to the issues posed for the Hebrews by the proposal to adopt a hereditary king in place of charismatic leaders, but now the problems are almost infinitely more momentous. If, as the foregoing vignettes suggest, Jesus erases the distinctions by which moral attainment (involving legitimate concern for respectability) is defined and commended; if he disregards the conventions by which society creates and protects important values; and if he exemplifies a politics bordering on subversion, are we to take this behavior as offering definitive guidance?

There have been various answers given to this question throughout Christian history. Such answers have sprung from good faith and an earnest effort to take the New Testament seriously. The answers have stood on a spectrum between two poles—though the formulations given to the polar opposites have tended to frame the issue. On the one hand we find those understandings of Christian responsibility that say in effect, "By all means we are to follow the example of Jesus, even if that means going to the cross." At the other end, those understandings of Christian responsibility that declare, "Jesus cannot be a model for our action. The behavior of Jesus helps us to realize the terrible compromises that we must make to achieve tolerable order in human affairs, but we cannot tear apart the fabric of the social order in order to emulate Jesus." According to this view the behavior of Jesus is not a pattern to follow, but a revelation that alerts us to the ambiguous and tragic necessities enmeshed in every human effort to create and maintain structures of justice and order in a fallen world. Both of these poles have been embraced in earnest good faith by Christians, and the contrast between them has been a perennial feature of theological reflection about morality in almost every age.

The answers to this question bear careful examination. For instance, people may give (and indeed have given) one or the other answer and lived out what they have taken to be the implication of their choice without realizing its radical implications. Some, for example, have professed to take Jesus as an example yet missed the radical implications of his behavior. They think of Jesus more like a first-century boy scout or a member of some local service club (such as a first-century Rotary or Jaycees) rather than as one who challenged the very conventions upon which the good order of society normally depends. That may be a comforting tack, but it is based on moral confusion and obfuscation of a high order, to which Kierkegaard's characterization is apt: "the extraordinary degree of dullness so commonly found in Christendom." Conversely, people may say that the behavior of Jesus is not intended to be a moral guide for persons caught in the fallen conditions of humankind and that his actions cannot in themselves be a yardstick for actual practice. But this group may act as though all sorts of normal social practices, many of which do run counter to the behavior of Jesus, are thereby legitimized and thus completely overlook the moral problematic involved. When so used, the position of this second group undercuts the moral significance of the life and ministry of Jesus and flies directly in the face of his admonitions to the disciples that they live as he lived. Perhaps even more significantly, to suggest that the behavior of Jesus is not to be taken as a constraining example is to open the floodgates to new forms of the very attitudes and stances that were characteristic of the groups most at odds with Jesus and most instrumental in bringing about his downfall. Embraced emphatically, the second option often erases the necessary reservations that keep religious devotion from becoming fanatical, and opens the way for the very truculence that makes religious persons morally worse (at least as measured by the behavior of Jesus) than they would be if they had never attempted to be righteous.

Perhaps we cannot answer the question as to how far the behavior of Jesus offers moral guidance in the abstract, as though we should first decide whether or not it is or is not possible to take the behavior of Jesus as a guide and then proceed to look at the way Jesus lived and act accordingly. The use of Jesus as a model may depend upon the particular issue being dealt with and the social circumstances in which we have to function. Some concrete examples will help to show why this is the case.

After the Gulf War I had letters from former students that described to me their actions in response to the issues it posed. One of these letters was a request that I sign a manifesto declaring that war has ceased to be politically productive or morally acceptable—that failure to repudiate it entirely was tantamount to apostasy and clearly a case of infidelity to the ethical stance of the New Testament. The letter that accompanied this request contained arguments clearly akin to those of Yoder—contending that the moral mandate for Christians is clear and unambiguous. The opposite view appeared in a letter from a former student, enclosing a copy of a memo that he had prepared as a member of the White House staff in which he used traditional just-war criteria for demonstrating that the Gulf War was clearly legitimate. President Bush used this memo in giving a speech before a group of religious broadcasters to justify his decision to undertake military action in this instance. This writer also believed that it is possible to make a morally correct Christian judgment about such a political matter.

A third letter came from a student who had been called back as a reservist because he had attended college on an ROTC scholarship and had accepted a commission in the regular infantry before enrolling in seminary. Now he found himself conscientiously opposed to participation in what he regarded as morally illegitimate military action. Although he was exempted because he had since become ordained, that merely offered an administrative solution to an issue that was troublesome both to him and to the armed forces.

One reaction to this group of letters is to assume I had not been a very effective professor of ethics! How could former students come to such divergent judgments? But another reaction was to realize that here in microcosm is the situation of the Christian movement today, lacking a common mind about a perplexing issue—in part, at least, because it does not know for sure how to take the behavior of Jesus as a touchstone for making moral choices about deeply perplexing social issues. This second reaction suggested to me that I should maintain supportive contacts with all of these individuals, respecting them and their decisions, even urging them to stay in conversation with each other (at least in a public sense) and not to destroy community because of those differences. Such a position, however, was least likely to commend itself to the writer of the first letter, who certainly would be likely to regard it as a moral "cop-out," nor can it be taken as permanently satisfactory.

Then my thoughts ranged back to my own experiences with disagreements about the proper Christian stance toward the use of military coercion for socially important objectives. As a young CO during the World War II, I discovered there were those who agreed with me, those who disagreed but supported me, and those who regarded my stand as totally despicable. Indeed, because of my position I became persona non grata in the house of very close relatives for years. Then I chose a seminary in which the most impressive and popularly admired teacher was perhaps the most visible vocal critic of pacifism—though I have since been told by those who were fellow students that he admired my willingness to hold to a position that differed from his and to try to spell it out in dialogue with the way he developed his thought.

Considerably later, as an older scholar during the Vietnam War, I was interviewed for two positions teaching Christian ethics, and was pressed to indicate what I took to be the proper Christian stance toward that troublesome conflict. I answered that, while as a person who had always doubted the legitimacy of personal participation in war I would have serious doubts about its legitimacy, I could see how Christians could come to differing judgments about it and would need to respectfully treat their position in my teaching. I later learned through the network of my professional associates that there were members of both those faculties who stonewalled my invitation precisely because I was unwilling to declare that opposition to the Vietnam War was a necessary Christian stance, amounting to a matter of confessional correctness.

But while I think there are difficulties in obtaining a clear moral mandate about matters of participation in war—a moral mandate requiring a single Christian judgment—I am not sure there is equal latitude about according women an equal role in the life and leadership of the church.

The place of women in the early Christian movement does not present the same problems as would a consistently applied pacifism. They already have had a place, a strong and central place, in the early church. Their subsequent exclusion and subordination constitutes an aberration. Unlike the troublesome arguments about proper ways to deal with international conflict, the arguments for maintaining an all-male clergy are based on ideological contentions rather than profound concerns for procedural viability and social responsibility. In this case there is every warrant for regarding the newly appreciated role of women in the Jesus movement as a compelling model.

Does such a contextually governed concept of how we are to use the behavior of Jesus for moral guidance undercut the significance of Jesus and wreak havoc with moral integrity? Some would argue that it does; others would contend it is the necessary condition of remaining faithful to some of the very values of openness that Jesus himself exemplified. We must keep the conversation between these responses alive and well, for it is the very stuff on which life in a viable community of faith depends. It is probably important to be contextual about embracing contextualism, to know when such a stance is a crucial ethical move that serves important values and when it is a flight from obligation. But it also suggests that the moral correctness by itself is not a sufficient expression of Christian fidelity and that obedience to moral law is not salvific. That Jesus shared this view and so taught his hearers is the burden of the reflections in the next chapter.

13

The Teachings of Jesus

Moral Wisdom Beyond Legal Obligation

The focus in this chapter is on what Jesus taught, and more particularly on what he said. The difference between living and teaching, between behavior and speech, is impossible to draw clearly in actual life. Nevertheless, the categories provide a legitimate analytical way to look at different aspects of the "historical" (or what Borg calls the "pre-Easter") Jesus. The difference between behavior and teaching is helpful in distinguishing between the significance of Jesus as a pattern/example for ethical choice and the significance of Jesus as a teacher of ethical requirements or ideals.

Jesus did not give us a single coherent "systematic" discourse in which he carefully set forth a perspective on the nature and function of moral reasoning. He was even less discursive than Socrates, and certainly offered nothing remotely akin to treatises such as the *Nichomachean Ethics* of Aristotle or *The Critique of Practical [i.e., Moral] Reason* by Kant. Nevertheless, we do have clues as to how Jesus himself thought about, not merely moral requirements (such as the substantive provisions of the Law), but the function that morality itself should have in the life of his followers. These clues are found in many of the things he said as well as in many of the things he did.

Although Jesus provided helpful guidance for judging what is morally correct behavior in some instances, he did not so much lay down a law or a code in all its detailed specifics as he probed the complexities of moral choice and aimed a penetrating scrutiny upon the various ways by which people shirk or misapply their moral impulses. It is misleading to place the significance of the teaching of Jesus upon a contention that Jesus enunciated strikingly different or utterly new moral standards, as though plucking them out of nowhere in some pristine act of revelatory uniqueness.

Much of the specific content of Jesus' teaching was already found in ancient Near Eastern cultures or in the Hebraic heritage.[1] Thus preaching that tries to suggest that Jesus is unique in the standards of moral behavior he taught can easily be misguided (the usual item mentioned is the admonition to love our enemies, but that can be found in the Old Testament). Yet Jesus offered remarkable insight about the moral life in what he taught and how he taught it. He worked with aphorism and parable to illuminate what it means to be faithful to God and responsible to the neighbor.[2]

Marcus J. Borg has recently offered us a suggestive way of thinking about the impact that the teaching of Jesus has in the situation of his time (and, by inference, can have in our common life). According to Borg the teachings of Jesus "invite his hearers to *see* in a radically new way. The appeal is to the imagination, to that place within us in which reside our images of reality and our images of life itself; the invitation is to a different way of seeing, to different images for shaping our understanding of life."[3] According to Borg the newness offered by Jesus consists of an "alternative wisdom" that contrasts decisively with the conventional wisdom that was present in the culture of his time (and that is just as strongly evident in the ordinary morality of our time). Conventional wisdom is concerned with manners; is bound up with a "dynamic of rewards and punishments;" and encourages persons to be concerned with how they measure up to society's expectations. Such conventional wisdom imagines God "primarily as lawgiver and judge." It can be found in every religious tradition—in contemporary Christianity as much as in the religion of Jesus' day. Conventional wisdom uses morality to divide good people from others, encouraging smugness in the first group and self-doubt or self-negation in the second.[4] Borg indicates how Jesus brought about a transformation in the understanding of wisdom and morality. For one thing, Jesus reverses the judgments upon which conventional moral comparisons are made. He makes a Samaritan (who belongs to a group despised for its heresy and impurity) the hero of a parable; the meticulous Pharisee the moral antimodel. "He directly attacked the central values of his social world's conventional wisdom: family, wealth, honor, purity, and religiosity."[5] Moreover, "Jesus invited his hearers to see God not as the judge, not as the one whose requirements must be met, not as the legitimator of conventional wisdom—but as gracious and compassionate."[6]

In the last chapter we noted how the behavior of Jesus modeled compassionate inclusiveness in the place of self-protecting purity and emancipating unconventionality in the place of bondage to manners and traditional mores. Here we will see how the teaching of Jesus provides an alternative wisdom that contrasts with the understanding of morality of which Proverbs and Deuteronomy, for example, are representative. It should not surprise us that the sayings of Jesus were not accepted with widespread enthusiasm, particularly among those who were moral by the customary standards of the time. We must understand how such teaching engenders fear—particularly in those who think of themselves as defenders of righteousness. Such fear results in hostility. It happens no less in our day than it did in the time of Jesus. Think how quickly even those among us who would extend freedom and fellowship to groups now considered careless, delinquent, or perverse (we don't generally use the term "impure") are looked upon as dangerous. Religious moralism associated with conventional morality renders people intolerant and prompts them to the very attitudes and actions that become a terror to those whose behavior is unconventional or whose creative and imaginative ways of looking at life challenge the security of so-called "good folks."

We can understand the teachings of Jesus by asking how (as far as can be discerned from the record) Jesus aligned himself in the contrast between the tendencies to precise legalism that grew out of Ezekiel's response to the Exile and the efforts to build upon the suffering servant material in the latter part of Isaiah. Jesus never addressed this issue in quite those terms, but his teaching contains a highly plausible indication of what his answer might well have been. For instance, we come to realize how Jesus was distinctly at odds with the scribes and Pharisees over the purpose and meaning of the Law. It is on the basis of such a premise that we offer the following interpretations of the teaching of Jesus.

We will look at this issue first by examining a pivotal portion of the Sermon on the Mount, or that collection of the teachings of Jesus collected by Matthew in the fifth, sixth, and seventh chapters of his Gospel. It is placed there by Matthew as the counterpart to the Mosaic Torah—as the new law that replaces the old law. But the Sermon on the Mount is not a single coherent discussion of morality that Jesus himself delivered as a learned discourse. That is one of the reasons its interpretation is difficult and has prompted a great variety of understandings.

Probably no part of Scripture receives greater lip service and doting adulation than the Sermon on the Mount. President Harry Truman once declared that he ran American foreign policy in accord with its teachings; and when the Iranagate/Contra episode broke in February of 1987, Colonel Oliver North, the White House military aide who was deeply involved in the diversion of funds secured from selling arms to Iran to back the Contras in Nicaragua, appealed to the Sermon on the Mount as a warrant for contending he shouldn't be persecuted for whatever violations of law he may have perpetrated. That kind of pious confusion doesn't aid in understanding ethical matters.

But even among serious exegetes and scholars the Sermon on the Mount has been interpreted in many ways. It has fascinated and confounded Christians throughout the whole history of the church.[7] One modern writer can deem it a "design for living, and write about it as offering a practical and effective guide to moral behavior."[8] Another, in a work also written for lay persons, declares that it is a document with revolutionary implications, in the sense that it turns values upside down.[9] Some scholars have suggested that the Sermon on the Mount was a catechism that, used in conjunction with the Epistle of James, furnished a set of guidelines for the behavior of early Christians.[10] But even supposing this to be the case, questions arise whether its moral injunctions apply to individuals or to group life, or whether these injunctions are intended to be an interim ethic or a guide for ordinary conduct in the world as we know it and have to live within it. Still others have argued that the Sermon on the Mount sets forth a series of impossible ideals, and therefore prepares the way for the repentance that leads to forgiveness and grace. And so the overview might go on.

Each of these options (and others that might be mentioned) has some bearing on how to understand the ethical stance in the teachings of Jesus. The interpretation that sees the Sermon on the Mount as a perfectionistic code would treat the teachings of Jesus as a refined and amplified continuation of the Jewish Law—noteworthy for its intensity and stress on inward attitude as well as outward act, and designed to provide guidance for living in conformity to God's will. The interpretation that regards the Sermon on the Mount as setting forth an interim ethic would make those teachings a prolegomenon to a new way of behaving, one suitable for use in a community waiting for some new kind of history to be established by a sudden value-altering act of God. The view that the Sermon sets forth demands impossible of fulfillment has been advanced with special earnestness by those whose theology stresses the need for repentance and forgiveness and whose morality includes an assumption that living in a fallen world entails compromises with an ethic of love.

The interpretation that we offer here (bracketing a judgment as to whether or not other interpretations are valuable for other purposes or compatible with this interpretation) may offer a glimpse of how Jesus looks at the relationship between the old law as it was used to sustain a conventional morality and the new law as the basis for an alternative community. It sheds light on how Jesus positions himself over and against the priestly and legalistic approaches that were built on the paradigm advanced by Ezekiel. This interpretation draws heavily on the contrast between the old law and the new law as set forth in the beginning of Matthew's Gospel at verse 5:17.

First, however, let us consider the passage in which Jesus begins the comparisons involved:

> Do not think that I have come to abolish the law and the prophets; I have come not to abolish but to fulfill. For truly, I tell you, until heaven and earth pass away, not one letter, not one stroke of a letter, will pass from the law until all is accomplished. Therefore, whoever then breaks one of the least of these commandments and teaches others to do the same, will be called least in the kingdom of heaven; but whoever does them and teaches them shall be called great in the kingdom of heaven. For I tell you, unless your righteousness exceeds that of the scribes and Pharisees, you will never enter the kingdom of heaven. (5:17–20)

Jesus here denies he is advancing a different morality, one that abrogates the basic moral stance of the Jewish Torah. His teaching doesn't substitute the approval of treachery for the condemnation of murder, the approval of false witness for the respectful treatment of others; or freewheeling for marital fidelity. Even its admonition to love both neighbor and enemy alike is not, despite the inference, a reversal of the Torah tradition as much as a repudiation of conventional morality (as it prevails both in that time and ours). W. D. Davies, whose study of the setting of the Sermon on the Mount is considered a classic, has pointed out that the Sermon on the Mount underscores the fact that faith and morality are considered to be inseparably tied together in the New Testament.

> To examine the setting of the S[ermon on the] M[ount] is to be compelled to recognize that "these sayings of mine," "the law of Christ," "the new commandment" played a more significant part in the New Testament as a whole than is often recognized. The faith of early Christians rested, not on a mime, but on a drama, and in this drama the words of the chief protagonist on morality, as on other subjects, were essential to the action. For some in the primitive Church,

if not for all, the penetrating demands of Jesus, no less than the great kerygmatic affirmations about him, were part of "the bright light of the Gospel," that is, they were revelatory.[11]

The comparisons, then, between the old law and the new are not comparisons between different moral standards or ideals, but they are comparisons of the extent to which such standards are to be considered obligatory. Let us look at the contrasts from this perspective:

In verse 21 of chapter 5 we read, "You have heard that it was said to those of ancient times, 'You shall not murder' and 'whoever murders shall be liable to judgment,'" whereas in verse 22 we read, "But I say to you that if you are angry with your brother you will be liable to judgment; and if you insult a brother or a sister you shall be liable to the council, and if you say, 'you fool!' you shall be liable to the hell of fire." It is reasonably possible to obey the old law—in this instance to avoid premeditated murder. The great majority of people are worthy of being considered morally good as judged by that standard. But it is less easy—perhaps even impossible—to obey the new law, to keep free of anger, to refrain from implying insulting things about others (or even thinking them), and to resist deeming others to be fools. Most people have not, and will not, successfully live up to that kind of a requirement. It might even be legitimate to suggest that it is impossible to do so, or at least virtually impossible to do so.

Or, take another contrast. In verse 27 we read, "You have heard that it was said, 'You shall not commit adultery.'" In contrast, verse 28 says, "But I say to you that every one who looks at a woman with lust has already committed adultery with her in his heart." It is possible to obey the old law that prohibits sexual infidelity in marriage—but it is less easy, perhaps even impossible—to obey the law that prohibits even the contemplation of adultery. Even stating the moral obligation as the prohibition of a certain action brings that action to mind.

Similarly, verse 31 indicates, "It was also said, 'Whoever divorces his wife, let him give her a certificate of divorce.'" But verse 32: "But I say to you that everyone who divorces his wife (except on the ground of unchastity) causes her to commit adultery; and whoever marries a divorced woman commits adultery." The old law merely tempered the harsh practice of divorce as considered to be legitimate at the time. It allowed the husband to call off the marriage upon impulse, but required him to furnish a written release that helped the wife to maintain some standing in the community and be eligible for another partnership. In the place of this somewhat humane provision (although one distorted by sexism) Jesus enunciates a new requirement that makes the obligation to remain married unconditional. This can be recognized as the case especially if the phrase placed in parentheses above, which is believed by many authorities to have been added later, was not in the original. Marriage is an unconditional obligation. No one can ever come to the place of breaking off a marriage, no matter what the circumstances, with a complete sense of innocence. If the new law, however, is taken as a rigid prescription that prohibits all divorce, then the freedom to deal helpfully with miserable situations when they arise between marriage partners may be curtailed in new ways. Divorce may be more humane than suffering or hostility. But if the new law is understood as a statement of the ultimate nature of the obligation against which all failures in marriages are judged, it functions to reveal the limitations of legalism rather than to create a new code. Divorce may be the only way to deal with a tragic breakdown of the matrimonial relationship; but it isn't free of moral problems even if it seems to be a preferable alternative.

The contrasts continue in verse 33: "Again you have heard that it was said to those of ancient times, 'You shall not swear falsely, but carry out the vows you have made to the Lord.'" Verse 34: "But I say unto you, Do not swear at all, either by heaven, for it is the throne of God, or by the earth, for it is his footstool, or by Jerusalem, for it is the city of the great King. And do not swear by your head, for you cannot make one hair white or black. Let what you say be simply 'Yes,' 'Yes' or 'No,' 'No'; anything more than this comes from evil." At stake here is the extent of the obligation to be true in our words and to our commitments. Does that obligation cover only statements made under oath, or only to contracts that are notarized, or does it apply to all the statements and all the commitments one makes— whether or not explicitly declared to be binding? The new law makes all obligations unconditionally important, not something to be observed only under special circumstances. Although it may be legal to do so, morally it is just as wrong to weasel out of agreements clearly but casually made as to break contracts solemnly sealed and delivered.

And finally, the very famous contrast: Verse 38 reports, "You have heard that it was said, 'An eye for an eye and a tooth for a tooth.'" [which was, when first promulgated, a humanitarian limitation on unrestrained revenge]. But verse 39 declares, "But I say to you, Do not resist an evildoer. But if any one strikes you on the right check, turn to him the other also; and if any one wants to sue you and take your coat, give your cloak as well; and if any one forces you to go one mile, go also the second mile. Give to him who begs from you, and do not refuse him who would borrow from you." As anyone realizes who has read Harry Emerson Fosdick's book *The Sec-*

ond Mile, which sold thousands of copies when it was published in the 1930s, this part of the Sermon on the Mount can be the basis of a powerful vision that can transform behavior. But that benefit would be mocked if the new requirement were "relegalized," as for instance, if the requirement of Roman law that an able-bodied person carry the soldier's pack one mile (one thousand paces of 0.296 meters each) were to become a Gospel requirement of two thousand paces *and not one step more!*

Each of the obligations as specified under the old law has a ceiling on what is required. That ceiling constitutes a prudent expectation that can be met by the average person of good intentions. The ceiling is part of conventional moral wisdom, which has to hold that the requirement can be fulfilled. The obligation connected with the new law is much higher—so much higher in fact that one can never be sure of having done enough to claim to have lived up to the moral expectations. In summary: The prohibition against an adversarial relationship to another includes not only the prohibition of murder, but the preclusion of anger and dislike; the prohibition against adultery precludes not only sexual activity outside wedlock, but even the contemplation of doing so; the prohibition of divorce is complete—ruling out a loophole of convenience (for males) by which the obligation to stay married can be set aside on technical grounds; the obligation to be truthful and to respect commitments knows no limitation and would never countenance the ways in which courtroom lawyers often say almost anything they want for the press, whereas witnesses have to be accurate; the obligation to serve persons in need is without a ceiling and knows no distinctions between those who deserve it and those who don't; and the obligation to live at peace with others cannot be circumscribed by prudence.

The new law as set forth in the Sermon on the Mount removes the ceiling on the requirement for righteousness in such a way as to render it impossible ever to say one has done enough to be good. That effectively destroys the major condition necessary for a legalistic morality to work, namely, an ability to know when one has been righteous enough to be worthy and able to make a claim on God's grace. Under the new law there can be no boasting about having achieved sufficient fidelity. Every claim to moral adequacy is demolished. That clearly puts the moral stance of Jesus at fundamental odds with that of legalistic schemes—past and present—for guiding and measuring attainment.

If we look at another part of the Sermon on the Mount, the Beatitudes (5:1–12), we can observe the same reversal in the understanding of the purpose of morality that we have examined in both the behavior of Jesus and his comparison of the old law with the new. Who is blessed? Not those who are proud or confident of their virtue, but those who mourn; not those who hold themselves up as paragons of purity and are critical of those who do not have it, but those who are poor in spirit; not those who are prudently careful to marshal their resources and tend to their obligations, but those who hunger and thirst for righteousness; not those who foment conflict even in well-intended efforts to uphold standards of decency, but those who make peace; not those who are tough on crime, but those who are merciful. In summary, not those who are good according to conventional wisdom. The Beatitudes portray an alternative measure of fidelity in which it is better to fall short of what is morally required than to be judgmental of others; in which sinners who know they are inadequate are better than so-called good people who harshly condemn them; in which religion is a source of humility and penitence rather than a psychic club with which to bludgeon others into conformity.

We turn attention now to the way in which the attitude of Jesus toward morality is evidenced in the parables. Here we are dealing with narrative rather than with admonitions, with story rather than aphorisms, but the implication is no less compelling.

We begin with the parable of the Prodigal Son. Our minds have become hardened to the thrust of this story because we have read it too often and too casually. Suppose it had been written this way:

There was a man who had two sons. The younger of them said to his father, "Father, give me the share of property that will belong to me." So he divided his property between them. A few days later, the younger son gathered all that he had and traveled to a distant country, and there he squandered his property in dissolute living. When he had spent everything, a severe famine took place throughout that country, and he began to be in need. So he went and hired himself out to one of the citizens of that country, who sent him into his fields to feed the pigs. And he would gladly have filled himself on the pods that the pigs were eating; and no one gave him anything. But when he came to himself he said, "How many of my father's hired servants have bread enough and to spare, but I am dying of hunger! I will get up and go to my father, and will say to him, 'Father I have sinned against heaven and before you. I am no more worthy to be called your son; treat me as one of your hired servants.'"

So he set off and went to his father, and when he came to the house he knocked at the door. When the father finally answered he said, "Aha, I thought you would be back. There's a job for you in the barns cleaning the stables. When you have earned back the money you have squandered, we'll have a conference of the family to see whether or not you are ready to rejoin us as a son rather than as a servant. If you are not ready then, we'll set up another trial period to get you ready." (Luke 15:11ff., with apologies to both Jesus and Luke)

A father who acted that way would qualify as a loving father, a believer in a moral order, and a parent capable of forgiveness but wise enough not to dispense "cheap grace." He would exemplify all schemes of religion in which salvation is tied to a penance and satisfaction cycle that the sinner can utilize to reestablish the relationship of acceptance. He would have upheld family values understood in moralistic terms. Had Jesus told the story that way it would have made sense to those seeking to preserve covenantal fidelity by legalistic means. But Jesus didn't tell the story that way—which is one of the factors that must be considered in determining what he intended to convey about the moral situation.

Let us try again to see what the story as Jesus told it suggests by imagining an imaginary alternative that Jesus might have told to convey yet another meaning.

There was a man who had two sons. The younger of them said to his father, "Father, give me the share of property that will belong to me." So he divided his property between them. A few days later, the younger son gathered all that he had and traveled to a distant country, and there invested the inheritance wisely. He got a good job, lived frugally, speculated successfully, and became a young upwardly mobile professional. Whereupon he wrote back to his father and said, "I want you to come and see what I have accomplished. I am now comfortably successful. I have more than you ever got together through your country bumpkin ways of doing things, and I hope you will be thrilled to see what I have done. Moreover, I am getting in a position to be sure that you will not need to have financial worries in your final years.

But, if you do come, at least get yourself a new suit and leave that farmer's hat back home. You might not be let into my condominium if you were to arrive looking as you often do. (with even more apologies to Jesus and Luke)

Why didn't Jesus tell the story that way—or in a first-century equivalent? Had he done so he would have suggested the possibility that human success can have saving significance apart from a divinely bestowed redemption. This version describes a life of human success—a morality that denies the need of divine involvement and may even result in a kind of rebellion in which the son presumes to tell the father about his shortcomings. Those who think Jesus simply overlooked the possibility of writing this kind of success story should consider the parable of the rich fool in Luke 12:16–21!

Now consider the ending of the parable as it was written:

> But while he [the son] was still far off, his father saw him and was filled with compassion; he ran and put his arms around him and kissed him. (Luke 15:20)

The son confesses his wrong—but it seems as though the father hardly even hears him—he certainly does not seem interested in whether or not the son grovels enough—so joyful is he about the son's return. The father welcomes the son back—with a ring on his hand, a robe, shoes, a fatted calf to feast on, and great merriment, "for this son of mine was dead and is alive again; he was lost, and is found" (v. 24).

One of the important aspects of the parable is the ending, which is an account of the resentment shown by the elder son who had stayed at home and been an exemplary paragon of fidelity and virtue. He refuses to join the festivities, and the father comes out to entreat him to come in. The parable ends without revealing whether or not the elder son goes in and joins the festivities. The implication may well be that the virtuous prigs of this world are cut off from God by their own refusal to participate in the forgiveness of others. Only those who have "done life aright" are tempted by that mode of rebellion. That ending to the parable, in its own way, implies a devastating criticism of works/righteousness even without having to be explicit about it.

I clearly remember a conversation I had many years ago with a very sensitive yet proper gentleman who was deeply devoted to being morally correct in all of his relationships with others. He was a very good and gracious man. Even so, he expressed exasperation with the sermons to which he listened that (as he heard them) castigated the older brother. That older brother, he argued, deserved the benefits he enjoyed and was also entitled to be a bit resentful of the ease with which the father welcomed back the younger son. And from the standpoint of the very conventional morality that is so valuable in ordering commonplace social relationships, that gentleman was right.

The things that Jesus taught suggest some of the same conclusions as to the nature of faithful morality as the way Jesus behaved and carried on his ministry. Jesus taught that people should be treated on the basis of need even as he responded to persons on the basis of need, not on the basis or status or virtuous achievement. He taught about the importance of accepting outcasts and sinners even as he inspired them to newness of life by compassion and concern rather than by condemnation or moralistic scolding. He developed a set of understandings about the importance of putting human concerns above legalistic requirements even as he cared for human beings. He suggested that if some unusual action is required to meet a specific situation, it is legitimate to do something that is expressly prohibited by the law in order to meet human need.

It is not difficult to see this by reading the New Testament. Jesus often failed to observe the laws of purity and righteousness that were the defining measures of fidelity for his time (Matthew 9:14; Mark 7:1–8). He healed the sick, even on the Sabbath (Mark 2:1–12; 3:1–6; Matthew 9:1–8; 11:9–14). And Jesus recognized the increasing breech between his way of looking at the nature and purpose of moral earnestness and that of the religious authorities.

The collections of sayings in Matthew 23 reflect this growing tension. It is doubtful that Jesus delivered all the strictures recorded here in one sweeping denunciation of those who trusted in their own moralistic righteousness and sought to impose it on others. But the denunciations of those who were making the Law a means of proving their own virtue and insisting that obedience to the Law is necessary to social stability and religious purity allow us conclude that the tension was very great between Jesus and those whose views about the place and purpose of morality were very different.

A winsome comment in Matthew 23:37 may be more consistent with the spirit of Jesus.

> Jerusalem, Jerusalem, the city that kills the prophets and stones those who are sent to it. How often have I desired to gather your children together as a hen gathers her brood under her wings, and you were not willing!

In this verse the whole city refuses to accept the moral stance of Jesus, thus seeming to act much like the elder brother acted toward his father in the parable of the two sons. This passage may indeed be more authentic than the polemical material in the rest of the chapter, but every part of the chapter indicates the same dynamic in the situation. Hence groups as well as individuals can allow moral rigor to become a source of self-confidence and of intolerance toward those who are less impressive in their virtue. Both may cut themselves off from the saving power of the Gospel. If they do so, they bring judgment upon themselves. Such judgment occurs, not by the vindictive anger of God, but by the self-generated resentment that cannot subordinate morality to grace.

The teachings of Jesus have fascinated people across the centuries and will continue to fascinate people long into the future. Jesus is less patient with those who are morally judgmental of others than he is with those who fall short of what might be morally expected. So-called good people are more harshly criticized than sinners; those who use religion as a club over others are treated more severely than those whose religion is a source of penitence and humility. All of this is crucially important for understanding Christian morality. It renders repentance more significant than moral resolve for the Christian life. It abolishes the assessment of moral achievement as the basis for standing and acceptance without making morality unimportant. It prompts a new ditty: How odd, of God, to choose sinners.

But it does not render moral requirements meaningless! Instead of being preconditions for being accepted by God they become a grateful way of responding to the divine grace. Instead of being determining factors in a merit-badge race for virtue they become means of creating community between persons committed to accepting one another. Instead of the preconditions for an earned reward they become the fruitful expressions of gratitude for a bestowed salvation. Instead of worrying about the fact that freedom entails the hazards of doing wrong, they point to the possibility of being free to do the right in unexpected and imaginative ways. They even offer the possibility that some untested and flexible response to a moral vision may be a more humane achievement than perfect obedience to a code.

This is liberating. It frees the inner as well as the outer self, embraces rather than condemns the oppressor, produces newness of life as well as a possible change in the external conditions of existence. This gives morality a liberating significance. It is consistent with Exodus and all that it means as a symbol of liberation. Without Exodus as starting point there would be no Christ figure and no Christ event, no possibility of moving to reconciliation and redemption. It is also consistent with exile, without which the group that is free might forget its own shortcomings and be too sanguine about its moral achievements. Just as there could be no covenant fidelity without liberation, so there can be no covenant without nationhood, prophecy, punishment, and repentance. The first liberation is essential to the second, but the second is the culmination of the first. To know that and to realize its implications, however dimly, is to move toward an adequate understanding of the role that Christ plays in the biblical drama.

14

Ethics in the Thought of Paul the Apostle

Sanctification, Justification, and Openness to Other Cultures

The disciples were in a position to observe the behavior of Jesus and to hear his teaching. But Christianity cannot be explained as a movement that arose simply and solely out of enthusiasm for a leader known only for a temporal career. Christianity emerged from a more momentous experience, namely a belief in the Resurrection that followed the Crucifixion. Hence what Marcus J. Borg has called "the post-Easter Jesus"[1] becomes essential for our reflections. The disciples did experience the Resurrection, and accounts of the Resurrection do appear in the Gospels (which would not have been written without it), but the power of the resurrected Christ is interpreted most fully in the thinking of Paul. In contrast to the disciples, who were acquainted with the historical Jesus, Paul was not a participating witness of the ministry of Jesus but was an architect of a massive and decisive understanding of Jesus Christ as the Messiah. He struggled to understand how the Christological event in its totality could be appropriated within and in relationship to many currents of thinking swirling through the ancient Near Eastern world in his time. Although Paul's letters are not next in the canonical ordering (the Book of Acts immediately follows the four Gospels), they probably predate the Gospels and reinforce that aspect of the narrative that deals with the post–Easter Christ.

Paul formulated several theological ideas that have crucial significance for much subsequent Christian thinking. Whether one views those ideas as having decisive importance or regards them as distortions of the Christian message (as do some), one has to realize that they are central to many theological movements in the history of the church and are pivotal for a complete range of thinking about how faith relates to moral decision making. The ideas of Paul shift the focus from "The Ethics of Jesus" (Pattern and Teacher) to "The Power and the Righteousness of God as Manifested in Christ" (Sanctifier, Justifier, and Creator/Redeemer). The focus of moral faithfulness changes from discerning the requirements of discipleship to being transformed by the power to live a new life in Christ.

Granted, Paul's writings consist more of analysis and argument than narrative and parable. They often employ turgidly complex formulations that put some people off because they are discursive and confuse others because they are so complex. His writings also offend a few because they make sense only from a faith perspective informed by a belief in the significance of the death and resurrection of Christ. We must also realize that Paul's writings are no more a lengthy coherent discourse about ethics than are the teachings of Jesus. Contained in letters written to individual churches, their treatment of moral issues is very often situation-specific rather than being organized into a massively abstract ethical system. They even include petulant reactions to some of his followers and diatribes against his opponents, and frequently admonish one group to do one thing and another group to do something quite different.[2]

Although it is often suggested that the teachings of Jesus and the theological formulations of Paul belong to two different worlds—that, as I often heard it expressed by theologically liberal friends during my youth, "There once was a man named Jesus, who taught a simple message of love and trust, and then along came a man named Paul who spoiled it all"—it is the contention of this chapter that Paul's understanding of the Christological event represents more continuity than discontinuity with the rest of the biblical drama, and that the moral teaching of Paul picks up basic themes from the biblical story as a whole, and at some significant places even bridges some of the polarities that are contained in that story.

To show this we will offer a list of key points that indicate the significance of Paul for thinking about the nature of the ethical enterprise.

The Universality of Sin. Paul forcefully examines the universal presence of sin and guilt in human experience and recognizes sin to be the fundamental problem of human experience. His interpretations here are the warp and woof of many later interpretations of Christian faith in terms of justification, particularly that of the Protestant reformers. But Paul roots this contention in the Old Testament, which was his scripture.

Paul argues that bondage to sin is universal; it affects Jews (who are under the Law) and Gentiles (who are not) with the same devastating consequences. Sin came into the human situation with the disobedience of the first human being (Paul says "with the first man.") Sin involves a self-confidence that leads to the repudiation of dependence on God and turns quickly into moral wrongdoing. Sin is an attitude of rebellion that eventuates in deliberate malfeasance (misconduct). Paul speaks about sin as having an almost independent status—it is not merely the misdeeds people do but a condition in which they are caught. It brings death to all because it is a reality that affects, or is found in, all persons. It is manifested as a repudiation of the creative purposes of God that is so deep it is impossible to rise above it, or overcome it—at least without God's help as offered to us by the work and righteousness of Christ.

Paul's presentation of these faith perspectives is stated most fully in Romans, particularly in the fifth chapter. That chapter begins with a treatment of justification by faith as a free and marvelous gift of God, but it includes an analysis of the origins of sin—an analysis obviously informed by the story of the fall.

> Therefore, as sin came into the world through one man and death came through sin, and so death spread to all because all have sinned— sin indeed was in the world before the law, but sin is not reckoned when there is no law. (Romans 5:12)

Paul's language here is consistent with those understandings of sin that point to a condition that is deeper and more complex than moral misconduct. This is the doctrine of original sin in substance if not in name.

It is important to bear in mind that Paul's treatment of sin is set in the context of his argument for sanctification and justification. The good news of saving grace is coupled with the portrayal of the "bad news" of depravity. Paul's is the first of many theologies with deep doctrines of the human predicament that strongly affirm the power of grace. A. C. Purdy was correct in noting, "We do scant justice to Paul's thought, if we fail to note that every statement about the reign of sin and death and about man's helplessness and hopelessness in the grip of sin is set in immediate and vivid contrast to the reign of life through the one man Jesus Christ."[3]

Christ's Healing Power. Paul contends that the power of sin and guilt has been overcome by a divine power to heal and redeem the human enterprise—and that this saving power is manifestly operative in the work of Jesus Christ, the risen Lord. In the same chapter that talks about the overwhelmingly universal presence of sin and death in the human situation, Paul says, "Therefore, since we are justified by faith, we have peace with

God through our Lord Jesus Christ" (Romans 5:1). This is a cause for joy and hope, a ground on which we can rejoice even in the suffering we must endure in this world. Paul's declaration about the good news of justification comes before his declaration about the bad news of sin. (This is the order in which these two matters are always treated in thinking about justification—it is the good news about salvation that makes it possible to hear and accept the bad news about sin.) This is the fundamental truth, and Paul declares it with brazen confidence.

The Continuing Struggle. But alongside of this confidence Paul realizes that the experience of being saved or converted is marked by an ongoing tension between the joy of the new being in Christ and the persistence of the old person. Paul never portrays his life following conversion as an experience of idyllic bliss. While he rejoices in the confidence he has in Christ, he is well aware that the ambiguity that plagues every historical achievement is not eliminated. Paul doesn't say very much about "going on to perfection." Rather, he describes the tension that dominates his experience—a tension present even as he writes about living the justified life. While he is grateful, profoundly grateful, he is not proud or triumphalist. He rejoices in the confidence he has in Christ, but he is well aware that the ambiguity of historical achievement is not eliminated. Thus he describes the tensions that are present even in the life of the justified.

> So I find it to be a law that when I want to do what is good, evil lies close at hand. For I delight in the law of God in my inmost self, but I see in my members another law at war with the law of my mind, making me captive to the law of sin that dwells in my members. Wretched man that I am! Who will rescue me from this body of death? Thanks be to God through Jesus Christ our Lord!
>
> So then, with my mind I am a slave to the law of God, but with my flesh I am a slave to the law of sin. (Romans 7:21–25)

Predestination. A fourth understanding of the Christian life is found in Paul's discussion of predestination in its "single" form, i.e., declaring God to be the author of saving faith wherever it is found. In Paul's own words:

> We know that all things work together for good for those who love God, who are called according to his purpose. For those whom he foreknew he also predestined to be conformed to the image of his Son, in order that he might be the first-born within a large family. For those whom he predestined he also called; and those whom he called he also justified; and those whom he justified he also glorified.
>
> What then shall we say about these things? If God is for us, who is

against us? He who did not withhold his own Son but gave him up for us all, will he not with him also give us all everything else? Who shall bring any charge against God's elect? It is God who justifies; who is to condemn? It is Christ Jesus, who died, yes, who was raised, who is at the right hand of God, who indeed intercedes for us? Who shall separate us from the love of Christ? Will hardship, or distress, or persecution, or famine, or nakedness, or peril, or sword? As it is written,

> "For your sake we are being killed all the day long; we are regarded as sheep to be slaughtered."

No, in all these things we are more than conquerors through him who loved us. For I am sure that neither death, nor life, nor angels, nor rulers, not things present, nor things to come, nor powers, not height, not depth, nor anything else in all creation, will be able to separate us from the love of God in Christ Jesus our Lord. (Romans 8:28–39)

This passage contains the very affirmations that later come to be called the doctrine of assurance—one of the ideas frequently associated with predestination, and one of the clues to the power of the doctrine in the lives of the faithful. It is not boasting of being chosen, but confidence in God and God's enduring purposes that gives the proper meaning to the saving relationship between God and the believer. This passage also, in its way, is an expression of gratitude for liberation from bondage to sin. Paul's formulation of the idea that grace is a gift leaves unsaid anything about the cause of unbelief in persons who seem to lack faith. The assertion that God is also responsible for the condition of the reprobate is the seemingly offensive premise of the double form of the doctrine, which came about in later, more speculative and/or logically consistent formulations of the doctrine.

Although Paul's formulation of the idea of predestination avoids the difficulties that later double forms present, it raises certain problems. There is something of a parallelism between the scandal of particularity that attends the experience of Exodus—where by God's choice and by the divine initiative a particular group is brought out of a situation of oppression—and the idea that by God's choice and by the divine initiative particular individuals are destined for salvation. In the initial presentation of each idea, there is an arbitrariness that affronts the notion of justice as impartial (as seen from a universalistic perspective). That issue has to be worked through—and interestingly enough it is worked through in biblical faith in surprisingly similar ways in each case—by treating the experience of being chosen as a call to service rather than to privilege.

Being justified by faith means being treated as though righteous even if one has not achieved purity under the Law. Paul is in the very same stream of thought here as Jesus was—whose treatment of the old law/new law distinction guards against a scheme of works righteousness and whose parable of the lost son clearly infers that salvation is an act of grace, not a reward for righteous living.

Paul went back to the patriarchal stories to defend his interpretation of the Promise. He suggested that Abraham was justified by faith—that if Abraham had depended on works, "he would have nothing to boast about." It was Abraham's faith in God, not his accomplishments, that saved him (see chapter 4 of Romans). Abraham is "the father of us all." Paul utilizes the term "adoption" as well as the term "election" to describe the consequences of being objects of God's saving love and grace.

> Abraham believed God and it was reckoned to him as righteousness. . . . Now the words, "it was reckoned to him," were written not for his sake alone but for ours also. It will be reckoned to us who believe in him who raised Jesus our Lord Christ from the dead, who was handed over to death for our trespasses and raised for our justification. (Romans 4:3b, 4:23–25)

If what we said earlier about the Exodus representing God's free grace is correct, Paul could have gone back to Moses/Exodus as well as Abraham to make his case—but it would probably not have been as effective, since at the time Paul is writing there is much more emphasis on obedience to moral law associated with the Mosaic tradition than is the case with respect to Abraham.

Paul holds that the power of Christ, working through justification and adoption, liberates us from the tyranny of law without destroying the importance of moral fidelity. This is an experience of being set free. It contains, therefore, a strong element of liberation—a liberation from bondage and slavery to the power of sin. It is by the power of Christ we have been set free of sin (Romans 6:22a). In the Epistle to the Galatians Paul declares, "For freedom Christ has set us free; stand firm, therefore, and do not submit again to a yoke of slavery" (5:1).

Whereas the law is a tyrant to those without the power to fulfill it (since they have no hope of being accounted as righteous if they do not), when we are related to God in this new way the law is holy and just and good. It offers guidance for freedom, peace, and love. In Galatians the fruits of the spirit as listed as "love, joy, peace, patience, kindness, generosity, faithfulness, gentleness, and self-control" (5:22).

The impulse for moral living is changed, but it is not diminished in importance or intensity. Instead of seeking to do right because we fear adverse consequences for doing wrong, we seek to do right because of gratitude. The indicative posture is connected to respect for the Law. Paul creates the same sense of joy and gratitude that was present when the Law was first given by Moses. The "I am your God . . . therefore" of Exodus becomes "We have become new beings in Christ . . . therefore" in Paul.

The Law is useful as guidance for those who are alive with the spirit—the moral significance of the Law can be freely and joyously embraced because dependence on law as a way of earning (or meriting) salvation has been annulled (i.e., transcended). The freedom from the Law not only allows the works of the spirit to supersede the works of the flesh, but it allows the Law to be embraced in order to be helpful to others rather than to acquire righteousness for ourselves. Indeed, we can even decide it is well to disobey the Law, from which we are already set free, if by so doing we will help someone else. In 1 Corinthians 8 Paul considers the question of whether Christians can eat the meat that came from the animals used in sacrifices to idols. He points out there is nothing to prevent us from doing so even though the act itself is considered wrong by the law; but there is much to prevent us from doing so because the exercise of the liberty in which we stand can be a stumbling block to the weak. "All things are lawful, but not all things are helpful." Morality, therefore, is not a schema for the determination of our own destinies by intense obedience to the Law, but a means of becoming a support and a help to others. The Christian is free, not only to disobey the Law if that serves the neighbor's good, but even to obey the Law if that serves the neighbor's good.

Here Paul stands in the strand of biblical thinking that is found in the servant poetry of Isaiah. The liberty with which we are set free by Christ is a liberty that is validated in service to the neighbor. Election is to discipleship, not to license. Of course it is a scandal if it is election to special privilege! Of course it is a scandal if the idea of being a believer is a life of self-esteem, peace of mind, confident victory for self-defined achievements, and a cushy niche in the suburban sprawl. But it is not a scandal to be chosen for service because that is a destiny that can benefit others.

According to Allen Verhey the ethical thinking of Paul brings together the indicative and the imperative ways of thinking about ethical obligation. This is not so much a present achievement as the ultimate basis of confidence, and because it is the ultimate basis of confidence it does have consequences for living here and now.

> The indicative mood has an important priority and finality in the proclamation of the gospel, but the imperative is by no means merely an addendum to the indicative or even exactly an inference drawn from the indicative. Participation in Christ's cross and resurrection (the important priority of the indicative) and anticipation of the new age of God's unchallenged sovereignty (the important finality of the indicative) are *constituted* here and now by obedience to God's will (the imperative).[4]

Another accomplishment of Paul was to open the possibility of embracing Christianity to people of different cultures and backgrounds. Not only did he interpret moral obligation so as to bridge the gulf between indicative and imperative moods with respect to the Law, he bridged the gulf between the particularistic/exclusive and universalistic/inclusive understandings of community. Paul wrestled with the question of how the understanding (or the understandings) of morality wrought out within one community of shared experience could be related to different cultural and social worlds.

He gave shape to Christianity as a new religious movement rather than as a mere extension or modification of Judaism. This is seen in how he responded to the question of whether the ceremonial decalogue is to be considered binding on the Christian as well as the ethical decalogue. Paul contended this is not required, and he sided with those who felt it possible to bring Gentile converts into the Christian movement without demanding that they be circumcised and keep the Law of Moses.[5]

Paul also struggled to understand the relationship of Christian faith to the intellectual and social forces of the Hellenistic world. In this connection he looked at the Greek philosophical enterprise—especially its search for wisdom as a clue to dealing with life. A passage in 1 Corinthians 1:17ff. relates Greek philosophical wisdom to the message of the Gospel much in the same way the material in Romans deals with the Law of Moses in relationship to the Gospel. Both law and wisdom have a legitimate subsidiary place in the Christian experience, but each easily slips into a stance that blocks the understanding of the Gospel whenever it is made into a sole source of confidence or trust.

Hence, according to Paul it is not necessary to be a Jew, but neither is it sufficient to be a Greek. Greek wisdom is no more an adequate and self-sufficient vehicle for Christian faith than Jewish ceremonial legalism, yet neither is it any more of a barrier. All have sinned and fallen short of the glory of God, and all can correct that situation: "since God is one; . . . he will justify the circumcised on the ground of their faith and the uncircumcised because of their faith" (Romans 3:30). That justification, however, cannot be received any more adequately by those who make wisdom the source of confidence than it can be received by those who make the Law the source of confidence. The trust of the Christian must be in the power of Christ.

The openness of Paul toward the wider world of his time came to a particularly sharp focus in his acceptance of the political authority of Rome. A passage of great influence in subsequent Christianity is found in Romans 13:

> Let every person be subject to the governing authorities. For there is no authority except from God, and those authorities that exist have been instituted by God. Therefore whoever resists the authorities resists what God has appointed, and those who resist will incur judgment. For rulers are not a terror to good conduct, but to bad. Do you wish to have no fear of the authority? Then do what is good, and you will receive its approval, for it is God's servant for your good. But if you do what is wrong, you should be afraid, for the authority does not bear the sword in vain! It is the servant of God to execute wrath on the wrongdoer. Therefore one must be subject, not only to avoid God's wrath but because of conscience. For the same reason you also pay taxes, for the authorities are God's servants, busy with this very thing. Pay to all what is due them—taxes to whom taxes are due, revenue to whom revenue is due, respect to whom respect is due, honor to whom honor is due. (Romans 13:1–7)

This passage has been taken by many Christians as calling for complete obedience to civil authority—at least in political matters. Such Christians have recognized that unless they relate in some way to the social structures that surround them, the effectiveness of their witness is sharply limited. But the passage has given other Christians much grief and difficulty, because this second group recognizes the tensions that can arise between the implications of the Gospel and the demands of political rules and cultural pressures. There are branches of the Christian movement—the left-wing reformers, for instance—who have found that the advice inferred from Romans 13 leads to highly problematic consequences, undercutting their effort to take the radical demands of the Gospel seriously. The Christian tradition in the aggregate has never resolved the problem created by the demands of civil authorities, particularly when these run counter to important moral mandates found in the Gospel. The problem is unresolved because the historical fortunes of the Christian movement may actually depend on the support that comes from cultural dynamics it cannot admire. A separatist response generally avoids idolatry but fails to greatly influence or to transform culture, whereas the strategy of cooperation may effect a Christian impact on society at the price of compromising some of Christianity's most crucial moral stances. The argument between those who hold that compromise with culture is a necessary price to pay for being effective, and those who argue that Christians must live apart and distinct from the world if they are to be loyal to Christ's guidance, will probably be with us for a long, long time.

This issue is frequently discussed in relation to a historical turn of events that occurred long after Paul offered his admonition to respect civil authority. For three centuries Christians were subject to persecution at the hands of Rome. They lived as a largely pacifist minority in the cultural and political worlds of the time, though they did not rebel. Then, early in the fourth century of the common era, under the Emperor Constantine, Rome officially recognized the church. The Emperor himself became a convert. But the church also made its compromise with the empire. Thereupon, Christians began to act more and more like the other members of society. Instead of a pacifist, persecuted, minority they occupied state offices and became soldiers and officials who sought to use political power for the advancement of the Christian cause. The acceptance of official positions in the political order replaced a high moral visibility in the marginalized minority. And the debate goes on whether this change is best described as one in which the Christian movement finally conquered the empire (and thus perhaps ensured its own survival) or a development in which the empire conquered the Christian movement (thus destroying the moral uniqueness of the church and its members). If a person believes that the Constantinian revolution saved Christianity from extinction, the pressure to embrace the cultural dynamics of the world is great. If one holds that such a concordat diluted or so altered the unique morality of the Gospel as to destroy essential Christianity, then a return to the pre-Constantinian conditions of the early church is indicated as a necessary strategy for maintaining the moral integrity of the Gospel.

But the discussion today, while not necessarily neglecting the questions of political loyalty, deals with a very broad set of issues. It concerns not merely obedience to civic authorities but a whole range of cultural dynamics. A long process of acculturation and assimilation has taken place that has brought about what may well be a close association between Christianity and Western cultural values. Missionary work can face difficult decisions as it takes the Gospel into cultural settings in which the mores and practices differ from those in Western culture. Is adoption of Western cultural patterns necessary for acceptance of the Gospel? Does becoming a Christian—as a humorous ditty once suggested—involve being washed (by Baptists), educated (by Presbyterians), and starched (by Episcopalians)? Paul struggled against those who insisted that acceptance of all the cultural mores of Judaism was a necessary precondition for becoming a Christian. Does his example warrant the conclusion that it is possible to be faithful Christians within a variety of cultural patterns?

There are people today who would align Christian faith to a capitalistic/free entrepreneurial system, while others believe that only a Marxist social system can embody a concern for economic justice. Many representatives of these positions act like the Hebrews and the Greeks—each wanting Christian faith to conform to their own perspective. The term "Marxist atheism" is used by the exponents of one view to read the others out of the fold. Terms like "capitalist exploiters" are used by the other group to do the same thing with their opponents. Paul might very well feel that both are making the identification too complete. While he was willing to cooperate with Rome, he never saw Rome as the central object of loyalty.

The characteristics of Rome as a major political entity at the time of Paul present us with an interesting model with which to think about the characteristics of Western society, and particularly its American component, and how religious faith and practice is shaped and expressed by being associated with these social systems. Rome enforced a peace across the whole known world by the use of relatively well-disciplined and omnipresent military power. Rome was noted for her engineering achievements—such as roads, aqueducts, and bridges—rather than for culture or for religious sensibilities. Rome entertained her population with bread and circuses—gladiatorial encounters in huge amphitheaters designed for the spectatorship of combat. The similarities between Roman culture and contemporary public life (particularly in America) should give us pause. To an extent that has often been overlooked, it has been Roman cultural patterns—not the Hebraic and not the Greek—that have functionally amalgamated with Christian faith to produce much contemporary American religiosity and which even today are largely intermeshed with the North American versions of theology that (at least until quite recently) have been so triumphalist in their dominance. Not covenant or moral law as known by the Hebrews, not wisdom as sought by the Greeks, but material achievements, athletic circuses, and military armies have often been the most evident features of the culture with which Christian faith is presumed by so many to be a partner. Often it is the Christian right wing, which professes to be uniquely faithful to the Bible, that buys into this neo-Roman acculturation without realizing what it is doing. Sometimes it seems to give the impression of being more eager to be American than to be biblical.

Can it be that Paul, who did so much to free Christians from bondage to legalistic religion and to warn them against the hubris of the purely intellectual solution to the human predicament, can also warn us against the very forms of idolatry that have been so prevalent in Christendom ever since, especially in American society? It is hard to believe that Paul, while he indicated that Christians should be subject to Roman authority, really meant they were to become blissfully like the Romans, or that Roman culture is an entirely satisfactory one through which to embody Christian impulses. Would not Paul's far profounder significance prompt a multicultural openness that would relate Christianity today to many other cultures, each perhaps in a slightly different way, even as he opened the religion of his time to the Gentile world? Paul would remind us that the important factor is God's work and not worldly systems that offer the power to transform the realities of life in the particular circumstances in which people live.

15

Early Christian Communities

Piety and Fidelity in Boundary Conditions

The life and teachings of Jesus exploded into a Palestinian world in which many different understandings of what it means to be religiously faithful already vied for allegiance. Numerous groups within Judaism offered a range of opinions as to how religiously faithful people should live together and how they should relate to their surrounding culture. Some, for instance the Sadducees, favored cooperation and accommodation on all such matters as the Law does not explicitly proscribe, and they defended their position as the most sensible way to survive as Jews in Greco-Roman culture. Others, such as the Essenes, in not inconsiderable contrast to the mainstream of Hebraic thought, moved to asceticism and withdrew into special enclaves where they developed a set of unique practices as marks of fidelity. Paul's views of Christ's redeeming work also impacted a diverse cultural situation that included Hellenistic patterns of thought and Roman political power. Religious movements in the Greco-Roman complex offered still other options. We have already taken note of Paul's attitude toward Gentiles and his willingness to acknowledge the legitimacy of Roman authority in political matters.

As the early Christian community struggles to find its modus vivendi amid the many options open to it, the biblical narrative presents a complex saga as the teachings of Jesus and the theology of Paul furnish the bases for the formation of new communities—communities composed of persons committed to a new set of beliefs and a lifestyle that harmonizes with them. Such individuals are called followers of "The Way," but even they do not all share the same understanding of what it means to be faithful in such complex circumstances. Consequently, it is impossible to delineate a clear and simple pattern of essential Christianity by looking at the life of the early Christian communities. Wayne

A. Meeks suggests how difficult it is to discern all the features of early Christian practice.

> Stalking the early Christians, [it is required that] we draw concentric circles. In the world of the Greek-varnished culture of the eastern Mediterranean, transformed by the power and order of Rome, the Jewish communities of homeland and Diaspora were a special case. Within the manifold adaptations of Judaism to that larger world, a small circle of Jesus' followers appeared, spread, and quickly became multiform itself. That meaningful world in which the earliest Christian lived—the world which lived in their heads as well as that which was all around them—was a Jewish world. But the Jewish world was part of the Graeco-Roman world. If therefore we are looking for some "pure" Christian values and beliefs unmixed with the surrounding culture, we are on a fool's errand. What was Christian about the ethos and ethics of those early communities we will discover not by abstraction but by confronting their involvement in the culture of their time and place and seeking to trace the new patterns they made of old forms, to hear the new songs they composed from old melodies.[1]

Early Christians felt powerful incentives to live as communities of new beings in an existing and complex cultural setting—what John's Gospel, in particular, calls "the world." "Christians," as one common way of putting it declares, "live in the world yet are not of the world." Another way of saying it would be to suggest that the early Christians practiced piety and fidelity from the sidelines. Their relationship to Judaism, seemingly clear at first, proved increasingly tenuous; their relationship to Greco-Roman society, while inescapably real, was not without difficulties. This did not make for an easy time of it.

The condition of the early Christians is probably best described by the term "marginal." The early Christian communities existed at the edges of cultural situations that were largely shaped and driven by other influences. Christ's Resurrection did not miraculously establish an entirely new order of things or eliminate the countervailing forces that were so powerful in the Middle East of the first century. While the early Christians firmly believed that the sovereignty of Christ ultimately transforms the human prospect, they could not escape the fact that it does not entirely alter an existing society at the center nor place them in positions of power and influence from which they can transform the social order.

Considered in worldly terms, the historical circumstance of the new

Christian communities was only provisionally more satisfactory than the situation that confronted the Hebrews when they were held in Egyptian bondage; it was only provisionally better that the situation experienced by the Jewish exiles living in Babylon. None of these groups—captives, exiles, or marginals—enjoyed an enviable prospect as measured by worldly measures of well-being. None of these groups were "established" in the sense of exercising control over their social and political "worlds." To be sure, the particulars differ between ancient Egyptian and first-century Roman rule. The early Christians faced more complex circumstances than the conditions faced either by Israel in Egypt or Jewish groups in exile, and any strategy for overcoming them had to take into account the fact that possible ways of responding must be different. Rome ruled over most of the known world. The early Christians could not pack up and leave (or even leave without packing up!). Hence there is a difference between the narrative that had already unfolded under Moses and the narrative that loomed under the leadership of the apostles. In the case of Moses, leaving Egypt was a way of opening up new sociopolitical possibilities for a covenant people that acquired a land base in which to live; but in the case of the earliest Christians, discipleship was a way of adjusting to sociopolitical realities that they had little possibility of escaping and had little standing to transform. For the exiles the yearning to return to Jerusalem provided a symbol that generated hope for a historical restoration, but for the early Christians there was neither a single place nor a vivid sociopolitical prospect to give concrete potentiality to their aspirations. The early Christians simply could not go home again in historical terms; hence they looked toward a home that was not of this world and become numbered among the apocalyptic groups of the time.

The Book of Acts, which was authored by Luke, carries the story of early Christianity from the Resurrection (where the Gospels leave it) to Paul's arrival in Rome to establish a community of faith. It offers important information about Paul's career beyond that found in the letters. But the Book of Acts is also instructive because it sheds light on the ways in which the early Christians wrestled with the task of living in relationship to their world. Acts contains various literary genres that help us to understand how many of the first Christians viewed the obligations of Christian discipleship. The book gives us important (although by no means the only) clues as to how "the Christian communities transcended religious, social, economic, and sexual barriers in the dominant society of the time."[2]

Understanding that set of developments helps us to think about what it means to live faithfully on the margins. Acts offers clues as to what it means to live on the margin of Judaism, on the margin of Hellenistic culture, and on the margin of the Roman Empire. Each margin presented its own particular problems and its own unique opportunities. Each margin indicated that those committing themselves to the Gospel must struggle with the continuing presence of the world (or worlds) within which they have been placed. Each margin also represented an intersection where the redemptive power of the Gospel could interact with a wider world that did not share the experiences that engender the new faith and may not even have been particularly interested in understanding them.

Many of the earliest Christian groups arose within Jewish communities and consisted of Jews who were attracted to the Christian saga. This made the proto-church something of a Jewish sect. As a marginalized subgroup within Judaism, the early Christians shared certain convictions with Judaism: They believed in one God yet also in the reality of other supernatural beings having the power to affect human life; they believed that the Hebrew Scriptures offer adequate moral guidance; and they believed that history has a purpose that will be consummated according to God's standard of righteousness.[3]

Although early Christianity shared many aspects of the Judaism that was, in effect, its parent, it developed distinguishing features of its own: It believed Jesus is the fulfillment of the messianic hope; it anticipated a new age, and hence had an eye to an imminent and radical conclusion to history; it very quickly required baptism as a ceremony of entrance; and it was relatively free of geographical restraints on where it could carry on its life. At first, it did not seem primarily concerned with what is involved in sustaining an officially organized movement or what it owed to the dominant culture.

To describe the early Christian communities as marginalized is not to say that they consisted only of the economically dispossessed or downtrodden. Although the early Christian communities shared the view found in Judaism that orphans and widows and other disadvantaged groups deserve special support, the early church was not a movement composed only of economic and social outcasts. It included persons of some wealth and sometimes of some social standing. According to Wayne Meeks, while the early Christian community cannot be classified as ascetic (rejecting the acquisition of goods altogether), it did exhibit a mutual supportiveness not generally typical of the affluent.

At least potentially, however, the developing Christian movement had some very specific assistance to offer in the economy of the weak. To travelers in a dangerous world, it offered a network of hospitality among "brothers and sisters." To vulnerable people it offered the support of small, intensely connected groups, mutual care, mutual admonition, mutual assistance. With few exceptions it did not try to dismantle the common Graeco-Roman structures of patronage, friendship, and affiliation, but worked out its own special variations on those patterns.[4]

It is quite clear that membership in this early Christian community was not a casual matter. Careful instruction (as well as baptism) came to be required as a condition for joining. Once identified as belonging to the new group, the early Christians were subject to possible ridicule, and even hostility (Acts 6:8–15). They were often required to defend their allegiance to the faith, and they were not always honored for their efforts. Tensions developed between the Jewish community in Jerusalem and the early Christians. This is not surprising. Similar suspicions occur whenever a new group arises within a religious establishment and somehow implies that the current practice of the tradition is no longer adequate.

We must look very carefully at what was taking place. The newly forming Christian communities were not ascetic in the sense of calling for the repudiation of all possessions. They were not rural in the sense of romanticizing pastoral scenes in favor of living in hurly-burly cities; indeed, Christianity spread throughout the Greco-Roman world because its evangelists used channels of commerce and culture to carry their message to centers of population across the known world. But the early Christian communities were intentionally confessional and morally rigorous. They were often marked by radical practices—so radical, if fact, that (as we can learn from Acts 4:32–37) members were expected to share possessions with one another. In the story of Ananias and his wife that begins the fifth chapter of Acts, it is suggested that those who fail to share their possessions completely in the commonality of ownership will suffer the gravest consequences. The early church was both a demanding and a supportive community.

The dialectic between demand and support that operated in these early Christian communities is instructive. The early Christians shared not only their property but a deep concern for one another. Moreover, by requiring new converts to undergo preparation as a condition of joining, the early Christian communities indicated that membership was something to be taken seriously. We can learn something for social ethics from this. Communities that are entered casually, without a ritual of passage, without instruction or testing, are more likely than not to have half-hearted members whose commitment is tenuous and whose morale tends to sag. Communities that make but minimal requirements on their members, and that have little discipline seldom prove to be significantly supportive. But communities that require much of their members commonly offer them much.

But such communities are not necessarily blissfully harmonious. The early Christians themselves were not of a common mind in thinking what their relationship to Judaism should be. Some believed it was first necessary to be a strong Jew, obedient to the Torah, before becoming a Christian. Others wished the church to start afresh, to be available to the Gentiles who did not live according to Jewish law.

These two groups eventually had to resolve their differences and agree on a working policy. We have already mentioned the conference in Jerusalem at which the relationship of members of the Christian communities to Jewish faith and practice was discussed.[5] This is a pivotal event for it greatly helps to set the framework for defining the conditions by which Gentiles can become members of the Christian communities. The actual decision focuses on release from the obligation to be circumcised, but that was to evolve into the eventual understanding that Christians are bound by the moral/ethical but not by the ritual aspects of the Law of Moses. The agreement of the Christians to refrain from things polluted by idols can very well belong to the moral and not merely ritual category, for it is a provision for not submitting to the demands of the Roman civic cultus.

As long as the early communities of Christians were considered to be subgroups within Judaism, they enjoyed much of the same immunity from persecution by the Roman authorities as the Jews had come to enjoy. But as the distinction between the Jewish and Christian communities became increasingly evident, Christians began to suffer opposition (read: painful marginalization). As their independent status became clearer, the Christians were not particularly welcomed by Jewish authorities, who were displeased with groups that did not fully follow the Law. Even more severe persecution developed as Roman political authorities came to realize that the new religious group stood on its own and was not, therefore, covered by the policy of begrudging toleration that enabled the Jews to be uniquely faithful to their tradition while under Roman rule. The persecutions to come after the New Testament period would be even more severe, as post-biblical materials attest.

The life and practices of the early Christian communities furnish us with grounds for additional reflection on the nature of voluntary associations and their place within the public sphere. These communities were brought together by a common set of convictions about the redeeming power of Christ. Nobody was forced to join such communities by sociopolitical pressures; they were prompted to join as they embraced a new worldview. If anything, all the sociopolitical pressures of the time ran counter to the formation of such communities. There is little in the first-century world that made joining an early Christian community religiously respectable, socially advantageous, or politically strategic.

As it became less and less possible for the early Christians to gather at the Temple in Jerusalem or in synagogues elsewhere, the early Christians came to meet in the houses of their members. This was not, as it is interpreted by the Gospel of Thomas (which did not get into the canon) an ascetic means of renouncing the world as much as it was a means of coping with the suspicion and frequent rejection that was visited on the early Christians by those in positions of power and influence. Ironically, the move to meetings in private households increased the suspicion, particularly as the meetings became more and more private and more and more concerned with claiming the full loyalty of those who attended.

This means that the devotion and commitment tended to be high. Marginalization tends to filter out the merely curious, the half-hearted, and those who desire easy benefits without price. But the communities did not deliberately seek to be marginalized. The marginalization as such was not the occasion or the instrumentation for their formation, but a set of consequences that attended membership in these particular groups at this particular time.

Marginalization is not identical with deliberate isolation. Living on the sidelines is not to be equated with seeking to be separatist. Early Christianity, unlike some contemporary groups that come into conflict with the law, did not aim to be secret, nor choose marginalization as an end in itself. Moreover, although there was a strong sense of community, this was created out of common loyalty and not by arbitrary control. One indication, ironic though it may be, of the fact that these early Christian groups did not exercise complete and total control over their members, is the presence of conflicts and controversies that have to be addressed. Several of Paul's letters indicate the existence of such controversies.

We can empathize to some degree with the Jews and the Romans as they face the rise of such new groups. Even today, in a land that officially embraces the idea of religious freedom (as Rome did not), the rise of new religious groups can present a quandary. Is such a society called to tolerate all such groups regardless of their beliefs and their behavior? Is it to refrain from judgment (or from intervention) simply because groups purport to be religious in nature? Groups that exercise total control over the life of their members naturally create suspicion and distrust, especially if their activities are carried on in enclaves from which the public is excluded. Societies need to hold religious groups to some degree of public accountability. As long as groups are marginalized they do not need to be concerned about restraining religious practices of others that are a menace to human well-being. But as religious groups become part of the established order, or attempt to participate responsibly in the decisions of that order, they can no longer avoid such responsibilities.

There is a story in the fifth chapter of Acts that highlights the problem of the Jewish authorities. The high priest and those associated with him arrest the apostles because they are violating an order not to proclaim the Gospel. Thrown into prison, the apostles escape but are captured and are brought again before the council, which is inclined to kill them. But Gamaliel, a Pharisee on the council, observes that if this new movement is of human making it will fail of its own accord; if it is of God it will succeed no matter how strongly it is opposed. After flogging the apostles (a less than ultimate discouragement) the authorities release them with the admonition to desist in their preaching.

Free societies require the likes of Gamaliel—persons who trust events to unfold according to a purpose—who believe that freedom is more to be trusted as a condition for God's creative ends to be achieved than coercive restrictions are to be trusted as means of guarding correct beliefs God has already mandated. But free societies also need the likes of the apostles, whose preaching was available to all, done without secrecy, and espoused without malice or violence. If groups on the fringes cease to act like the apostles, then it becomes increasingly difficult for authorities to take the advice of a Gamaliel. The interaction between toleration and marginalization produces creative possibilities—possibilities that are easily endangered when clandestine intrigue invites oppressive counterthrusts.

Another way to keep marginalization from becoming purely idiosyncratic is to maintain communication between the various communities having a common profession of faith in Christ. Even in the early period the various Christian communities were interconnected through the ministry of leaders like Peter and Paul. That served to head off purely localized and idiosyncratic innovation. Christian groups in one location offered hospitality to members of Christian groups from another location. One way to deal with the differences and disagreements that were found in the early church, even with its enormously supportive practices of sharing and mutual support, was to commend the power of love as the moral foundation of community. A special term, *koinonia*, emerged to denote the mutual supportiveness of the early Christian communities. This term has become a favorite one for use in contemporary Christian movements that are especially interested in communal life, in re-creating in our time some of the sustaining togetherness that is attributed to the early Christian church.

This exercise of charity and supportiveness was not left to mere spontaneity or chance. A special group, seven in number, was specifically appointed to the task of distributing food to the needy (Acts 6:1–6). This move was not seen as a contradiction of the voluntary nature of the new community, but as a necessary step to care for the responsibilities of the community in a more deliberate way. In the next chapter we will see how the impulse to give increasingly organized form to the Christian movement carried this process to much greater lengths.

The fervor of the early Christian was sustained by a strong belief in the power of the Spirit. This is apparent in the story of Pentecost in the second chapter of Acts, which has often been cited as a reversal of the story of Babel. In the case of Babel the people's languages were confounded because they sought to engineer their own salvation; at Pentecost the differences in languages were superseded by a momentous common understanding that took place among persons who were caught up in the redeeming power of a new faith. Repentance leading to conversion is thus seen as having a central role in the creation and sustaining of the new community.

It is probably no less the case today than it was in the days of the early church that the fundamental moral orientation of people is more a gift of the Spirit than a consequence of purely logical reasoning and coolly calculating wisdom. This does not make it irrational (or antirational), but rather transrational. Our reason must become enthralled by conversion before we can understand the power and the promise of moral discipleship. The reason is redirected, not negated. When we think of something as "making sense," we are taking as sensible that to which our hearts (which are thinking/willing gestalts) are drawn. That involves the fundamental outlooks that we have embraced, the impulses we take as guiding, and the loyalties that tug at our entire being. Pentecost stands for the possibility— yes, only a possibility—that the ethical confusion that Jeffrey Stout has identified as the moral discontents of the world after Babel[6]—can be eventually transcended by the power of the Spirit. We are, of course, still waiting for Pentecost to be enacted, not within the confines of a small marginalized group that lived in the past, but as the foretaste of a universal transformation that yet must come. We need to ask, not how people can be pressured into conversion in the narrow sense of deciding to become religiously correct, but how the public mind of the whole human enterprise can be brought to the point where the substance of just practice can be agreed upon, and the claims of compassion can be controlling.

This involves working with the same dialectic between the particular and the universal that formed such a large aspect of the Old Testament narrative. The Book of Acts contains further evidence of this dialectic. At places it declares that Jesus is crucial to salvation (4:12), as though to imply that people with other beliefs have to abandon those beliefs in order to become disciples; at other places it suggests that the practices of people who, like the Athenians, had a vague sense of ultimacy can take that belief and bring it into fuller richness by understanding it in relationship to Christ (17:16–28).

In Acts, as in Paul, the cultural features of the Greco-Roman world are accepted without rancor. The inclusive outlook overrides the particularistic. As the early Christian community worked out its relationship with Greek thought, it sought to appropriate what was valuable from that thought and use it in the service of new commitments. Conversion does not need to mean total repudiation of an entire old life. Evangelism need not be harshly judgmental, but is compatible with compassionate and embracing impulses and even with the requirements of a pluralistic society.

All of this involves a narrative in which the Jesus movement struggles with its relationship to the Judaism out of which it has sprung and the Greco-Roman world to which it is increasingly related. By the sixth decade it had become increasingly evident that the Christian communities could not be contained within the parent group. One of the momentous factors that led to this state of affairs was the refusal, on the ground of Jesus' teaching, of the early church to participate in the Holy War of the Jewish groups against Rome in 66–70 C.E. This did not endear the early Christians to the militant parties in Judaism, nor, ironically, to the Romans. Within a decade the new Christian community had to define itself more explicitly as a movement and to face the problem of living under still more outcast conditions. As the Christian movement became larger and more diverse, the voluntary associationalism on which the earliest church depended was no more able to sustain its life than the amphictyony was able to sustain the Hebrews once they entered into their new Palestinian home after the Exodus. The institutionalization of Christianity ensued, attended by all the benefits and all the problems that involved.

Some of the most troublesome issues in contemporary church life revolve around questions of how churches should relate to public life. The New Testament offers very little direct guidance on this issue, since the New Testament church was in no institutional position to make a corporate witness to the Roman Empire. However, the combination of holy discontent with patient endurance may provide the basis for some indirect guidance. Holy discontent can keep Christian communities from being satisfied with reflecting only the values of their surrounding world—letting the culture shape their commitments and behavior. Patient endurance should keep Christian communities from thinking their life can be so separated from the culture as to escape the moral ambiguities that membership in a civic order is bound to involve. One of the most important of all of the tasks for the churches is to make people sensitive to the complexities involved in public policy making rather than to engender simplistic partisanship.

Churches can and ought to try to influence political and social conditions in the civic orders of which they are a part. They can engage in study and issue documents that look at the issues in prophetic ways. Although they are not generally well-known and have not been universally acclaimed, many of the study documents on public issues done by the churches are remarkable for the depth of their analysis and the uniqueness of their perspectives. Across the years these have ranged over many important issues, from consideration during the Second World War about ways to establish a just and durable peace to the study of numerous public issues by many denominations in more recent years. Such studies are less important as manifestos or as instruments of political effectiveness than as documents deserving of discussion in the public realm. Used properly and widely (which, alas, they often are not) they could do much to raise the level of moral and political thinking in society.

Church groups can also undertake pilot projects that point the way for more broadly sponsored programs and activities to develop. The Salvation Army has often done this, with a host of social services that are helpful models for more widely based efforts to be of service to the needy. A few churches have been involved in constructing low-cost housing that encourages pride of ownership yet makes such ownership available to the very persons who generally could not hope to have it. Even if churches do not undertake such efforts on their own, it is possible for Christians to participate in programs carried on by special groups, like Habitat for Humanity. Even more significantly, some parishes have arranged housing for those with AIDS. Some denominations have developed retirement centers for the elderly, though they have not necessarily been sufficiently concerned with the task of alleviating the financial problems of the indigent and therefore have often created what may be enclaves of affluence. On the frontier, when there was no general public education, churches often started the only available schools. Church-related colleges played a very important role in the latter part of the nineteenth century and today may have a unique opportunity to exemplify how genuine community rather than a callous scramble for what is taken to be prestige may be the most important goal of higher education. Perhaps churches ought to think about ways with which to deal with the health care cost crisis, perhaps by devising alternative models for care that are neither profit-driven nor closed to those in greatest need. These are crazy and impossible ideas, of course, but is not the unconventionality of the Gospel a warrant for such kinds of innovation?

One of the most socially effective and morally impressive actions of the churches to have taken place in this century occurred under the Nazis, when Christians voluntarily began to wear the Star of David to confound the Nazi persecution and the annihilation of the Jews. This is social effectiveness of heroic proportions. Similar, but perhaps less heroic, are actions that Christians have taken across the years: setting up underground railroads for transporting slaves from the south to the north during the Civil War; working with the freedom riders and engaging in sit-ins to combat segregation during the 1960s; creating sanctuaries for the harboring of political refugees from oppressive regimes in Central America, even when contrary to public law. Such actions tend to be honored after they have been effective, or when done in another place or another country. They are controversial when done in one's backyard or one's own country. These things require people to act in public and in organized ways but are unique because they are public without succumbing to the domestication of Christian morality to the merely conventional mores of society. They are rooted far more profoundly in a sense of the biblical narrative in all of its liberating and redeeming power than are hortatory calls for conventional moral correctness—which alas are often touted in our time as biblical. All of these actions, however, are feasible and effective when they can utilize the resources of a religious body that draws upon institutionally managed resources and makes possible organized activity. The pastoral Epistles, to which our attention will now turn, are valuable in alerting us to the possibilities of institutionalization, but that should prompt us to go beyond the conventional morality that institutionalization tends to engender and to ask how the radical unconventionality by which Jesus offers liberation can be encompassed within institutional endeavors that advance God's purposes.

16

The Pastoral Epistles

Structure and Leadership in
Confessional Communities

The institutionalization that took place in the ongoing life of the church occurred for some of the same reasons that prompted Israel to deal with the problems of governance by moving from charismatic judges to kings. But the formal structuring of the church differed in some important ways from the manner by which Israel after the Exodus dealt with problems of governance. In New Testament times the problem was how to organize and structure a special community, whereas in the Old Testament the problem was more how to deal with the governance of an entire sociopolitical unit. Moreover, the narrative material in the New Testament dealing with the organizational structuring of Christianity does not examine the problems and difficulties involved to the same extent as the Old Testament materials worry about the establishment of the monarchy in Israel. For instance, there does not seem to be any New Testament passage that poses questions about the legitimacy of structured church life to the same extent that Jotham's fable posed questions about the establishment of the monarchy. Even so, the impulses to give structure and order to common life are quite analogous, and the moral issues that grow out of them are not dissimilar.

As many parts of Paul's letters suggest, the internal affairs of early church life did not go smoothly. There were divisions and controversies. There were arguments about claims to leadership. There was hostility from outsiders. There was embarrassing misbehavior. There were perplexities as to how the new communities were to be related to the Jewish heritage from which some of them sprang or to the Gentile culture to which many of them had to relate. There were strained relations between the new communities and their founders, especially Paul, who started many of them.

Just as the Exodus was followed by wandering in the wilderness, so the mighty freedom proffered by Christ's redeeming work was followed by difficulties and disorder. The early church was no exception to the pattern in which a major consequence of liberation is to create the need for new patterns of governance and order.

But we do find materials in the New Testament, particularly in the pastoral Epistles (1, 2 Timothy and Titus) that indicate, however obliquely, that attempts were getting underway to give order and structure to the new Christian communities. From this material we realize that the Gospel does not eliminate the need to be concerned about problems of governance any more than the Exodus from Egypt resulted in an existence for the Hebrews that eliminated the need to be concerned with problems of social organization.

There are a number of reasons why pressure to institutionalize appeared in the early Christian communities. The possibility of spontaneous gatheredness based on an experience of having been saved has little more staying power than does liberation that results only in amphictyony. Just as there is an inevitable historical logic to the move from amphictyony to kingship, so there is an inevitable historical logic to the move from spontaneity to polity, from gatheredness to institutionalization.

Sooner or later churches find it imperative to institutionalize. They face this necessity for several of the following reasons.

The Need to Own Property. They come to possess property—even if they have a theoretical aversion to the idea of acquiring earthly possessions. A vow of poverty is possible for individuals (most readily if they have someone else or an institution to support them), but it is almost impossible for a group—certainly for any group that is more than a temporary gathering without any intention of remaining together for any length of time. Institutionalization is necessary in order to determine the ownership of property. Some legal entity has to hold the deed.

Society demands that ecclesiastical bodies be clear about this matter; e.g., if they apply for exemption from taxes, an institutional identity is necessary to indicate that a particular organization is an ecclesiastical body. This may work out differently in the case of local property taxes than in the case of the Internal Revenue Code—but the necessities involved are similar. For instance, exemption from real estate taxes often requires specific application, or certainly a classifiable institutional identity; receipts for charitable deductions can be issued only by groups having a definite polity that attests to their philanthropic or religious purposes.

Moreover, to dispose of property (whether as a beneficial act during the life of the group or as a remainder upon the dissolution of a group) requires legal standing, which is dependent on institutionalization. It is just as impossible to write a check from an organization if there is no polity as it is if there is no money. Moreover, it is always wise to be clear about ownership, even within religions groups. I was once employed by a retreat center that was founded by some well-meaning people who felt it was "too worldly" to draw up a set of legal agreements defining the financial interests of the various individuals who formed it. So the founders each poured their personal resources into the venture on the assumption each was to commit as much as possible to its support. Then, after a brief time, one of them decided to pull out for valid personal reasons. There was no contractual agreement defining the respective interests of the founders. They probably had as their ideal something like holding all things in common. They ended up needing outside adjudication about the division of the assets—a situation hardly exemplifying New Testament ideals, and rendered very difficult precisely because of the way they had dealt (or, more precisely, failed to deal) with the matter of ownership.

Moreover, churches must be accountable for negligence or other torts. They must carry liability insurance. Claiming to be a spiritual institution is hardly a defense in the case of a lawsuit. Moreover, if negligence on the part of a church by its staff or members is involved, claiming to be a "spiritual" body would be a morally indefensible way of escaping responsibility, leaving the injured party without redress.

The Need to Identify Members. A second reason to institutionalize religious communities stems from the need for voluntary groups to be able to identify their members. Some groups, particularly in the phase of initial mass response, may not need to do this. Those attending a revival meeting do not need to be listed in any official records and most probably should not be. Similarly, it might not be necessary to have an official set of membership standards in the case of a prayer group consisting a half dozen members who know each other intimately and meet only for inspirational purposes (but unofficial membership standards are clearly functioning in such a situation). But in time (and that time is usually not very long in coming in the experience of any group) it becomes important to have an identity and to know who shares responsibility for the group's life.

Polities develop in which the conditions that determine membership and its obligations are spelled out and provisions are made for making decisions in an orderly fashion. Churches may need these definitions for internal reasons; the culture may expect/require them for external reasons. However, patterns by which membership in churches is defined may vary widely—in some polities joining is a long, deliberate, and qualifying process; in such instances membership tends to be attended by strict requirements and conformity to demanding obligations. In other polities it is quickly obtained and may involve few overt commitments. (The Community Church in New York City in the 1950s simply kept a book at the front of the meetinghouse and a person might become a member merely by signing.) Offering membership through a quick and easy action is appealing, but churches in which there are few if any stipulated requirements for being on the rolls may face problems if individuals wish to claim benefits from belonging or be involved in decisions regarding the life of the community. A decision to be a member of a community has greater significance if matched by a conscious, deliberate, and formal acceptance of the member by the community. That helps to keep clear who is entitled to participate in the decision making of the community about matters of institutional life, such as budgets, group commitments, and the like. Moreover, it increases the significance of belonging.

There may even be greater need for knowing the conditions and obligations of members if a group finds it necessary to censure a member (that is, either to discipline or ban someone). Any actions of this sort call for due process, and due process depends on formal institutionalization. Otherwise, groups can easily operate in merely *ad hoc* ways, by impulse and perhaps by what almost seems to be intrigue. Discipline by impulse is more likely to occur in groups that proceed without becoming formally structured—and failures to establish careful and thoughtful polities often plague the life of fringe groups, with bizarre and sometimes tragic consequences.

The Need to Choose Leaders. Institutionalization also provides criteria by which leaders are to be chosen and their authority specified. The most easily identified systems for achieving these results are hierarchical in form. Today, there is a great deal of criticism of hierarchical ordering of ecclesiastical life—not ill-taken. But problems do not evaporate if hierarchy is merely repudiated unless careful thought is given to providing alternative structures. Moreover, leadership roles that are established by careful procedures agreed to on the basis of a group polity are often less dangerous than leadership roles that come about by accident or clever individual conniving.

Persons who come to leadership roles without institutional legitimation may be less subject to control and less accountable than hierarchical figures even though they do not presume to wield as much institutional authority. The contrast between hierarchical bishops (or cardinals) who can be rigid and/or possibly "officious" and some TV evangelists who can be tempted to personal indiscretion or cult leaders whose power is not carefully limited offers instructive comparisons. Billy Graham, in contrast to a number of others, has probably avoided scandal precisely because he has institutionalized his enterprise.

Paul Harrison has examined how mainline church officials whose roles are not institutionally defined often acquire more functional power than do officers in churches having a clear and centralized structure of authority. Since their roles are not institutionally circumscribed, they can write their own tickets so to speak, and in so doing acquire powers according to their own capacity to engineer them.[1] To remove or curtail those who misuse their office when there is no specification of the duties of, and limits on, the office frequently involves incredible infighting. Having to endure such infighting may possibly be preferable to being subject to the unilaterally exercised authority of a monarchial ecclesiastical official, but it is no guarantee of escape from potential moral corruption in the exercise of leadership.

The Need to Settle Disputes. Another function of institutionalization is to provide some agreed-in-advance procedures for settling disputes. If there are no such procedures, then disputes became brawls—fought with intrigue and with scheming, somewhat as gang wars are fought with bloody threats. It is well to count on the inevitability of disputes—no group ever avoids them, even if it thinks that it is such a spiritual enterprise, such a truly special community, as to leave no room for disagreements. If disputes can't be brought into the open and adjudicated fairly according to rules agreed to in advance of the conflict—they will likely be carried on covertly and with ugly overtones.

The courts, for instance, when they do have to deal with cases involving churches, will first determine (if they can) what the controlling polity of the ecclesiastical body involved requires. They usually do not interpose their own independent judgment as to what is most wise for the group in question—but seek to determine what the church's internal rules would require (even if seemingly less wise or prudent than some alternative the courts might consider). The most difficult time to draw up rules for deciding how to adjudicate a conflict is after the conflict has arisen. Then every move is suspect, and the effort to define suitable procedures may be as controversial as the conflict that must be resolved.

All of these aspects of institutionalization have potentially ethical implications—not merely operational significance. How does one hold property as a faithful steward, seeking to make it benefit the group without harming those whose lives are affected by what the group does? How does one define membership in ways that protect the identity and purposes of a voluntary association but do not become instruments that unfairly exclude others? How can leadership be chosen and how can leadership act so as to avoid the misuse of authority and power? How can disputes be settled according to procedures that ensure the parties are fairly treated, or at least treated in accordance with policies they accept? There is no way to arrive at a single way of ensuring all these aims can be satisfied. There may be different polities, some of which are effective at dealing with one issue or set of issues, and others that do better with different obligations. Institutions do not have to be alike to be valuable or cut from the same ecclesiastical cloth to be legitimate. The New Testament does not provide a blueprint for any one single ecclesiastical polity. But we can find in the New Testament grounds for being concerned about having a helpful and decent ordering of the church's life.

Of the four reasons why institutionalization is important the New Testament seems to pay special attention to the task of identifying and ordering leaders and to indicating how they should behave. The primary patterns that leadership took in the early church began with apostolic standing, moved through heroic witness, and eventually entailed ecclesiastical office.

The term "apostle" was used in the early Christian church to identify persons with a special connection to the life, death, and Resurrection of Jesus. It included those, like the disciples, who were associated with Jesus during his lifetime. It included those who had personally witnessed the Resurrection. It included those, such as Paul, who seemed to have been endowed with a special quality of spirit that made them uniquely powerful witnesses to the Gospel. All of these criteria for thinking about what constitutes an apostle depend on some status or gift of grace that has been bestowed on the person. In some instances this standing comes from the historical circumstance of association with Jesus; in other instances it comes from the possession of abilities and gifts that stand out in an unusual way. However, the qualifications of an apostle are not understood, most certainly at first, as being created by some institutional process that bestows a special standing by special ordering.

Leadership in apostolic terms should be understood as a gift, bestowed by circumstance rather than achieved by effort, engendered by the Spirit rather than created by some institutional action. But it is difficult, if not impossible, to create or to continue institutional life in charismatic terms alone. Just as amphictyony gave way to kingship, so the idea of apostolic leadership gave way to ecclesiastical office. Because this happened, the subsequent Christian movement developed elaborate mechanisms for claiming to hold on to the apostolic charisma in more institutionalized ways. The most noteworthy of these mechanisms was institutionalized under the rubric of apostolic succession. This doctrine institutionalizes the apostolic charisma by claiming to possess the power to bestow leadership roles in the Christian community from one generation to the next. The emphasis shifts to roles and functions rather than movements of the Spirit.

As we have already observed[2] it is clear that the concept of apostleship underwent changes that moved women from the central roles obvious in the New Testament to secondary roles in church life. Recently, with the benefit of new perspectives women scholars have come to see that women should be recognized as among those given the apostolic gift. The confession of Martha that Jesus is the Christ, the Son of God (John 11:27) is indisputably as clear as the confession of Peter (Matthew 16:16). We cannot undo the past, but we can make deliberate choices through formal procedures to reconstitute the present and the future. We can only do that institutionally.

Resisting the historical logic of institutionalization, some groups reject the idea of a professional or a permanent clergy. Such groups say in effect, "If kingship erodes covenantal responsiveness and hierarchy destroys charisma and breeds distortion, why then have them?" The Society of Friends has probably done this more successfully than other groups—with many beneficial consequences, but perhaps also with the result it has remained small. But even Quakers have elders and clearly respected ways of conducting their meetings and arriving at their decisions. In other groups that try to pattern their group life without creating officials, the role of preaching elder is chosen by lot, and all male members of the group deemed qualified must risk being chosen to exercise this function for a stipulated term. The use of the lot, based upon Acts 1:23–26 as the warrant, is really something of an institutionalized way of determining who should be selected to be the leader for a given moment in the group's life.[3]

Leadership roles became more specifically defined and the process for choosing leaders became more complex with the further development of the Christian communities. The leadership of the church seems to have been destined by the logic of history to become more formalized. Ecclesiastical officials appeared to take over the functions once performed by apostles. Spontaneous leadership or fortuitous choice gave way to patterns of authority and regularized methods for choosing leaders. The New Testament as such does not present just one clear picture of the forms that leadership roles took in the early church, but it does provide significant evidence that regular ecclesiastical offices developed and that they had an official quality about them that was different from that generally associated with the origin of the apostle's role.

The New Testament mentions the functions of teacher, of evangelist, of pastor. It also mentions the offices of elder, deacon, and bishop. But the relationships between these different functions and identities of leadership in the early church as portrayed in the New Testament itself are sufficiently fluid to have provided ample grist for the development of numerous polities in subsequent church history and even for controversies over which is the most legitimate. Indeed arguments regarding the way in which ecclesiastical offices should be structured have been among the most heated in church history, and they are still among the most contested aspects of ecumenical discussions about faith and order. Even today, the nature of the ministry—how it is to be structured, what are its sacramental powers, who is eligible for ordination, etc.—is a subject of great disagreement and continues to divide denominations one from another more than most other issues.

These arguments over the nature of governance in the church may be mainly disagreements about procedural matters. Polity may appear to deal less with ethical judgments than with logistical arrangements. Even those who prefer one form of church governance to another are not inclined to regard their way as the only moral solution (although they may try to claim it is the only biblical pattern). To be sure, moral questions do arise about how particular individuals exercise an office, but no pattern of office as such is *ipso facto* immoral; no office as such is *ipso facto* moral.

One of the interesting things about the New Testament's discussion of church leadership is how little the counseling role is emphasized. The therapeutic role of the clergy has become so important in our time as to make many of the other roles seem secondary. In our times management skills and institutional maintenance are often emphasized along with counseling, but solid pedagogical roles are given less and less weight. Perhaps the most tragic development in modern ministry is the loss of the expectation that ministers are called to teach and instruct congregations with skill and in depth. An equally serious development has been the tendency to resist, if not to punish, those ministers who attempt to exercise a prophetic role— a role that by its very nature means bringing both congregation and the civic culture under judgment.

In the pastoral Epistles considerable attention is given to the qualities of life that are to mark the leaders in the church (e.g., 1 Timothy 3:1–13). But these Epistles deal with church offices in a way that offers an interesting contrast with the attitude toward the office of the king in the Old Testament. In the case of the king the personal virtues of the individual holding the office are considered to be of only secondary importance, if that. Such is not the case concerning the holders of ecclesiastical office, though in some later Christian thinking the validity of the sacraments comes to be considered independent of the personal moral qualities of the priest—providing the sacrament is properly performed by a duly ordained individual.

According to Timothy, "A bishop must be above reproach, married only once, temperate, sensible, respectable, hospitable, an apt teacher, not a drunkard, not violent but gentle, not quarrelsome, and not a lover of money" (3:2). Similarly, "Deacons likewise must be serious, not double-tongued, not indulging in much wine, not greedy for money" (3:8). These descriptions of necessary qualities for holding office are descriptions of moral attitudes that can just as readily be expected from all the other members of the community.

However, churches have often tended to expect the ministry to exemplify higher moral achievements than those expected in the laity. This might, at first glance, seem far better than thinking of an officeholder as somehow exempt from requirements for personal integrity. Yet all branches of the church have been plagued by a tendency to think in terms of a double standard that has no warrant in the New Testament. In the case of the double standard the expectation of exemplary moral achievement gets subtly transformed into an expectation of different standards for clergy and laity. Whereas the New Testament does expect those who exercise leadership roles to exemplify in a special way those moral qualities that all Christians can be expected, or at least encouraged, to achieve, the double standards that have crept into thinking about the ministry are quite another matter.

The earliest and most enduring double standard is found in the development of priestly celibacy. While this is frequently defended on procedural and pragmatic grounds—married persons cannot devote themselves to the demands of an office as readily as single individuals—it institutionalizes a much deeper judgment, which considers the celibate life morally superior. Celibacy is an ideal for a special class. Indeed, laity are expected to behave in quite a different way, to marry and to procreate. Only an occasional figure in the history of the church has urged that celibacy be made a universal requirement, and faced up to the stark consequences that this would bring the human odyssey to a fairly decisive halt.

But Protestants have created their own versions of the double moral standard. For many years, a number of denominations, either by explicit obligation or by implicit inference—required their clergy to refrain from the use of tobacco and alcohol, although no such requirement was made on laity. Langdon Gilkey has described the consequences of this double standard in the Bible Belt of the South during the 1950s. A ministerial student having a church in Tennessee while studying at Vanderbilt Divinity School was invited, somewhat to his surprise, to accept a drink at the home of the chief lay officer of the parish he was serving. He did so, having been accustomed to the somewhat more lenient attitudes of the North, where he had previously studied. Almost immediately thereafter, apparently as quickly as the grapevine could spread the story, he was asked by the official board to relinquish his ministerial position. This may be an extreme example, but it vividly and pathetically reveals the extent to which a double standard can exist in Protestantism and the way such a double standard can be misused.[4]

Although it has not, as far as I am aware, been widely examined as such, the present tendency of many denominations to reject certain sexual lifestyles as a condition for ordination or for the ratification of a call of an already ordained person to a charge constitutes a new form of the double standard. This is especially the case if the same denominations explicitly admonish their member churches to accept persons of such sexual lifestyles as members and to render them full pastoral care. In arguing about these matters, appeals to isolated biblical passages are hurled about vehemently in the debate, but the far profounder biblical perspective that the moral expectations of church officers should be but a rigorous application of the same standards that can be expected of all devoted Christians seems not to be recognized.

Although the pastoral Epistles do not explicitly reject the radical implications of other New Testament writing, they present a far more traditional and conventional picture of moral obligation than that found in either the Gospels or the other Epistles. Institutionalization has already begun to domesticate the ethic of the New Testament. The writer of the second letter to Timothy tells him to give this advice to the members of the community: "Remind them of this, and warn them before God that they are to avoid wrangling over words, which does no good but only ruins those who are listening" (2:14). Self-control is emphasized in Titus (2:3–8). Indeed, in Titus the conventional subordination of women to men and slaves to masters is cited as the paradigm of proper faithfulness. Under the pressures of institutionalization conventional domestication has overridden the emancipating unconventionality of Jesus.

As religion institutionalizes it often tends to conventionalize morality; it tends to take the edge off the prophetic thrust; it comes to honor conformity and dutiful loyalty rather than innovation and unconventional actions, no matter how emancipating. Yet, if institutionalization is seemingly necessary to the survival and continued existence of ecclesiastical groups, the pressure toward conformity is likely to be inescapable. To be sure, in early and preliminary stages of any movement it is possible to be innovative, to avoid the entanglements that go with structuring for social stability and public responsibility, to rattle the rafters and "shake the foundations."[5] But a persistent iconoclasm is more effective for the purposes of demolition than for the task of construction, and demolition alone is not enough. Nor can we demolish some oppressive situation once and for all, and then build a perfect and enduring social edifice. We have to live in a continuous tension between these two stances, and a host of complex mixes that entail both at once. To do so calls for holy discontent combined with patient endurance, and patient endurance chastened by holy discontent—all rolled into a discipleship that struggles constantly to be both radically loyal to the Gospel and effectively responsible to institutional structures.

17

The Revelation of John

Fidelity Under Duress, the Powers and Providence

The last book of the canon is one of the least understood, often misunderstood, and yet potentially one of the most fertile sources of moral insight found in the Bible. I would not have said that in my early years, when I jokingly referred to Revelation as Saint John's nightmare. Some of my attitude may well have consisted of a reaction to ways in which my grandmother—prompted by the radio "voices of prophecy" that she followed "religiously"—predicted all sorts of immediate culminating disasters to come upon the earth momentarily on the basis of clues derived from Revelation. But youthful years that know no sense of possible doom, that are buoyed up by promises of a rosy future all celebrated enthusiastically in a display of technological grandeur in World Fairs of Tomorrow, differ from seasoned years that have stared the possibility of atomic/nuclear holocaust in the face, and seen the spread of wanton and apparently meaningless violence into almost every aspect of our common life. Nor is my ambivalence regarding the usefulness of this book a personal idiosyncrasy. Speaking of the difficulties interpreting the book, Elisabeth Schüssler Fiorenza has found no surprise in the fact that "many exegetes and Christians throughout the centuries have relinquished an understanding of the book in despair while others have found it to be a source not only of spiritual but also artistic inspiration."[1]

The Revelation of John was redacted into its present form late in the first century of the common era, when conditions for the early Christians began to be nerve-wracking and unsettling. As the status of Christianity changed from that of a protected sect within Judaism to that of an independent religion, the begrudging toleration afforded Judaism by the Roman rulers covered Christians less and less. The Roman authorities began to treat the Christian movement with suspicious hostility, as a new and threatening development. Their attitude reflects both the suspicion that is normal to officials and a more general distrust of a new and strange religion by the wider public. The officials of the empire realized that it is prudent to placate such distrust.[2] Specifically, the early Christians refused to show the Emperor Domitian (81–96 C.E.) the proper deference (that is, they refused to address him as Lord and God and to worship his image), but this is a symbolic part of a larger pattern of distinctiveness that caused them to be distrusted as nonconformists. The result was persecution, sometimes involving exile; sometimes martyrdom. Like any political hegemony, Rome wanted unity and loyalty. Although some interpretations picture the demands of the Roman emperors merely as blatant efforts to extract a narrowly defined political allegiance, the problems of civic religiosity (and Christian refusal to adapt to it) are present here even as they were present for the Jews under the Hellenizers. Consequently, the Book of Revelation is not dissimilar to the Book of Daniel. Each was written to instill fidelity under duress, utilizing the classic mode of apocalyptic literature.

If anything, Revelation is more highly imaginative than Daniel and uses more code symbolism to convey its message so as not to flatly declare its purposes and intentions to those whose hostility it does not wish to arouse. Although the book contains numerous allusions to Old Testament passages, it is addressed to contemporaries (seven churches in Asia Minor living under Roman rule). Chapters 2 and 3 cite the strengths and weaknesses of each of those churches in a series of letters marked by a strong approving/criticizing dialectic. The letters to those ancient churches certainly pose questions that modern Christian groups might well ask about their life today, but that does not provide the main locus for the moral thrust of this book.

The next part of the book is devoted to a vision of God on a heavenly throne, accompanied by the Lamb, who now exists in resurrected glory (chapters 4 and 5). The imagery of these chapters is clearly dependent on a belief in the efficacy of Christ's death and Resurrection. Christ is able, as is no one else, to open the seals to make the message of God known to humankind. The opening of the seals, seven in number, provides the dramatic action for unveiling the future, a future preceded by many trials and tribulations that correspond to the conditions of the present. Imagery from the first four seals, involving the four horsemen of the Apocalypse, has furnished interpretive categories for a variety of purposes—some of them quite different from the actual conditions that prompted the writing of this book.[3] The opening of the fifth seal presents a vision of the souls of the martyrs living in heaven and asking how long it will be until their blood is avenged, their fidelity vindicated. That of the sixth foretells great upheavals that will come. Although portrayed as natural calamities, these upheavals signify social dislocations as well (6:9–17).

Chapter seven, offering an interlude between the opening of the sixth and the opening of the seventh seal, sets forth two visions. One indicates that God's faithful servants will have a mark of protection (7:1–3) affording escape from the coming doom. This chapter contains one of the coded symbols that has been so frequently seized upon to interpret the seemingly esoteric messages of this material. It numbers those to be protected at 144,000, drawn from the twelve tribes of Israel. The significance of the number is completeness—all the tribes are to be equally protected. However, the number has frequently been used to connote exclusion. The number has a quite different moral thrust when seen in the context of first-century Palestine and symbolizing all the tribes of Israel than it does when seen in the context of a very much more populous twentieth-century world. In the first instance it is big enough to cover everyone; in the second it is but a piddling remnant that easily lends itself to exclusion on the basis of moral differentiation.

The opening of the seventh and last seal (chapters 8–10) is attended by a series of momentous consequences: angels blowing trumpets, calamities affecting nature, plagues, demonic beasts and galloping steeds, and so on. Those who are to escape these calamities are again assured that they will be saved, although the message is basically one of judgment and doom upon those who do wrong. Chapter 11 continues the prediction of woes, foretells a beast who will come up from a bottomless pit, and ends with an account of the victory of God and the vindication of the faithful. Chapter 12 portrays a continuing struggle between the forces of good and those of evil, personified as a woman about to bear a child, and a dragon. Chapter 13 portrays two beasts, one arising from the sea, the other from the earth. The contemporaries of John could read the symbolism and know that the first beast represents the Roman Empire; the second, the emperor, whose terrible actions are enumerated and whose identity is coded with the number 666.

Here is the place to pause for some initial ethical reflection. Revelation 13 is a counterpoint to Romans 13, though the numbering of the chapters is undoubtedly coincidental. Whereas Paul advised his followers to be obedient to existing Roman authority as ordained by God, the Seer of the Apocalypse makes unmistakably clear (at least to those who can read the coding) that the faithful should be leery of the Roman authorities and not submit to them in ways that compromise their convictions. Although

Romans 13 opens with a convenient proof text that again and again has been cited as an admonition to be unquestionably obedient to political authority, a reading of Revelation 13 depends on a more complex and sophisticated understanding that can, at appropriate times and places, legitimize resistance. On balance, therefore, the New Testament (both in this comparison and elsewhere) offers legitimation for both submission to civil authority and noncooperation, and casts us back upon faithful responsiveness in particular circumstances to decide when one is appropriate and when the other is called for.

It might be easy to deal with the relationship between Christian faithfulness and political authority if only one of these chapters were in the canon, or if the rest of the New Testament offered a clear and simple view of civil authority. But the problem of relating Christian fidelity to political obligation cannot be so readily resolved. Moreover, it is wrong to assume that the state is always the source of the problem, as though the church's only task is to decide when obedience is called for and when resistance is appropriate. After Constantine later recognized Christianity as the official religion of the empire, the very church that was the victim of persecution when Revelation was written not infrequently became the handmaiden of persecutors. Christianity across its history is just as frequently associated with the reigning sociopolitical establishment as it is separated as a persecuted minority. That enables it to participate in the benefits Paul sees in ordered authority, but also entangles it in the moral difficulties John sees in the exercise of authority.

In considering whether civil disobedience is legitimate, for instance, one cannot merely decide in the abstract whether or not it is right to disobey authorities and then deal with particular circumstances according to that abstract conclusion. One must not use either Romans 13 or Revelation 13 as an all-embracing model. The obligation to uphold "law and order" is a conditional one, not an absolute principle. An obligation to resist wrongful authority is situation-determined, not a general rule. Many Christians in Germany before and during the rise of Hitler used Romans 13 uncritically, but then discovered that they had to move to Revelation 13 (or complex equivalents) in order to say no to Hitler. Many Christians in America have considered loyalty to the state an important obligation, but under the pressures of events like the struggle to overcome segregation, to stop the race to nuclear annihilation, or to protest immigration policies that are inhumane, they have come to realize the legitimacy of civil disobedience.[4] More recently, at quite the opposite end of the usual scale of political postures, some Christians are citing civil disobedience to sanction the use of coercive means to prevent abortions.

In making moral decisions we must scrutinize not only the legitimacy of obedience in comparison with civil disobedience but also our involvements in a society that treats many groups with contempt. If Christians think of themselves only as possible victims of political "beasts" they miss an important point. As part of an establishment Christians have been parties to persecution as frequently as they have been its victims. Their record in relationship to Jews has often been shameful. The record with respect to Muslims may not be much better. In American history during the nineteenth century the Mormons suffered hostility and in many places so did the Roman Catholics (especially those associated with immigrant groups)—all at the hands of a professedly Christian establishment essentially Protestant in flavor. In the 1930s and 1940s Jehovah's Witnesses were the objects of much harassment, much of which was overcome, not by tolerance engendered by churches, but by a series of Supreme Court decisions that were as controversial in their day as the decisions about abortion and affirmative action seem to be in ours. Today the Unification Church (the Moonies) is often treated with suspicion and contempt—whereas the Mormons, Roman Catholics, and Jehovah's Witnesses are not only generally tolerated but have often come to represent the most stable and sometimes conservative parties in the civic religious establishment. In Korea, however, many people feel that the Unification Church is closely tied to a governmental structure that oppresses those who are engaged in a struggle for economic justice and greater political freedom—so these matters may differ from place to place as well as from time to time. The Book of Revelation is morally important because it furnishes a strong New Testament warrant for keeping Paul's idea of obedience to political authorities from chaining Christians into mere subservience.

Returning to the text of Revelation, starting with chapter 14 we find a continuing contrast between accounts of the glorious state into which the 144,000 chosen followers of the Lamb are to come and the horrible fate others can expect. The narrative picks up the contrast between the glory in store for the faithful and the agony and punishment destined for those who follow the beast. That contrast is repeated in many different ways, with changing imagery that emphasizes the contrast in great variety. In chapter 18 a dirge is sounded for fallen Babylon (Rome), whereas in chapter 19 the glorious reign of God is acclaimed with hallelujahs. The tension between the forces of evil and those of the Lamb continues until a final judgment of great decisiveness rewards one and casts the other into a lake of fire (20:11–15). Some of the imagery here undoubtedly has found its way into that popular piety that envisions the final judgment of individuals as the reading of a record book of deeds.

Such imagery may engender moral fidelity, but it is prone to considerable misuse. It can re-create the very sharp contrast between the righteous and the unrighteous that Jesus sought to undercut. It can lend itself to visionary hyperboles that turn the biblical narrative into a set of destiny-predicting signals that have little more theological depth than fortune-telling. It can engender contemptible hatred for those who are considered beyond the pale of grace, whose foreheads do not bear the right sign. And yet these materials can be constructive ingredients for affirming the ultimate providence of God in historical circumstances. Without that premise history can easily engender nihilistic cynicism. By affirming significance for the end of temporal existence as presently experienced, assurances of God's victory over evil can be a source of confidence and hope. In answer to the query, "Is there any basis for hope?" the Book of Revelation offers a resounding confidence in the eventual establishment of a new heaven and a new earth (21:1).

In the Book of Revelation the tensions and contrast between moral faithfulness and its opposite is clearly acknowledged, but in such a way as to avoid a sharp, immutable dualism. According to Leonard Thompson,

> [T]here is no spatial or temporal dualism between the kingdom of the world and the kingdom of God. God creates and sustains all things. Transformations and changes permeate every boundary and break down every distinction because there is an underlying dynamic system into and out of which all distinctions fold and unfold. God's dynamic power may flow into rebellious vortices and opposing whorls, but ultimately everything and every power derives from and depends upon God.[5]

The discussion of the dynamic interplay to which this passage points is found in many biblical materials, and is designated by the rubric eschatology. Eschatology affirms an eventual destiny that finishes the ongoing course of history with a decisive culmination rather than a whimper, with fulfillment rather than mere indeterminacy. Eschatological thinking always wrestles with the question of why the present is not a fuller and more adequate embodiment of the divine work of Creation than it appears to be from present signs. Revivals come, but produce no lasting utopias; crusades are undertaken but seldom liberate the Holy Land; traditions seek to hold on to the values of the past but often merely create the rigidities of a new present that is no better than the old. Liberations take place, but yield to wilderness as soon as they are significantly functional. Even moral reflections about the biblical drama offer more questions than assurances! Without some way of thinking of a culmination that is a break with the ongoing routines of common experience, it is difficult to feel confident of moral fulfillment. Eschatological affirmations are efforts to affirm the possibility of a meaningful closure without denying contemporary ambiguity, to affirm that historical experience is to be valued without regarding it as self-vindicating, and to see transformation as a promise that will not be endlessly defeated.

We must inquire, therefore, concerning the biblical understanding of how nature and history are to reach fulfillment even as we earlier inquired as to how they originated. A doctrine of creation logically requires a doctrine of consummation. It will not do merely to eliminate or to repudiate the idea that a consummation is significant. The materials in Revelation help us to think about these issues and their bearing on moral reflections and moral action, but it is possible to understand their importance if we look at them in comparison with alternative views of time and destiny.

The Cyclical View. One possible view of the relationship of time and destiny is a cyclical view, charted below.

This view suggests that nothing is ever permanently changed for good; what goes up (as a moral achievement) comes down (as a moral disaster); what is made better at one time will sooner or later turn worse. In this view history has no value-preserving or value-supporting dimensions.

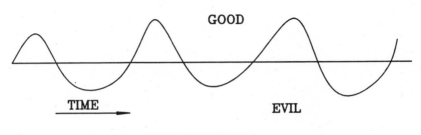

CYCLICAL VIEW

Morality is accidental, episodic, always tentative, and ultimately defies a premise of purpose. We have seen something very close to this view in the Book of Ecclesiastes (at least before it was edited); this view is found in much Greek mythology, especially the account of Sisyphus, who is condemned to roll the stone up one side of the mountain only to have it roll down the other side. The Hindu doctrine of karma with its indeterminable reincarnations can be understood this way, although it gets modified in many strands of Hindu thought to avoid the most dismal implications. A cyclical view of history breeds despair; it is akin to punishment. In certain military disciplinary barracks one of the most demoralizing punishments is to be required to shovel dry sand all day long from the outer bottom of the pile to the top. If we think history imposes a similar requirement on us, who will take moral obligation as challenge or possibility?

The Idea of Progress. A contrasting view is found in the modern idea of progress, which comes in both religious and nonreligious variations. In such a view history has no decisive end, but the process itself provides some significance for life and action. The dead bones of one generation make a pathway for the advancement of the next generation—which supposedly will move a little further along the way to something better. We are always in an Exodus rich with possibilities, but never translated into a land flowing with enough milk and honey to assure we have gotten to a place of refreshment or fulfillment. A doctrine of progress can be diagramed as follows:

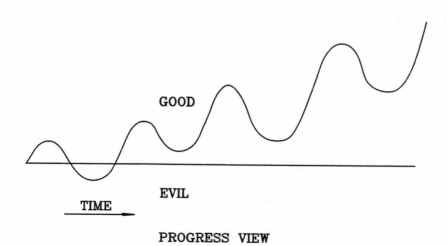

PROGRESS VIEW

To be sure, a doctrine of progress helps to overcome cynicism. It is provisionally closer to the biblical perspective than a cyclical view, but it makes a significant place for God's action only in an ongoing created order. It does not deny the possibility of a consummation but simply provides no place to put it, no way of giving it symbolic significance. We encounter the idea of progress in much of the culture about us, where we are reminded, even as technological warfare grows increasingly horrendous, that "Progress Is Our Most Important Product," or that we benefit from "Better Things for Better Living Through Chemistry."

Belief in progress can provisionally encourage and sustain moral endeavor. We can be faithful to positive impulses if we believe that our accomplishments, while not yielding a consummation, do work for the benefit of those who follow in our path. Arnold Toynbee, in his book *The Study of History,* combined elements of the cyclical view with aspects of the progressive view by suggesting that history moves something like a wagon wheel. Civilizations come and go, as though on the outer rim of a moving wheel, but the hub traces an upward path evident in the development of high religion.[6] All of this is provisionally helpful but not ultimately satisfying. It is more a product of rationalist thinking than of the biblical narrative.

An Eschatological View. Another view, found in apocalyptical and eschatological literature, in both Old and New Testaments, can be diagramed as follows:

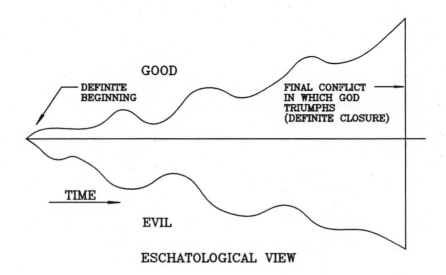

ESCHATOLOGICAL VIEW

According to this understanding both goodness and evil grow and expand within history until at some cataclysmic end-time God consummates the purpose of Creation and removes the ambiguities that persistently plague historical existence. In this understanding of time and destiny a decisive divine action is needed to consummate history just as a decisive divine action was needed to begin it. The endurance under stress that we talked about earlier in this chapter is premised, if only implicitly, upon something akin to this affirmation. Belief in moral order can help, but moral order as a natural reality is too easily questioned to make heroic resistance to evil likely. Martyrdom makes relatively little sense on merely human or natural premises, although it sometimes does occur. It is given much greater impetus by a belief in God as the effective sovereign of a history in which a consummation is possible.

Abstractly stated, this sounds plausible enough. Problems come in making it meaningful and avoiding its misuse. Literature like that found in Revelation is both profoundly helpful and subject to serious distortion. It can energize the saints; it can produce religious lunacy.

Let us clear away some distortions first. One of the most obvious misuses of apocalyptic literature is for the purpose of making specific predictions of events to come within the historical process itself—albeit at the very end. In a certain sense this is not eschatology at all, but a presumptuous employment of religious symbolism to manipulate history or at least to triumph over its vicissitudes. To return to my grandmother: She used the number of the beast to prove that Adolph Hitler was the anti-Christ and therefore the end was very near. She was convinced, not merely that he was a demonic figure whose policies were profoundly evil, but that he was the figure predicted by the Bible to arrive in connection with the millennium. She thus awaited the end, much to the discomfort of some of her family, whose understandings of life's purposes were essentially modern and premised on accomplishment rather than informed by an understanding of biblical eschatology. How did my grandmother come to her opinion? The name Führer Adolph Hitler has 6-6-6 letters! He must be the beast. But, alas, history did not end in her lifetime. Comrad Joseph Stalin followed; and while my grandmother did not live to see them in office, so did Lyndon Baines Jonson and Jimmie Plains Carter (a little fudging needed to give each of them the code number), and Ronald Wilson Reagan. Such uses of futuristic eschatology as event prediction discredit the idea by attempting to render something literal and certain that must be a approached through interpretation and understood by faith.

An almost equally questionable use of eschatology in futuristic terms is to take some threatening escalation of evil as a sign that the end is near at hand. Some people even think that helping evil to intensify may be a way of hastening the final great battle between Gog and Magog. Such thinking can be frightening because it attempts to manage the eschaton rather than trust in God's providence. Were human beings, for instance, to bring about the end of history as we know it by some foolish nuclear conflagration, that would be gross betrayal, not eschatological fulfillment.

Another, somewhat less problematic, form of eschatology centers on the idea of a millennium—a thousand years of revised but not truly consummated historical existence. Millenarian thinking is founded on the passage in 20:1–3 that speaks about a thousand years associated with an earthly return of Christ. But millennialists divide into two groups: those who believe that the thousand years will begin with the appearance of Christ (pre-millennialists) and those who believe it will end with the appearance of Christ (post-millennialists). Millennialism is often associated with a particularistic exclusivism that asserts that the benefits of Christ's reign are to be reserved only for the faithful.

Eschatological thinking does not well serve the life of faith when it is used as a means of attempting to control the future or even of predicting what is truly a matter of God's way of working out the divine purposes. Those concerned to predict the future seek to domesticate the manner in which God works. But this does not mean eschatological thinking has no moral significance. It is a profound way of affirming that the moral enterprise is upheld by the ultimate intentionality of God and is consistent with the most fundamental purposes of reality. Such an affirmation is a crucial foundation for a theology founded on hope.

Alternative ways of using eschatology provide a transforming power for the moral enterprise without seeming to invite the misuses to which predictionist eschatologies are prone. One of these is denoted by the term "realized eschatology"; another, to use the rubric suggested by Thomas Ogletree, by the term "dialectical eschatology."[7] These forms of eschatology are more subtle, yet morally more significant, than those we have been describing.

Realized eschatology finds the assurance of God's victory over the forces of evil already demonstrated. Christ has conquered the principalities and powers. All that follows is transformed by that confidence. Such confidence has operational significance for Christian behavior. The war has already been won. All that now needs doing is to "mop up" the pockets of continuing resistance to which the word about the armistice has not yet arrived. Such operations, as in real military experience, may be difficult and dangerous, but they can be undertaken with a quite different sense of what has to be done than if the main battle is still undecided.

The power of realized eschatology to transform life can be illustrated with quite different imagery. Those who live in temperate climates know that the shortening of the days, the coming of cold, and the onslaught of snowstorms are not the harbingers of a sudden inevitable movement to oblivion. The experience of these events is made quite different by the very fact we have confidence that spring will come, and summer. If we had to think that the sun had gone off course, or that the cold would continue to intensify indefinitely, then living through late fall into winter could bring panic. While the limitation of this illustration is the fact that seasons are cyclical, since we must realize cold will come again, the analogy is helpful within its own confines. In moral terms, realized eschatology helps us to recognize that the continuance of evil, even an increase in the seeming amount and intensity of evil, is not a cause for panic.

Dialectical eschatology, as Ogletree conceives it, allows communities to participate in the realities of a present imperfect age without having to capitulate to the norms and practices of that age. It permits communities of faith to recognize the worth of human institutions that serve human needs even if they are not entirely free of moral problems. Such institutions "are relative and provisional, not absolute and final; yet in their relativity they are suitable spheres for living out one's call in Jesus Christ."[8] Or, to state it differently, eschatology makes sense of the admonition to live in the world but not be of it. It legitimizes hope without requiring capitulation.

In the case of Abraham, as we have seen,[9] hope was wedded to risk. In the case of eschatology the dialectic between hope and risk is caught up and then transcended by assurance. The affirmation that undergirds this perspective is at heart of the fifth model offered by Gustafson for thinking about the relationship of Christ and the moral life, the model of Christ as the Lord of History. Eschatological thinking is the ultimate way of affirming that God reigns as Sustainer, Redeemer, and Comforter and of declaring that Christ's consummating work will not suffer ultimate demise or defeat.

Thus eschatological thinking helps us to remember that we wrestle, not merely against an ignorance of what is right, or against the perverse intentions of merely willful individuals, but against the principalities and the powers that provide such momentous impetus to moral wrongdoing.[10]

These powers seem to have a self-generating dynamic that far exceeds the capacity of well-intentioned idealism to stem. Moreover, Christians (as all others) are sometimes caught by the dynamic of these powers and carried along by their influence. But that is only the provisional assessment, the interim judgment, the seeming evidence as understood without the benefit of an eschatological assurance. The more ultimate judgment is that Christ's empowerment is operative in a history through which God's purposes will be constructively consummated in all good time. Such a conviction keeps moral faithfulness from being wishful thinking.

If victory over evil is assured then the moral life can be understood as a creative venture rather than as a compulsive necessity. The difference between these stances can be represented symbolically by the contrast between power boating and sailing. Power boating usually involves having a known goal, a place to reach, often on a fixed schedule. It is a form of management, of control, of resolute fixation with results. It engages in a drive that is primarily meaningful in terms of obtaining a consequence. A power boat is designed to run entirely by virtue of the resources it carries on its own. Power boating may well involve ignoring surrounding circumstances, except to avoid collisions, and not infrequently (despite the rules of the waterways) makes others move aside to allow the boat to remain on course.

But sailing entails responsiveness. It is a form of dependence on givens, on unseen powers that blow according to their whims rather than in obedience to human demands, that is truly a gift, but a gift that must be accepted on its terms, not bent to ours. It is gift that is responded to rather than grasped; something to be appreciated not subjugated. In sailing, a goal is still sought, but seeking it may involve some moving back to get ahead; sailors can greet circumstances that change with gratitude and sometimes even with surprise, but they are not offered immunity from temporary disappointment. Sailing understands promise as assurance yet not as guaranteed triumph, and it requires the utmost sensitivity to everything that is going on about it—knowing the wind and its vicissitudes, caring for the environment and its fragility, continuing in companionship with others on board, with whom conversation is not prevented by the roar of a motor running a top speed. Years ago many people put bumper stickers on their cars that said, "I'd rather be sailing." That phrase should not be understood as merely a yearning for aesthetic pleasure with a yuppie hobby. It is a way of pointing out how the moral life may be most richly understood and lived. Realized eschatology ensures that the goal is secure even if the venture of getting there is marked by vicissitudes and strategic tacks. It gives meaning to the very venture itself and not merely to the end result. Sailing involves serious dedication and creativity, but it is acceptable only to those who will embrace fulfillment with an element of faith, not demand it as an assured given. Sailing is a way of cooperating with all of the forces that affect us rather than countering them in an expenditure of energetic determination. It weds hope with trust and depends on grace. In a quite profound sense, when one relinquishes the helm of the power boat and becomes involved in the rigging of the sails, a new heaven and a new earth unfold.

Eschatology permits hope to be realistic without embracing cynicism. We must live in hope. Against hope, the realism of this world always says, as it seemingly must: "Not yet, if indeed ever." These "not yets" can destroy us if allowed to become the final word, since fulfillments indefinitely postponed are destinies destroyed. But if realism writes "not yets" in blazing letters across the face of every human aspiration, Christian hope writes "The time has been fulfilled" against those same experiences when understood in light of God's incessant tugging for our loyalties. We can afford uncertainty because we have been redeemed by a power that does not depend on correctness; we can afford to be tolerant because we are not required to protect our purity; we can afford to be patient because we are not required to assure a particular outcome by our own efforts alone. That is the confidence that brings the moral meaning of the biblical drama to a close, and it is the heart of what it means to believe in the good news of God's involvement with us in the ongoing events of our lives.

Epilogue

The Bible does not solve our moral problems, or offer ready made dicta as to what is morally required. Rather, it poses issues, illumines the human situation, and offers valuable resources for moral reflection. The Bible can be read most profitably with a hermeneutics of tension, a dialectical hermeneutics that acknowledges the contrasting moral implications of the narrative. These contrasts include: freedom from oppression in tension with the need for law and order; charismatic judges in comparison with hereditary monarchs; the moral calculus of Ezekiel in contrast to Isaiah's suffering servant; spirit-led apostles and appointed church officials; serious concern for present nature/history and eschatological hope. The Bible does not say that one side of these contrasts can stand alone and is always right. Rather, it suggests that these pairs encompass the range of issues that make claims on us, and it offers resources for thinking about ethical decisions that must be made afresh in every generation, in ever new and changing circumstances.

Two images or models stand out as especially instructive and decisive: the experience of Exodus and the experience of the Exile. Two massive and impressive understandings of the role of faith and morality flow from these models: Exodus models an oppression/liberation understanding of human destiny and opportunity. The Exile, in contrast, models a sin/redemption understanding of Christianity. Both of these have strong biblical warrant and impressive contemporary advocates, though it may be ironic that the first model to appear in the biblical narrative has been the last to receive emphasis in twentieth-century Christianity.

Sin/redemption understandings of Christianity are embodied most impressively in the theological formulations of so-called North American theology; oppression/liberation understandings appear more frequently and are articulated more forcefully among Christians in the Third World, or in those groups within the First World that have been marginalized or oppressed. One way of doing theology is usually associated with privileged males, though women of a traditional and conservative bent may embrace it with equally strong commitment; the other way of doing theology is more compatible with the approach of Hispanic, black, and feminist theologians, but it has importance for all persons of faith. Although there are many understandable and cogent reasons why these two ways of thinking about the moral implications of the Gospel are aligned as they are with contemporary identity groups, such alignments are contingent and situation-bound rather than necessary and perennial.

Those who are in a contemporary "Egypt" are bound to think in terms of an oppression/liberation model and should be encouraged to do so. Those who sense themselves in a situation that imposes upon them more ambiguous responsibilities will more likely think of themselves in a sin/ redemption model and should be honored for doing so. But neither position by and in itself can claim to have the only clue to being faithful to God. A full-orbed understanding of a faithful moral stance can be had only by somehow making creative use of both of these models and thinking very carefully about how they are related. To take either of them as a sole sufficient basis of moral action is to miss the grandeur, profundity, and dialectical richness of the biblical understanding of God's encounter with the human situation. The oppression/liberation model alone can very easily become the basis of a politicized ideology; the sin/redemption model alone can very easily become a tool of theological triumphalism that oppresses others in the name of offering them salvation.

But how, indeed, can these models be related? There are potentially three possibilities.

1. *Sequential Relationship*. The first possibility is to relate them sequentially, as they seem to be related in the biblical narrative understood chronologically. That is to say, we can begin by sensing oppression and seeking liberation. Then, as we move through the stages that follow, we will recognize the enormous problems that attend such a movement and come to see the need for and benefits of a sin/redemption understanding of the human situation. The thinking of those who relate these models in such a manner, which places them in one or the other model at this particular time and place, is not to be repudiated because it does not include the other model. Yet neither can these thinkers be allowed to insist that their standing ground is alone legitimate and the place to which all others must come. There is, of course, more warrant from the biblical record under-

stood chronologically for honoring those who believe in the sufficiency of the liberation model than for those who would embrace the sin/redemption model with total disregard of the liberating experience that was its forerunner, but that does not warrant regarding the Exodus standing ground as an entirely adequate way of understanding the Bible.

2. *An Episodic/Situational Relationship.* A second possibility is to relate these models episodically or situationally. That is, to see the relevance of one at a particular time or in a particular set of circumstances and the relevance of the other at a different time and set of circumstances. This is to be contextual in method, and may well offer significant resources for overcoming the problems that inhere in taking just one of these models as the definitive stance for a Christian ethic. To take the episodic or situational approach requires that we think about the range of situations we face, the myriad moral problems and demands on us, and that we realize that a major aspect of the ethical task is to recognize when one of the models offers greater wisdom and leads to more emancipating and redeeming consequences than the other. To be sure, such a situational or episodic possibility depends on acknowledging the validity and potential relevance of both models rather than being fixated upon just one of them. It does not, however require that they be given equal weight at any one time.

3. *A Dialectical Relationship.* A third possibility is to think of these models as dialectically related, each offering something crucial for understanding moral responsibility and each also offering a check on any effort to embrace the other without reservations. A dialectical approach suggests that the tension between these models must be felt and taken seriously in every set of circumstances rather than applied to only some of them. Those who find the traditional formulations of Christian faith in sin/redemption terms to be persuasive must look with more sensitive and empathetic eyes on what prompts people to think in terms of liberation. They must recognize the many Egypts that still oppress people and must understand why the people who are caught in those Egypts hurt so much that they can think only in terms of release and liberation. Conversely, although it is more difficult, those who are seeking liberation must imaginatively recognize that release alone is not a sufficient model, that getting out of Egypt opens the possibilities for adequacy of life but does not by itself bring about its consummation.

All of this is to insist that faithful appreciation of the biblical narrative is complex and difficult and that faithful action responses to it are even more so. There is no warrant in the Bible for any other conclusion. The biblical materials undercut any and all pretensions to quick, simple, or unambiguous solutions to the human enterprise. But they also reveal to us a promise that the difficult and demanding complexities through which we move by faith will not defeat us because the power that is revealed in the biblical story has triumphed over every alternative that might thwart the final outcome of God's intentions for the people. It is in that confidence we can rest our trust that even our partial and inadequate efforts to be morally faithful are regarded as adequate.

Notes

Preface

1. Edward LeRoy Long Jr., *Conscience and Compromise: An Approach to Protestant Casuistry* (Philadelphia: Westminster Press, 1954).

2. This is the traditional translation for 1 Corinthians 13:12. The New Revised Standard Version says "For now we see in a mirror, dimly." The new wording is, perhaps unconsciously, more compatible with a modern realization about the partiality of knowledge. Mirrors reflect back what is before them rather than transmit images having a standing of their own. Moreover, they often distort imagery more radically than do translucent panels.

Introduction

1. This is not to suggest that the Westminster Confession of Faith is misleading as a portrayal of biblical faithfulness. The Westminster Confession, like many efforts of the church to define its faith, presents a profound system of doctrine that stems from the Bible. But the validity of its understanding is not necessarily authenticated by its myriad references to specific texts; it lies in its overall understanding of the human condition in ways that are consistent with the biblical story in its wholeness. It is worth noting that many of the ancient Creeds of the church, which surely are significant statements of the same biblically informed faith, were not prooftexted, but they are not therefore less useful or less legitimate as embodiments of the church's understanding of biblical truths than the Westminster Confession.

2. For a helpful elaboration of this point see Walter Wink, *The Bible in Human Transformation: Toward a New Paradigm for Biblical Study* (Philadelphia: Fortress Press, 1973), chap. 1.

3. Presbyterian Church USA, *Keeping Body and Soul Together: Sexuality, Spirituality, and Social Justice*. A document prepared for the 203rd General Assembly of the Presbyterian Church USA, 1991. See pages 18–37. The discussion in this report of the way to use the Bible as a guide for making moral decisions is especially helpful. It is unfortunate that the hermeneutical perspective offered by this paper has been overlooked in a debate that has been focused on a narrow specific practice rather than on more fundamental matters of theological reflection.

4. Harry Emerson Fosdick, *The Modern Use of the Bible* (New York: Macmillan, 1925), 8.

5. To describe an Episcopalian as a "person of the Book" usually means that such a person is a stickler for the patterns of worship described in the *Book of Common Prayer,* whereas the same terminology used to describe a Baptist or a Presbyterian usually means that the person is a biblical literalist.

6. Stanley Hauerwas, *Unleashing the Scripture: Freeing the Bible from Captivity to America* (Nashville: Abingdon Press, 1993), 38.

7. See Elisabeth Schüssler Fiorenza, *But She Said: Feminist Practices of Biblical Interpretation* (Boston: Beacon Press, 1992); *In Memory of Her: A Feminist Reconstruction of Christian Origins* (New York: Crossroad, 1983).

8. For a helpful exposition of this kind of hermeneutics, see Nancy J. Duff, *Humanization and the Politics of God: The Koinonia Ethics of Paul Lehmann* (Grand Rapids: William B. Eerdmans Publishing Company, 1992), especially chap. 3.

1. Egypt and Exodus

1. In his book *The Way of Israel: Biblical Faith and Ethics* (New York: Harper and Row, 1965) (which is an introduction to biblical thinking about ethics), James Muilenburg has written this:

> The hour of the Exodus was the birth of a people, the people chosen and called to a destiny. Israel's consciousness of being a people was first awakened at the Exodus; the event was the *fons et origo* of her life. The phenomenon of Israel in the world is not to be explained ethnologically in terms of race or blood, or culturally in terms of intellectual genius or "spiritual" aptitude, or mythologically in terms of a divine hero or demigod as progenitor, or geographically in terms of the strategic physical situation she came to occupy in the land of Palestine, or sociologically in terms of a peculiarly dynamic history during the first millennium B.C.E. No, her beginning belongs to a divine action in history. He who belongs to this people belongs to history because he belongs to a solidarity which confesses this God of the Exodus to be the Lord and King. (50)

2. Megan McKenna, *Not Counting Women and Children: Neglected Stories from the Bible* (Maryknoll, N.Y.: Orbis Press, 1994), 42.

3. Paulo Freire, *Pedagogy of the Oppressed* (New York: Herder and Herder, 1970), chap. 1.

4. See Dorothee Sölle, *Political Theology* (Philadelphia: Fortress Press, 1974); Johannes Baptist Metz, ed., *Faith and the World of Politics* (New York: Paulist Press, 1968); Johannes Baptist Metz, ed., *Faith in History and Society: Toward a Political Fundamental Theology* (New York: Seabury Press, 1980); and Jürgen Moltmann, *Religion and Political Society* (New York: Harper and Row, 1974).

5. One of the sobering consequences of the televising of court proceedings,

particularly of celebrity cases, is the degree to which it reveals that the administration of justice falls short of the ideal of procedural fairness. It becomes increasingly apparent that social standing and economic wherewithal have a great bearing on the way a given case is treated.

2. Genesis History

1. The reader who is interested in this process can consult books that deal with the literary origins of the Pentateuch, as do many general introductions to the Old Testament. I have found the treatment in Walter J. Harrelson, *Interpreting the Old Testament* (New York: Holt, Rinehart and Winston, 1964), 58–73, especially helpful. Knowledge of these origins can refine the manner in which the material is understood but does not radically alter the ethical import as presented in this discussion.

2. Paul D. Hanson, *The People Called: The Growth of Community in the Bible* (San Francisco: Harper and Row, 1987), 19.

3. Søren Kierkegaard, *Fear and Trembling and the Sickness Unto Death*, translated with introduction by Walter Lowrie (Princeton: Princeton University Press, 1968), 48.

4. "Creating a Jewish Feminist Theology," in Judith Plaskow and Carol P. Christ, eds., *Weaving the Visions: Patterns in Feminist Spirituality* (San Francisco: Harper and Row, 1989), 197.

5. Hanson, *The People Called*, 83.

6. Dolores S. Williams, *Sisters in the Wilderness: The Challenge of Womanist God-Talk* (Maryknoll, N.Y.: Orbis Books, 1993), 33.

7. Bruce C. Birch, *Let Justice Roll Down: The Old Testament, Ethics, and Christian Life* (Louisville, Ky.: Westminster/John Knox Press, 1991); Harrelson, *Interpreting the Old Testament;* and Hanson, *The People Called.*

8. Bernhard W. Anderson, *Understanding the Old Testament* (Englewood Cliffs, N.J.: Prentice-Hall, 1975); Harry M. Buck, *People of the Lord: The History, Scriptures and Faith of Ancient Israel* (New York: Macmillan, 1966).

9. Norman K. Gottwald, *The Hebrew Bible: A Socio-Literary Introduction* (Philadelphia: Fortress Press, 1985).

10. Harrelson, *Interpreting the Old Testament,* 71.

3. Exodus and Sinai

1. Deuteronomy was written for a different purpose than Exodus. Exodus is a narrative report on the founding experience in which the Ten Commandments are presented as a means of responding in gratitude for what has been done by God in the act of liberation. Deuteronomy, in contrast, is a document from a later attempt to reform the group after it has ceased to be loyal out of grateful response. It renders the Commandments (and other aspects of the Law) more a means to obtain a benefit than a guide to gracious responses for a benefit already experienced. But that, in a sense, is to anticipate the unfolding of the narrative.

2. Hanson, *The People Called,* 44.

3. This is the inference of Walter Harrelson's treatment of these verses (see *Interpreting the Old Testament,* 94).

4. Hanson, *The People Called,* 44.

5. Ibid., 45.

4. Promised Land and Holy Kingdom

1. Namely, Numbers, Joshua, Judges, 1 and 2 Samuel, and 1 and 2 Kings.

2. Bernhard W. Anderson, *Understanding the Old Testament,* 4th ed. (Englewood Cliffs, N.J.: Prentice-Hall, 1986), 111.

3. Walter Brueggemann, *The Land: Place as Gift, Promise, and Challenge in Biblical Faith* (Philadelphia: Fortress Press, 1977), 52.

4. See Douglas Sturm, *Community and Alienation: Essays on Process Thought and Public Life* (Notre Dame: University of Notre Dame Press, 1988), 55f.

5. E.g., J. Morgenstern, "Jubilee, Year of," in *The Interpreters Dictionary of the Bible,* vol. 2 (New York: Abingdon Press, 1962), 1002.

6. Arthur Waskow has been among those who have pointed to the relevance of both the sabbatical year and the Jubilee year as having important ecological ramifications. See "From Compassion to Jubilee [Contemporary Applications of the Jubilee]" *Tikkun: A Bimonthly Jewish Critique of Politics, Culture, and Society* 5, no. 2 (March–April 1990): 78–81.

7. See Hanson, *The People Called,* 22–23; and Walter Brueggemann, *The Prophetic Imagination* (Philadelphia: Fortress Press, 1979), 16, 17, 19.

8. Birch, *Let Justice Roll Down,* 178.

9. It is this kind of development that is involved in what Ernst Troeltsch called the "sect-cycle." See Ernst Troeltsch, *The Social Teaching of the Christian Churches,* trans. by Olive Wyon (New York: Harper and Brothers, 1960), especially chap. 9 of vol. 1 and chap. 4 of vol. 2.

10. Such "halfway" covenants were actually drawn up and explicitly utilized in the churches of second- and later-generation New England Puritans.

11. However, as we are coming to realize, there has to be at least a minimal public trust in the integrity of a police official for the authority to work. If the public believes the police official is corrupt or beholden to oppressive powers, the authority is severely eroded, and the structural scheme of justice breaks down into quasi gang warfare between the police and the segment of the public that has lost faith in them.

12. Incidentally, Catholic priesthood used to be authoritarian in governance even as its role was objectivized in the theory of the sacraments—but that has changed a great deal. The governance dimension could be modified, since it affects only the polity of the church, but the objectivity of the sacramental system seemingly cannot be as readily modified, since it is believed to be crucial to salvation. However, living through a transition in which even the governance function has come to be questioned has traumatic consequences for priests who were trained in the older pattern as well as for congregations who were accustomed to strong guidance from the clergy.

13. A somewhat truncated understanding of governance as a social ethical reality is conveyed by telling the first story to church school children but not the second.

14. Emil Brunner, *The Divine Imperative* (Philadelphia:Westminster, 1947), 222.

15. Reinhold Niebuhr, *Moral Man and Immoral Society: A Study in Ethics and Politics* (New York: Charles Scribner's Sons, 1932), 75.

16. John Howard Yoder, *The Politics of Jesus: Vicit Agnus Noster* (Grand Rapids: William B. Eerdmans Publishing Company, 1972).

17. For a statement of this position see Stanley Hauerwas and William H. Willimon, *Resident Aliens: Life in the Christian Colony* (Nashville:Abingdon Press, 1989).

18. Richard J. Mouw, Politics and the Biblical Drama (Grand Rapids:William B. Eerdmans Publishing Company, 1976).

19. Nicholas K. Wolterstorff, *Until Peace and Justice Embrace* (Grand Rapids: William. B. Eerdmans Publishing Company, 1983).

5. Affluence, Corruption, and Prophetic Response

1. Birch, *Let Justice Roll Down,* 221f.

2. See Murray Lee Newman Jr., *The People of the Covenant:A Study of Israel from Moses to Monarchy* (New York:Abingdon Press, 1962), 177.

3. See Birch, *Let Justice Roll Down*, 243.

4. Bernhard W. Anderson, *Understanding the Old Testament*, 4th ed. (Englewood Cliffs, N.J.: Prentice-Hall, 1986), 278.

5. Bernard Häring, *Free and Faithful in Christ: Moral Theology for Clergy and Laity*, vol. 1 (New York:A Crossroads Book, Seabury Press, 1978) 87.

6. The earlier materials portray a henotheistic perspective, one that insists Israel should worship only one God but does not deny the existence of others.

7. This connection is explicitly described in Hanson, *The People Called,* 167–76.

6. The Creation Stories

1. Lynn White Jr., "The Historical Roots of Our Ecological Crisis," *Science* 155, no. 3767 (March 10, 1967): 1203–7.

2. Rosemary Radford Ruether, *Gaia and God:An Ecofeminist Theology of Earth Healing* (San Francisco: HarperCollins Publishers, 1992), 3.

3. See Paul Santmire, *Brother Earth: Nature, God, and Ecology in Time of Crisis* (New York:Thomas Nelson, Inc., 1970), chap. 4.

4. E. F. (Ernst Friedrich) Schumacher, *Small Is Beautiful: Economics as if People Mattered* (New York: Harper and Row, 1973).

5. Matthew Fox, *Creation Spirituality: Liberating Gifts for the Peoples of the Earth* (San Francisco: HarperSanFrancisco, 1991), 10.

6. Ibid., 14–15.

7. Ibid., 33.

8. Ibid., 27.

9. Ibid., 31.

10. Elizabeth Dodson Gray, "Eden's Garden Revisited: A Christian Ecological Perspective," in Patricia Altenbernd Johnson and Janet Kalven, eds. *With Both Eyes Open: Seeing Beyond Gender* (New York: The Pilgrim Press, 1988), 54.

11. Sallie McFague, *The Body of God: An Ecological Theology* (Minneapolis: Fortress Press, 1993), 34.

12. Ibid., viii.

13. Ibid., 40.

14. The term "helper" is used in many translations of Genesis 2:18 and is often read as implying the subordination of women to men. This is, as Phyllis Trible has shown, a misreading (perhaps even a mistranslation) of the text. Moreover, the story of Creation in the first chapter of Genesis implies equality between women and men, an equality that has too often been denied. See Phyllis Trible, *God and the Rhetoric of Sexuality* (Philadelphia: Fortress Press, 1978), especially chapter 4.

15. Charles Hodge, *Systematic Theology,* vol. 3 (New York: Scribner Armstrong and Company, 1876), 323.

16. Abraham Joshua Heschel, *The Sabbath: Its Meaning for Modern Man* (New York: Farrar, Straus & Giroux, 1951), 28.

17. John C. Bennett, *Christianity and Our World* (New York: Association Press, 1936), 18.

18. John C. Bennett, *Social Salvation: A Religious Approach to Problems of Social Change* (New York: Charles Scribner's Sons, 1935), 192.

19. Georgia Harkness, *The Recovery of Ideals* (New York: Charles Scribner's Sons, 1937), 128f.

20. William A. Spurrier, *Natural Law and the Ethics of Love: A New Synthesis* (Philadelphia: The Westminster Press, 1974), 21.

7. From Garden to Tower

1. Gottwald, *The Hebrew Bible,* 473.

2. Ibid., 474.

3. The term covers those who, in the categories of chapter 4, argue that even the covenant group must install kings who will marshal the power to keep evil—particularly the evil of enemies—at bay.

4. Bernard Ramm, *Offense to Reason: The Theology of Sin* (San Francisco: Harper and Row, 1985).

5. Ibid., 82. The reference is to Pascal's *Pensees,* 695.

6. Ibid.

7. Vergilius Ferm, ed., *Encyclopedia of Religion* (New York; The Philosophical Library, 1945), 711.

8. Although this story presumes that only toy guns are involved in the incident, as of this writing the use of real guns by young people is assuming alarming proportions. The speed with which this phenomenon has escalated is hardly proof that human relationships are naturally constructive or becoming more so with the shedding of religious myths.

9. Instead of coming to church next Sunday look ahead to chapter 11, page

152, where some possible clues to this query are explored with another children's sermon.

10. For a balanced and helpful discussion of the various strands to this movement see Rosemary Radford Ruether, *Gaia and God: An Ecofeminist Theology of Earth Healing* (San Francisco: HarperCollins, 1992), especially chap. 5 and 6.

11. Ibid., 116.

8. Exile as a Crisis of Faith

1. See Gottwald, *The Hebrew Bible,* 420.

2. Birch, *Let Justice Roll Down,* 284.

3. W. Lee Humphreys, *Crisis and Story: Introduction to the Old Testament* (Palo Alto, Calif.: Mayfield Publishing Company, 1979), 177.

4. Bruce C. Birch may overstate the case when he declares that the view has been "largely discredited." See *Let Justice Roll Down,* 296. For a different treatment see Paul Joyce, *Divine Initiative and Human Response in Ezekiel* (Sheffield, England: JOST Press, 1989), chap. 3.

5. I resonate wholeheartedly with the observation made by Marcus J. Borg that this distinction cannot be used to distinguish between Judaism as an ongoing tradition and Christianity. See Marcus J. Borg, *Meeting Jesus Again for the First Time: The Historical Jesus and the Heart of Contemporary Faith* (San Francisco: HarperSanFrancisco, 1994), 78f.

9. Attempts at Restoration

1. Hanson, *The People Called,* 250. I confess that I, too, have been woefully guilty of this same error, and that an early draft of this manuscript did precisely what Hanson describes.

2. Birch, *Let Justice Roll Down,* 305.

3. See Hanson, *The People Called,* 255.

4. Anderson, *Understanding the Old Testament,* 4th ed., 532.

5. See Hauerwas and Willimon, *Resident Aliens.*

6. See Hanson, *The People Called,* 254f.

7. See ibid., 255.

8. Anderson, *Understanding the Old Testament,* 4th ed., 492. Interestingly, Norman Gottwald, in *The Hebrew Bible,* declares, "It is not difficult to imagine that this story was framed by a woman confident at home in her social world" (557).

9. The significance of the book for illustrating the tensions within Israel between exclusivism and inclusivism is not dependent on the date the book was actually written. Dating the writing of the book is a legitimate and important focus of attention by biblical scholars interested in literary criticism and historical accuracy, but the significance of the book for moral reflection lies in its inclusivism and universal perspective.

10. See a particularly insightful discussion of this in Gottwald, *The Hebrew Bible,* 560.

11. Birch's discussion of this material in *Let Justice Roll Down* (chap. 9) is particu-

larly clear and helpful and guides the reader to an important body of literature that has explored the nature and significance of wisdom approaches to morality.

12. According to Norman Gottwald these subcollections are introduced by headings that occur at 1:1; 10:1; 22:17; 25:1; 30:1; and 31:1. Gottwald further holds that "differences in form and content set off chapters 10–15 from 16:1–22:16 and chapters 25–27 from 28–30." See Gottwald, *The Hebrew Bible,* 571.

13. See Birch, *Let Justice Roll Down,* 323. Also, Walter Brueggemann has made a similar point. See *In Man We Trust: The Neglected Side of Biblical Faith* (Richmond, Va.: John Knox Press, 1972).

14. See Birch, *Let Justice Roll Down,* 333.

10. Estrangement and Resistance

1. Harrelson, *Interpreting the Old Testament,* 460.

2. One of the benefits of historical criticism is to show that both of these books came out of the period we are discussing even though they are written as though they were accounts of an earlier period.

11. Messianic Categories and the Christological Narrative

1. Howard Clark Kee, *Knowing the Truth: A Sociological Approach to New Testament Interpretation* (Minneapolis: Fortress Press, 1989), 22. Kee offers this warning in conjunction with a helpful and sophisticated overview of contemporary views of the problems in knowing, indicating that biblical interpretation is not exempt from a more general difficulty in getting at absolute truth.

2. Hence, Alan Verhey entitled his treatment of New Testament ethics *The Great Reversal.* In delineating the meaning of this term, Verhey suggests that Jesus broke from the apocalypticism of his time, which embodied a nationalistic hope for Israel's triumph over the other nations, but did not break from the belief that the reign of God would "bring judgment and salvation, liberation and security." This book, however, does not suggest a complete break between Old and New Testament understandings of the moral situation. See *The Great Reversal: Ethics and the New Testament* (Grand Rapids: William B. Eerdmans Publishing Company, 1984), 15.

3. James M. Gustafson, *Christ and the Moral Life* (New York: Harper and Row, 1968).

4. Thomas Jefferson in a letter to John Adams, October 12, 13, 1813. In Lester J. Cappon, ed., *The Adams-Jefferson Letters: The Complete Correspondence Between Thomas Jefferson and Abigail and John Adams* (Chapel Hill: University of North Carolina Press, 1959), 384.

5. See Introduction, page 6.

6. Reinhold Niebuhr, *An Interpretation of Christian Ethics* (New York: Harper and Brothers, 1935), 37.

7. Karl Barth, *Church Dogmatics,* vol. 2, part 2, second half volume (Edinburgh: T. and T. Clark, 1957), 688.

8. John Wesley, Sermon LXXXI "On Perfection," *Sermons on Several Occasions,* vol. 2 (New York: Carlton and Porter, n.d.), 175.

9. Martin Luther, "A Treatise on Christian Liberty [The Freedom of a Christian]," in Timothy F. Lull, ed., *Martin Luther's Basic Theological Writings* (Minneapolis: Fortress Press, 1989), 624f.

10. Reinhold Niebuhr, *The Nature and Destiny of Man: A Christian Interpretation*, vol. 2 (New York: Charles Scribner's Sons, 1939), 125f.

11. Gustafson, *Christ and the Moral Life*, 12f.

12. The observations of Carol Gilligan about these role differences are important to recognize, though they should not be applied without the realization that individuals do vary in the degree to which they exemplify the traits of their own gender group. See *In a Different Voice: Psychological Theory and Women's Development* (Cambridge: Harvard University Press, 1982).

12. The Behavior of Jesus

1. Marcus J. Borg, probably somewhat more accurately, makes this distinction in terms of the pre-Easter and the post-Easter Jesus. See *Meeting Jesus Again for the First Time: The Historical Jesus and the Heart of Contemporary Faith* (San Francisco: Harper, 1994), see chap. 1 and 2. Borg's discussion also provides a helpful overview of the scholarly scrutiny given and being given to the problem of the historical Jesus.

2. John Dominic Crossan, *Jesus: A Revolutionary Biography* (San Francisco: HarperSanFrancisco, 1994), 93.

3. This is the title of a book by Harry Emerson Fosdick that was widely read in the late 1940s and 1950s. Fosdick, recognizing the difficulties of writing a historical account of Jesus, used the interesting tack of looking at the New Testament and other sources to ascertain how the people who lived at the time of Jesus saw him. See Harry Emerson Fosdick, *The Man From Nazareth: As His Contemporaries Saw Him* (New York: Harper and Row, 1949).

4. Ibid., 123f.

5. The way Jesus shot back is evident is various places in his teaching. For instance, he told the parable of the Pharisee and the publican—a parable that is critical of those who trust in their own righteousness and make it an occasion for holding others in contempt (Luke 18:9–14).

6. Fosdick, *Man from Nazareth*, 127.

7. Crossan, *Jesus*, 71.

8. Borg, *Meeting Jesus Again*, 49.

9. The translation of Luke 6:36 used in the New English Bible, the Jerusalem Bible, and the Scholar's version. This term is judged by Borg to have richer meaning than the term "merciful" (which implies a relationship between superiors and inferiors, or "perfect" which is the translation of the term in Matthew 5:48. See Borg, *Meeting Jesus Again*, 46, 62.

10. See Fosdick, *Man from Nazareth*, chap. 6.

11. See Crossan, *Jesus*, 63.

12. This point is made by Megan McKenna in *Not Counting Women and Children* (see chap. 3 and especially page 67).

13. This discussion is found in Crossan, *Jesus,* 80–84.

14. See Fiorenza, *In Memory of Her,* 138.

15. Ibid., 152.

16. See, for instance, the discussion in Crossan, *Jesus,* 58–60 and 96–101.

17. Ibid., 60.

18. Yoder, *The Politics of Jesus.*

19. See ibid., 34.

20. Ibid., 27.

21. Ibid., 44.

22. Ibid., 43.

23. Ibid., 52

24. Ibid. 46.

13. The Teachings of Jesus

1. See the work by Chester Charlton McCown, *The Genesis of the Social Gospel: The Meaning of the Ideals of Jesus in the Light of Their Antecedents* (New York: Alfred A. Knopf, 1929).

2. See Borg, *Meeting Jesus Again,* 70f.

3. Ibid., 74.

4. This condensation of Borg's thesis is based on the material on pages 75–80 in Borg, *Meeting Jesus Again.*

5. Ibid., 81.

6. Ibid., 82.

7. See Warren S. Kissinger, *The Sermon on the Mount: A History of Interpretation and Bibliography* (Metuchen, N.J.: The Scarecrow Press and The American Theological Library Association, 1975).

8. See Thomas S. Kepler, *Jesus' Design for Living* (New York: Abingdon Press, 1955), chap. 1. The term "practicable" is taken from E. Stanley Jones, *The Christ of the Mount* (New York and Nashville: Abingdon Press, 1931).

9. Roger L. Shinn, *The Sermon on the Mount: A Guide to Jesus' Most Famous Sermon* (New York: The Pilgrim Press, 1962).

10. Joachim Jeremias, *The Sermon on the Mount,* trans. Norman Perrin (Philadelphia: Fortress Press, 1963).

11. W. D. Davis, *The Setting of the Sermon on the Mount* (Cambridge: Cambridge University Press, 1966), 437.

14. Ethics in the Thought of Paul the Apostle

1. Borg, *Meeting Jesus Again,* 16.

2. See Verhey, *The Great Reversal,* 102 and 103; also Victor Paul Furnish, *The Moral Teaching of Paul: Selected Issues,* 2d ed., rev. (Nashville: Abingdon Press, 1985), 17.

3. A. C. Purdy, in *The Interpreters Dictionary of the Bible,* vol. 3 (Nashville: Abingdon, 1962), 692.

4. Verhey, *The Great Reversal*, 104f.

5. See Acts 15, which is discussed more fully in the chapter 15.

15. Early Christian Communities

1. Wayne A. Meeks, *The Moral World of the First Christians* (Philadelphia: Westminster Press, 1986), 97.

2. Kee, *Knowing the Truth,* 50.

3. These points are rephrased from ibid., 100.

4. Wayne A. Meeks, *The Origins of Christian Morality: The First Two Centuries* (New Haven: Yale University Press, 1993), 129.

5. See chapter 3, page 37.

6. Jeffrey Stout, *Ethics after Babel: The Languages of Morals and Their Discontents* (Boston: Beacon Press, 1988).

16. The Pastoral Epistles

1. Paul M. Harrison, *Authority and Power in the Free Church Tradition: A Social Case Study of the American Baptist Convention* (Carbondale and Edwardsville: Southern Illinois University Press, 1971).

2. See Introduction, page 8.

3. For an account of this practice within the Amish community see James A. Hostetler, *Amish Society*, 3d ed. (Baltimore and London: Johns Hopkins University Press, 1980), 108–13.

4. Langdon Brown Gilkey, *How the Church Can Minister to the World Without Losing Its Life* (New York: Harper and Row, 1964), 38 n. 10.

5. The phrase is close to one used by Paul Tillich for the title of the book *The Shaking of the Foundations* (New York: Charles Scribner's Sons, 1946).

17. The Revelation of John

1. Elisabeth Schüssler Fiorenza, *The Book of Revelation: Justice and Judgment* (Philadelphia: Fortress Press, 1985), 182.

2. For a discussion of the social location of the Book of Revelation see Leonard L. Thompson, *The Book of Revelation: Apocalypse and Empire* (New York: Oxford University Press, 1990), especially chap. 11. Thompson helps us to realize that the conditions against which John is writing are not merely political persecution in a narrow sense, but cultural estrangement in a broad sense.

3. For example, Jaroslav Pelikan, in a literary conversation with John Henry Newman, employs this symbolism in a recent book on the university and its purposes to characterize the types of evil against which the university struggles. See *The Idea of the University: A Re-examination* (New Haven: Yale University Press, 1992).

4. Civil disobedience should not to be confused with conscientious objection. When the law provides for conscientious objection, it is a form of complete obedience to the law, and necessitates civil disobedience only if there is no provision for its recognition or if claims are illegitimately denied.

5. Thompson, *The Book of Revelation,* 91.

6. Arnold J. Toynbee, *A Study of History,* a new edition revised and abridged by the author and Jane Caplan (New York: Oxford University Press, 1972), p. 334.

7. See Thomas W. Ogletree, *The Use of the Bible in Christian Ethics* (Philadelphia: Fortress Press, 1983), 177–82.

8. Ibid., 180.

9. See chapter 2.

10. For a discussion of the Powers see a trilogy of books by Walter Wink, *Naming the Powers: The Language of Power in the New Testament* (Philadelphia: Fortress Press, 1984); *Unmasking the Powers: The Invisible Forces That Determine Human Existence* (Philadelphia: Fortress Press, 1986); and *Engaging the Powers: The Language of Power in the New Testament* (Minneapolis: Augsburg Fortress, 1992).

Selected Bibliography

Anderson, Bernhard W. *Understanding the Old Testament.* 4th ed. Englewood Cliffs, N.J.: Prentice-Hall, 1986.

Barth, Karl. *Church Dogmatics.* Vol. 2, part 2, second half volume. Edinburgh: T. and T. Clark, 1957.

Bennett, John C. *Christianity and Our World.* New York: Association Press, 1936.

———. *Social Salvation: A Religious Approach to Problems of Social Change.* New York: Charles Scribner's Sons, 1935.

Birch, Bruce C. *To Love as We Are Loved: The Bible and Relationships.* Nashville: Abingdon Press, 1992.

———. *Let Justice Roll Down: The Old Testament, Ethics, and Christian Life.* Louisville, Ky.: Westminster John Knox Press, 1991.

———. *What Does the Lord Require: The Old Testament Call to Social Witness.* Philadelphia: Westminster Press, 1985.

Birch, Bruce C., and Larry L. Rasmussen. *Bible and Ethics in the Christian Life.* Minneapolis: Augsburg, 1976. Revised and expanded edition. Minneapolis: Augsburg, 1989.

Borg, Marcus J. *Meeting Jesus Again for the First Time: The Historical Jesus and the Heart of Contemporary Faith.* San Francisco: HarperSanFrancisco, 1994.

Brueggemann, Walter. *In Man We Trust: The Neglected Side of Biblical Faith.* Richmond, Va.: John Knox Press, 1972.

———. *Interpretation and Obedience: From Faithful Reading to Faithful Living.* Minneapolis: Fortress Press, 1991.

———. *The Land: Place as Gift, Promise, and Challenge in Biblical Faith.* Philadelphia: Fortress Press, 1977.

———. *The Prophetic Imagination.* Philadelphia: Fortress Press, 1979.

Brunner, Emil. *The Divine Imperative.* Philadelphia: Westminster Press, 1947.

Buck, Harry M. *People of the Lord: The History, Scriptures and Faith of Ancient Israel.* New York: Macmillan, 1966.

Crossan, John Dominic. *Jesus: A Revolutionary Biography.* San Francisco: HarperSanFrancisco, 1994.

Crosscurrents: The Journal of the Association for Religion and Intellectual Life ("Returning to Scripture" issue). Vol. 44, no. 4 (winter 1994–1995).

Daly, Robert J. *Christian Biblical Ethics: From Biblical Revelation to Contemporary Christian Praxis, Method and Content.* New York and Ramsey: Paulist Press, 1984.

Davies, W. D. *The Setting of the Sermon on the Mount.* Cambridge: Cambridge University Press, 1966.

Deen, Edith. *All the Women of the Bible.* San Francisco: Harper and Row, 1955.

Duff, Nancy J. *Humanization and the Politics of God: The Koinonia Ethics of Paul Lehmann.* Grand Rapids: William B. Eerdmans Publishing Company, 1992.

Edwards, George R. *Jesus and the Politics of Violence.* New York: Harper and Row, 1972.

Enslin, Morton Scott. *The Ethics of Paul.* New York and Nashville: Abingdon Press, 1957.

Everding, H. Edward, Jr., and Dana W. Wilbanks. *Decision Making and the Bible.* Valley Forge, Pa.: Judson Press, 1975.

Ferm, Vergilius, ed. *Encyclopedia of Religion.* New York: The Philosophical Library, 1945.

Fiorenza, Elizabeth Schüssler. *But She Said: Feminist Practices of Biblical Interpretation.* Boston: Beacon Press, 1992.

———. *In Memory of Her: A Feminist Reconstruction of Christian Origins.* New York: Crossroad, 1983.

———. *The Book of Revelation: Justice and Judgment.* Philadelphia: Fortress Press, 1985.

Flew, R. Newton. *Jesus and His Way: A Study of the Ethics of the New Testament.* London: The Epworth Press, 1963.

Fosdick, Harry Emerson. *The Man from Nazareth: Jesus as His Contemporaries Saw Him.* New York: Harper and Row, 1949.

———. *The Modern Use of the Bible.* New York: Macmillan, 1925.

Fowl, Stephen E., and L. Gregory Jones. *Reading in Communion: Scripture and Ethics in Christian Life.* Grand Rapids: William B. Eerdmans Publishing Company, 1991.

Fox, Matthew. *Creation Spirituality: Liberating Gifts for the Peoples of the Earth.* San Francisco: HarperSanFrancisco, 1991.

Freire, Paulo. *Pedagogy of the Oppressed.* New York: Herder and Herder, 1970.

Furnish, Victor Paul. *The Moral Teaching of Paul: Selected Issues.* 2d ed. rev. Nashville: Abingdon Press, 1985.

Gardner, E. Clinton. *Biblical Faith and Social Ethics.* New York: Harper and Brothers, 1960.

Gilkey, Langdon Brown. *How the Church Can Minister to the World Without Losing Its Life.* New York: Harper and Row, 1964.

Gilligan, Carol. *In a Different Voice: Psychological Theory and Women's Development.* Cambridge: Harvard University Press, 1982.

Gottwald, Norman K. *The Hebrew Bible: A Socio-Literary Introduction.* Philadelphia: Fortress Press, 1985.

Gottwald, Norman K., and Richard A. Horsley, eds. *The Bible and Liberation: Political and Social Hermeneutics.* Maryknoll, N.Y.: Orbis Books, 1993.

Gustafson, James M. *Christ and the Moral Life.* New York: Harper and Row, 1968.

Hanson, Paul D. *The People Called: The Growth of Community in the Bible.* San Francisco: Harper and Row, 1987.

Häring, Bernard. *Free and Faithful in Christ: Moral Theology for Clergy and Laity.* Vol. 1. A Crossroad Book. New York: Seabury Press, 1978.

Harkness, Georgia. *The Recovery of Ideals.* New York: Charles Scribner's Sons, 1937.

Harrelson, Walter J. *Interpreting the Old Testament.* Hew York: Holt, Rinehart and Winston, 1964.

————. *The Ten Commandments and Human Rights.* Philadelphia: Fortress Press, 1980.

Harrison, Paul M. *Authority and Power in the Free Church Tradition: A Social Case Study of the American Baptist Convention.* Carbondale and Edwardsville: Southern Illinois University Press, 1971.

Hauerwas, Stanley. *The Peaceable Kingdom: A Primer in Christian Ethics.* Notre Dame: University of Notre Dame, 1983.

————. *Unleashing the Scripture: Freeing the Bible from Captivity to America.* Nashville: Abingdon Press, 1992.

Hauerwas, Stanley, and William Willimon. *Resident Aliens: Life in the Christian Colony.* Nashville: Abingdon Press, 1989.

Heschel, Abraham Joshua. *The Sabbath: Its Meaning for Modern Man.* New York: Farrar, Straus & Giroux, 1951.

Hodge, Charles. *Systematic Theology.* Vol. 3. New York: Scribner Armstrong and Company, 1876.

Hoffmann, R. Joseph, and Gerald A. Larue. *Biblical v. Secular Ethics: The Conflict.* Buffalo: Prometheus Books, 1988.

Hostetler, James A. *Amish Society.* 3d ed. Baltimore and London: Johns Hopkins University Press, 1980.

Humphreys, W. Lee. *Crisis and Story: Introduction to the Old Testament.* Palo Alto: Mayfield Publishing Company, 1979.

Interpreters Dictionary of the Bible. New York: Abingdon Press, 1962.

Janzen, Waldemar. *Old Testament Ethics: A Paradigmatic Approach.* Louisville, Ky.: Westminster John Knox, 1994.

Jefferson, Thomas. Letter to John Adams. In *The Adams-Jefferson Letters: The Complete Correspondence Between Thomas Jefferson and Abigail and John Adams,* edited by Lester J. Cappon. Chapel Hill: University of North Carolina Press, 1959.

Jeremias, Joachim. *The Sermon on the Mount.* Translated by Norma Perrin. Philadelphia: Fortress Press, 1963.

Johnson, James Turner, ed. *The Bible in American Law, Politics, and Political Rhetoric.* Philadelphia: Fortress Press; Chico, Calif.: Scholars Press, 1985.

Johnson, Patricia Altenbernd, and Janet Kalven, eds. *With Both Eyes Open: Seeing Without Gender.* New York: The Pilgrim Press, 1988.

Jones, E. Stanley. *The Christ of the Mount*. New York and Nashville: Abingdon Press, 1931.

Joyce, Paul. *Divine Initiative and Human Response in Ezekiel*. Sheffield, England: JOST Press, 1989.

Kaiser, Walter C., Jr. *Toward Old Testament Ethics*. Grand Rapids: Zondervan Publishing House, 1983.

Kee, Howard Clark. *Knowing the Truth: A Sociological Approach to New Testament Interpretation*. Minneapolis: Fortress Press, 1989.

Kee, Howard Clark, Franklin W. Young, and Karlfried Froehlich. *Understanding the New Testament*. 2d ed. Englewood Cliffs, N.J.: Prentice-Hall, 1965.

Kepler, Thomas S. *Jesus's Design for Living*. New York: Abingdon Press, 1955.

Kierkegaard, Søren. *Fear and Trembling and Sickness Unto Death*. Translated with introduction and notes by Walter Lowrie. Princeton: Princeton University Press, 1968.

Kissinger, Warren S. *The Sermon on the Mount: A History of Interpretation and Bibliography*. Metuchen, N.J.: The Scarecrow Press and The American Theological Library Association, 1975.

Long, Edward LeRoy, Jr. *Conscience and Compromise: An Approach to Protestant Casuistry*. Philadelphia: Westminster Press, 1954.

———. *A Survey of Christian Ethics*. New York: Oxford University Press, 1967.

———. *A Survey of Recent Christian Ethics*. New York: Oxford University Press, 1982.

Lull, Timothy F., ed. *Martin Luther's Basic Theological Writings*. Minneapolis: Fortress Press, 1989.

Manson, T. W. *Ethics and the Gospel*. New York: Charles Scribner's Sons, 1961.

Marxsen, Willi. *New Testament Foundations for Christian Ethics*. Translated by O. C. Dean Jr. Minneapolis: Fortress Press, 1989.

Maston, T. B. *Biblical Ethics: A Guide to the Ethical Message of the Scriptures from Genesis through Revelation*. Cleveland: World Publishing Company, 1967. Reprint, Macon, Ga.: Mercer University Press, 1982, 1988, 1989, and 1991.

McCown, Chester Charlton. *The Genesis of the Social Gospel: The Meaning of the Ideals of Jesus in the Light of Their Antecedents*. New York: Alfred A. Knopf, 1929.

McDonald, J. I. H. *Biblical Interpretation and Christian Ethics*. Cambridge: Cambridge University Press, 1993.

McFague, Sallie. *The Body of God: An Ecological Theology*. Minneapolis: Fortress Press, 1993.

McKenna, Megan. *Not Counting Women and Children: Neglected Stories from the Bible*. Maryknoll, N.Y.: Orbis Press, 1994.

Meeks, Wayne A. *The Moral World of the First Christians*. Philadelphia: Westminster Press, 1986.

———. *The Origins of Christian Morality: The First Two Centuries*. New Haven: Yale University Press, 1993.

Metz, Johannes Baptist, ed. *Faith and the World of Politics*. New York: Paulist Press, 1968.

————. *Faith in History and Society: Toward a Political Fundamental Theology.* New York: Seabury Press, 1980.

Minear, Paul S. *Commands of Christ: Authority and Implications.* Nashville and New York: Abingdon Press, 1972.

Mitchell, Hinckley G. *The Ethics of the Old Testament.* Chicago: University of Chicago Press, 1912.

Moltmann, Jürgen. *Religion and Political Society.* New York: Harper and Row, 1974.

Mott, Stephen Charles. *Biblical Ethics and Social Change.* New York: Oxford University Press, 1982.

Morgenstern, J. "Jubilee, Year of." *Interpreters Dictionary of the Bible.* Vol. 2. New York: Abingdon Press, 1962.

Mouw, Richard J. *Politics and the Biblical Drama.* Grand Rapids: William B. Eerdmans Publishing Company, 1972.

Muilenburg, James. *The Way of Israel: Biblical Faith and Ethics.* New York: Harper and Row, 1965.

Newman, Murray Lee, Jr. *The People of the Covenant: A Study of Israel from Moses to Monarchy.* New York: Abingdon Press, 1962.

Niebuhr, Reinhold. *An Interpretation of Christian Ethics.* New York: Harper and Brothers, 1935.

————. *Moral Man and Immoral Society: A Study in Ethics and Politics.* New York: Charles Scribner's Sons, 1932.

————. *The Nature and Destiny of Man: A Christian Interpretation.* Vol. 2. New York: Charles Scribner's Sons, 1939.

Ogletree, Thomas W. *The Use of the Bible in Christian Ethics.* Philadelphia: Fortress Press, 1983.

Pelikan, Jaroslav. *The Idea of the University: A Re-Examination.* New Haven: Yale University Press, 1992.

Plaskow, Judith, and Carol P. Christ, eds. *Weaving the Visions: Patterns in Feminist Spirituality.* San Francisco: Harper and Row, 1989.

Presbyterian Church USA. *Keeping Body and Soul Together: Sexuality, Spirituality, and Social Justice.* A document prepared for the 203rd General Assembly, 1991.

Ramm, Bernard. *Offense to Reason: The Theology of Sin.* San Francisco: Harper and Row, 1985.

Ruether, Rosemary Radford. *Gaia and God: An Ecofeminist Theology of Earth Healing.* San Francisco: HarperCollins Publishers, 1992.

Sandeen, Ernest R., ed. *The Bible and Social Reform.* Philadelphia: Fortress Press; Chico, Calif.: Scholars Press, 1982.

Sanders, Jack T. *Ethics in the New Testament: Change and Development.* Philadelphia: Fortress Press, 1975.

Santmire, Paul. *Brother Earth: Nature, God, and Ecology in Time of Crisis.* New York: Thomas Nelson, 1970.

Schrage, Wolfgang. *The Ethics of the New Testament.* Translated by David E. Green. Philadelphia: Fortress Press, 1988.

Schrey, Heinz-Horst, Hans Hermann Walz, and W. A. Whitehouse. *The Biblical Doctrine of Justice and Law.* London: SCM Press, 1955.

Schumacher, E. F. *Small Is Beautiful: Economics as if People Mattered.* New York: Thomas Nelson, 1970.

Selby, Donald J., and James King West. *Introduction to the Bible.* New York: Macmillan, 1971.

Shinn, Roger L. *The Sermon on the Mount: A Guide to Jesus' Most Famous Sermon.* New York: The Pilgrim Press, 1962.

Sider, Ronald J., ed. *Cry Justice: The Bible on Hunger and Poverty.* New York and Ramsey: Paulist Press, 1980.

Sleeper, C. Freeman. *The Bible and the Moral Life.* Louisville, Ky.: Westminster John Knox Press, 1992.

Sloyan, Gerald S. *Is Christ the End of the Law?* Philadelphia: Westminster Press, 1978.

Sölle, Dorothee. *Political Theology.* Philadelphia: Fortress Press, 1974.

Spurrier, William A. *Natural Law and the Ethics of Love: A New Synthesis.* Philadelphia: Westminster Press, 1974.

Stout, Jeffrey. *Ethics after Babel: The Languages of Morals and Their Discontents.* Boston: Beacon Press, 1988.

Sturm, Douglas. *Community and Alienation: Essays on Process Thought and Public Life.* Notre Dame: University of Notre Dame Press, 1988.

Thompson, Leonard L. *The Book of Revelation: Apocalypse and Empire.* New York: Oxford University Press, 1990.

Tillich, Paul. *The Shaking of the Foundations.* New York: Charles Scribner's Sons, 1946.

Toynbee, Arnold J. *A Study of History.* A new edition revised and abridged by the author and Jane Caplan. New York: Oxford University Press, 1972.

Trible, Phyllis. *God and the Rhetoric of Sexuality.* Philadelphia: Fortress Press, 1978.

Troeltsch, Ernst. *The Social Teaching of the Christian Churches.* Translated by Olive Wyon. New York: Macmillan, 1931.

Verhey, Alan. *The Great Reversal: Ethics and the New Testament.* Grand Rapids: William B. Eerdmans Publishing Company, 1984.

Waskow, Arthur. "From Compassion to Jubilee [Contemporary Applications of the Jubilee]." *Tikkun: A Bimonthly Jewish Critique of Politics, Culture, and Society* 5, no. 2 (March–April 1990): 78–81.

Wesley, John. *Sermons on Several Occasions.* Vol. 2. New York: Carlton and Porter, n.d.

White, Lynn, Jr. "The Historical Roots of Our Ecological Crisis." *Science* 155, no. 3767 (March 10, 1967): 1203–7.

Williams, Dolores S. *Sisters in the Wilderness: The Challenge of Womanist God-Talk.* Maryknoll, N.Y.: Orbis Books, 1993.

Wink, Walter. *The Bible in Human Transformation: Toward a New Paradigm for Biblical Study.* Philadelphia: Fortress Press, 1973.

————. *Naming the Powers: The Language of Power in the New Testament.* Philadelphia: Fortress Press, 1984.

————. *Unmasking the Powers: The Invisible Forces That Determine Human Existence.* Philadelphia: Fortress Press, 1986.

————. *Engaging the Powers: The Language of Power in the New Testament.* Minneapolis: Augsburg Fortress, 1992.

Wogaman, J. Philip. *Christian Ethics: An Historical Introduction.* Louisville, Ky.: Westminster John Knox Press, 1993.

Wolterstorff, Nicholas K. *Until Peace and Justice Embrace.* Grand Rapids: William B. Eerdmans Publishing Company, 1983.

Wright, Christopher J. H. *An Eye for an Eye: The Place of Old Testament Ethics Today.* Downers Grove, Ill.: Intervarsity Press, 1983.

Wright, G. Ernest. *The Biblical Doctrine of Man in Society.* London: SCM Press, 1954.

Yoder, John Howard. *The Politics of Jesus: Vicit Agnus Noster.* Grand Rapids: William B. Eerdmans Publishing Company, 1972.

————. *The Priestly Kingdom: Social Ethics as Gospel.* Notre Dame: University of Notre Dame Press, 1984.

Index of Names and Subjects

Index of Biblical References

Old Testament